SOCIAL JUSTICE THROUGH THE EYES OF WESLEY

To serve the present age,
   My calling to fulfill:
O may it all my powers engage
   To do my Master's will!
— *Charles Wesley (1707–1788)*

O thou God of Love,
… who art loving to every man,
   and whose mercy is over all …
   have compassion on these outcasts of men…
Arise, and help these that have no helper,
   whose blood is spilt upon the earth like water!
… O burst thou all their chains in sunder…
   make them free, that they may be free indeed!
— *John Wesley (1703–1791)*

I am happy to commend Dr. Brendlinger's wide-ranging study, *Social justice through the eyes of Wesley*. Dr. Brendlinger is not one of the commentators on Wesley who thinks that earnest application to the *Journal* and *Letters* exhausts his obligation to his hero, and has read widely in Wesley's own writings and the now voluminous literature on slavery and the social history of the century. Nor is he content to narrate the involvement of Wesley and his successors in antislavery agitations, but offers a personal attempt to elucidate the roots of his attitude in basic theological and spiritual make-up. This kind of detective work can always be done in more ways than one, but Dr. Brendlinger's successors will always be grateful for his pioneering approach. And the subject is an important one. Most of Wesley's views on public matters fell within the parameters of country party politics; but Bristol and Liverpool, the great strongholds of the slave interests, were bastions of the country opposition to metropolitan politics. Here it was Wesley's conscience which strayed 'off-message,' and it is all the more interesting for doing so. I wish the book every success.

W. REGINALD WARD
Editor, "The Journal of John Wesley," *The Works of John Wesley*, Abingdon

---

I'm impressed. This book gives us some much needed information thus far neglected, primarily the theological justification for Wesley's views on the subject. Brendlinger's research is thorough enough to give us some detail on matters previously quoted out of context or misunderstood. This book will be useful in the courses I teach on the life and theology of John Wesley.

ROBERT G. TUTTLE, Jr.
Professor, Asbury Theological Seminary, author of *John Wesley, His Life and Theology*

For too long John Wesley has been pigeon-holed as a social and political conservative, though an ecclesiastical radical. Irv Brendlinger's book challenges us to think again. He challenges us to put Wesley's attack on slavery into a central place in any attempt to understand his thought as it has not been hitherto.

ANDREW C. ROSS
Honorary Fellow, School of Divinity, University of Edinburgh

This valuable work is a useful and needed addition to the already immense literature on slavery and antislavery. Dr. Brendlinger traces Wesley's varied acquaintance with Africans of the Diaspora and his increasing knowledge of slavery in the course of his long life, and the contacts with major figures in the abolition movement that proved the catalyst for his emergence as a campaigner in the later phases of it. But it goes further, by analyzing Wesley's thinking as a whole to show how Wesley — unlike Whitefield, with whom he had so much in common — came to the conclusions about slavery that he did. Antislavery was integral, not incidental, to what he believed and preached. His effectiveness as a campaigner is reflected in the way in which antislavery became part of his legacy to the Methodist people.

ANDREW F. WALLS
Centre for the Study of Christianity in the Non-Western World,
University of Edinburgh

SOCIAL JUSTICE THROUGH THE EYES OF WESLEY

John Wesley's theological challenge to slavery

by Iru A. Brendlinger

press

Joshua Press Inc.
Ontario, Canada
www.joshuapress.com

© 2006 by Joshua Press Inc.
All rights reserved. This book may not be reproduced, in whole or in part, without written permission from the publishers. Published 2006

Distributed by
Sola Scriptura Ministries International
www.sola-scriptura.ca

Editorial director: Michael A.G. Haykin
Cover and book design by Janice Van Eck

The cover portrait of John Wesley is by Frank O. Salisbury (1874–1962). This portrait hangs in Central Hall, London, and is used with the kind permission of Rev. Martin Turner, Central Hall.

National Library of Canada Cataloguing in Publication Data

Brendlinger, Irv A., 1943–
    Social justice through the eyes of Wesley : John Wesley's theological challenge to slavery / by Irv A. Brendlinger.

Includes bibliographical references and index.
ISBN 1-894400-23-2   ISBN-13 978-1894400-23-7

    1. Wesley, John, 1703-1791. 2. Slavery and the church—Methodist Church—History—18th century. 3. Slavery and the church—Church of England—History—18th century. 4. Slavery and the church—England—History—18th century. 5. Church of England—Doctrines—History—18th century. I. Title.

BX8495.W5B74 2006   270.086'25092   C2006-906062-2

PRINTED IN THE U.S.A.

To Shirley, who has been my consistent and ardent supporter in this and all my projects. Her belief in the importance of the work has brought invaluable encouragement. Taking on the task of composing her own piano arrangements of black spirituals, *SpiritSong*, reflects her deep identification with my concern. Her insightful criticism has given practical help. Had Wesley enjoyed this kind of support from Molly, well, his life may have been quite different. Words only begin to hint at my gratitude for our relationship that not only brings delight and joy, but facilitates my best.

contents

	Gratitude	xi
	Foreword	xiii
	Introduction	xv
chapter 1	John Wesley in context: his century, relationships and spiritual journey	1
chapter 2	John Wesley's antislavery journey	13
chapter 3	A brief excursion into Wesley's position on slavery and Negro inferiority	45
chapter 4	The relationship between Wesley's theology and his position on slavery	73
chapter 5	The larger context: Wesley's social ethic and philosophy of social change	129
chapter 6	The significance of John Wesley's antislavery influence	147
	Epilogue	171
	Appendix 1	175
	Appendix 2	193
	Appendix 3	201
	Abbreviations	224
	Endnotes	225
	Select bibliography	263
	Index	267

gratitude

I am deeply grateful and indebted to many who contributed to this book. Andrew C. Ross first suggested that I explore the topic of John Wesley and slavery. He not only supervised my doctoral research, but became a dear friend and continued to show interest and support for my ongoing work. Dennis F. Kinlaw, mentor and friend over many years, gave enthusiastic affirmation at a crucial time in this project. I am indebted to W. Reginald Ward for his inspiring work in Wesley's *Journals* as well as his critical insights as the manuscript developed. These three have each been significant influences; their friendship is highly treasured.

I am grateful to my wife, Shirley, and children, Carol Joy and David. Our shared "Scottish experience," during my postgraduate years, was the beginning of this quest. Family times brought special joy to the process and those memories are alive and cherished.

The family support has continued to the completion of the project. My learning about response to human need has been enhanced by observing their sensitivity to those who have been hurt.

I am also thankful for the support of George Fox University through the sabbatical year when most of the work was accomplished. It was a great honour to spend part of that year as Visiting Fellow at New College, University of Edinburgh. John Rylands University Library was helpful in my research; the willing and scholarly assistance of Peter Nockles made it accessible and profitable. My student assistants, Carla Rich and Sean Merrick have been efficient with their many tasks: typing, proofreading, double checking sources and correcting computer glitches. I am also grateful for the very skillful editing of Janice Van Eck. Her encouragement was helpful in the final stages of the work. Their generous, encouraging spirits were an added benefit.

As I reflect on my interest in this topic over the last twenty plus years, I am grateful for Wesley's response to the plight of human beings. As the first highly visible Christian leader to challenge slavery, he both taught and modelled a compassion that made a difference. Willing to go beyond cultural norms and probe the profound application of true Christian theology, he gave voice to its relevance for genuine human need.

Finally, I express my respect for those who suffered the atrocities of one of the world's greatest social injustices. Amazingly, millions of black persons embraced the faith of those who enslaved them. They saw beyond the greed of humanity to the true love of God. In that they continue to influence all who will listen. They, along with Wesley, inspire and instruct us to confront whatever compromises human value.

Irv A. Brendlinger

foreword

James Denney, the Scottish theologian and biblical scholar, would have liked John Wesley. He would also have liked Irv Brendlinger. Denney was convinced that every evangelist should be a theologian and every theologian should be an evangelist. Brendlinger in this volume illustrates Denney's thesis but goes further. He insists that the evangelist-theologian, if his theology is truly biblical, will also be a voice and a force for social reform as well. In this valuable volume Brendlinger shows the remarkable interplay between Wesley's theology and the rest of his ministry, that his theology not only determined the character of his evangelism but was also the very basis for his social passion, which had such a redemptive influence on eighteenth century Britain and nineteenth century America.

What made Wesley, at the age of seventy, turn his attention to the question of slavery and throw much of his energy into support for those who were fighting the battle to free those trapped in what Wesley called "the sum of all villainies"? It was not a general evangelicalism that motivated him. It was his own distinctive mix of theological convictions that drove him. It was his theological differences from his friend George Whitefield and other evangelicals like John Newton that forced him into the battle.

Wesley was convinced of the doctrine of original sin and that no human person, black or white, was untouched by it. Therefore the slave owner was in as deep a need of salvation as the slave. He believed, not only that Christ died for every person alike but that the Holy Spirit is actively at work in that person, black or white, to restore the image of God lost in the Fall. He believed that the purpose of that prevenient work of the Holy Spirit was to restore the agape-love, lost in the Fall, to every human heart so that the redeemed person would actually love his neighbour as himself. In that theological ambience the thought of one human enslaving another for his own benefit was just unthinkable. The thought of the cross of Christ left Wesley with no option but to throw what energies he had against the whole institution. And, his influence made a difference.

Brendlinger has put us in his debt with a significant work. It should be of great interest to any of us who want to see the gospel whole. It should be of special interest, theologian or not, to every one who is a Wesleyan. My prayer is that this volume will have a wide reading.

Dennis F. Kinlaw
Founder of the Francis Asbury Society

introduction

John Wesley: the missing chapter

While it is well known and frequently stated that Wesley opposed slavery and was a significant influence in the fight against it, those facts have only been alluded to in broad strokes. His antislavery activity has never been developed either in detail or in relationship to his theology. His influence has been assumed, but not substantiated sociologically until the recent work by Robert Fogel.[1]

My introduction to this information gap occurred when I began my doctoral research on the antislavery movement of the eighteenth century. Consistently, books that traced the events and persons in the cause would mention Wesley, but only briefly. They would write in glowing terms of his influence, but only in a sentence or two, or at most a paragraph. Usually such comments would take the shape of broad generalizations, simply assuming that Wesley's influence was significant. The most specificity would be related to the fact that in 1774 Wesley wrote a tract, *Thoughts Upon Slavery*. It was the broad assumption without specific support or thorough development that enticed me to devote a substantive portion of my doctoral research to this topic. That exploration was informative, fruitful and enthralling. My work with slavery was both captivating and depressing, as I learned of the atrocities human beings committed against one another. Subjecting others to abuse and degradation was no obstacle to them if it led to their financial gain. I am confident that my response was not unlike Wesley's as he learned the truth about slavery and was drawn into the cause. My work with Wesley was intriguing and inspiring as I grew to know the man through his journals, sermons, tracts, letters and contemporaries. I came to realize that his stand against and his activities to end what he called the "sum of all villanies" were not unrelated to his major doctrinal distinctives, particularly his understanding of Christian perfection. But I also came to appreciate the uniqueness and wonderful humanness of Wesley.

He was a multifaceted and very colourful person, perhaps more so than many assume from his titles and reputation. Indeed, he came from an Anglican family out of the stock of Dissenters to become an Anglican priest and the founder of Methodism. He was a key voice in the Evangelical Awakening of the eighteenth century and (what seems most austere to many) the "father of the holiness movement." Though hard-working, driven and committed, he was not without humour as his journal clearly portrays:

> May 1742; On Thursday, 20, I set out. The next afternoon I stopped a little at Newport-Pagnell, and then rode on till I overtook a serious man, with whom I immediately fell into conversation. He presently gave me to know what his opinions were; therefore I said nothing to contradict them. But that did not content him; he was quite uneasy to know, whether I held the doctrine of the decrees [predestination] as he did; but I told him over and over, "We had better keep to practical things, lest we should be angry

at one another." And so we did for two miles, till he caught me unawares, and dragged me into the dispute before I knew where I was. He then grew warmer and warmer; told me I was rotten at heart, and supposed I was one of John Wesley's followers. I told him, "No, I am John Wesley himself." Upon which, — as one that has unawares trodden upon a snake, he would gladly have run away outright. But, being the better mounted of the two, I kept close to his side, and endeavoured to show him his heart, till we came into the street of Northampton.[2]

The incident reflects not only Wesley's sense of humour and how well known he was, but how firm he could be on important issues. For him important issues were not limited to "doctrines," foundational as they were. He was also committed to broad principles of truth. Wesley's deep spiritual principles related to human need and justice. Such concern spanned his entire life. Could he rest idly while human beings were being dehumanized and exploited? By no means. And so at the age of seventy (when the vast majority of his contemporaries were either dead or at best settled into a very sedentary life) he took up the cause to overthrow the institution of slavery. He pursued it to the end of his life, even to the last letter he wrote.

In the following pages Wesley's antislavery journey will be investigated with a close look at the persons he interfaced with and the activities he pursued. His theological distinctives will be grappled with to sort out whether his powerful antislavery commitment was merely a human concern, an important tangent, or was deeply rooted in his theology. Finally, Wesley's legacy will be suggested in the desire to carry forward his vision of bringing the "good news" of Christian truth to bear on the needs of humankind. It is hoped that this examination of Wesley's relationship to slavery will begin to supply the "missing chapter" on how his unusual and important life responded to one of the greatest blights on human history.

chapter 1

John Wesley in context: his century, relationships and spiritual journey

Many biographies have been written about John Wesley (1703–1791), so there is no need to plow the same ground again. However, for the purpose of this study, we shall briefly view him in the context of his age, note some relationships and revisit several formative experiences of his life which bear directly on his eventual interest in the problem of human bondage.

Spanning the eighteenth century, Wesley lived before the principles of sociology were understood and before the idea of Negro inferiority was propagated or generally accepted. He also experienced the societal transition brought about by the Industrial Revolution and witnessed the transformation of many in the lower and working classes as they adopted his values and discipline and worked their way into economic security.

He grew up in a home deeply committed to the Church of England. Both his father, an Anglican priest, and his mother had chosen the Church of England in their youth despite the fact that they came from staunch dissenting families. John Wesley considered himself a loyal Anglican for his entire life and viewed the explosion of Methodism as the bursting into flame of the coals of true Christianity *within* the established church. He did not consider himself to have separated from it.[1]

Committed to the life of the mind, he relished new experiences and learning opportunities throughout his life. He was awarded the baccalaureate degree in 1724 and the Master of Arts degree in 1727 from Oxford University. He studied for his B.A. at Christ Church, Oxford, and his M.A. at Lincoln College. He was elected Fellow of Lincoln College (1726), which most likely indicated ecclesiastical status.[2] This brought pride to his father and satisfaction to himself. "Fellow of Lincoln College" is inscribed on his tombstone. He demonstrated his commitment to learning as he made innumerable resources available to his followers and as he continued to write throughout his life. It is not surprising that he took on the cause of the slave so late in life, when he learned of the need.

It was during his years as a Fellow at Lincoln College (from 1729) that he first associated with and eventually became the leader of the Holy Club. This group would become the relational nucleus of his experience in America and the community in which he established the patterns and discipline which so influenced the development of Methodism. Many years later he would reflect on the good of the Oxford years, "Let me be again an Oxford Methodist! I am often in doubt whether it would not be best for me to resume all my Oxford rules, great and small."[3] Community, discipline, service and learning were key factors in those years, and would facilitate his effectiveness for the rest of his life.

An important outgrowth of the Holy Club was Wesley's involvement in compassionate ministries. In 1730 William Morgan, one of the original members of the Holy Club, began a number of charitable services to the needy. Wesley and the other members became deeply involved. In a literal response to the gospel mandate they "fed the hungry, clothed the naked, visited those that are sick, and in prison."[4] With scheduled regularity they visited prisons, bringing spiritual solace and providing money for those imprisoned because of small debts. In addition to prison work, they assisted the poor with food, medicine, clothes, Bibles, and even helped tradesmen to procure materials and tools. They were motivated simply by what they read in Matthew 25:40: "Inasmuch as ye have done it unto one of the least of these my brethren, ye have done it unto me."[5] The needy, desperate and helpless prisoners so captured their compassion that by 1732 prison work filled the bulk of their time.

Such ministry, from the same biblical injunction, would be a dominant theme throughout Wesley's life. Likewise, his response to the plight of the slave many years later is related to the sensitivity and compassion he developed during those early attempts to alleviate the suffering of the poverty stricken, the sick and especially those who were denied freedom, the prisoners.

The debt to Whitefield

The Holy Club was also the place where the important relationship between Wesley and George Whitefield began. While it was Charles Wesley that brought Whitefield into the Oxford group, the most lasting and intimate bond was forged between John Wesley and Whitefield. Near the end of the book I posit that the spread of Methodism created a climate that shaped the response of both lay people and politicians to the problem of slavery, and energized their efforts to end it. While Wesley's role in the growth of Methodism is beyond question, in fairness, the role of George Whitefield must also be considered. This should be handled carefully because while Whitefield was very important to the spread of Methodism, his views on slavery were sometimes quite different from those of Wesley. That will be developed in a subsequent chapter, but the nature of Wesley's and Whitefield's relationship and the possible role Whitefield played regarding slavery will be mentioned briefly here.

The lives of Wesley and Whitefield interfaced on many levels. Each had a strong influence on the other and they played off each other for mutual benefit and development of ministry. Their relationship included mutual instruction, deep, affectionate support and disagreement.

Whitefield began open air preaching before Wesley and introduced the idea to him. At first Wesley was appalled, but he soon adopted and excelled in this method which came to be a hallmark of Methodism. Open air preaching was an effective means of reaching thousands who would not have entered a church building — but would eventually become thronging members of Methodism. Just as significant, Whitefield left the care of his converts to Wesley when he left England for his preaching tour in America. Wesley took the task seriously and organized the new Christians into groups that would experience support, learning and discipline. It is apparent that the seeds of Methodist organization, group dynamic, stability and success were sown in this process. This may well be one of the most important outcomes of the relationship between Wesley and Whitefield. It would certainly play a part in how ideas and values were transmitted, and how the masses were later organized to have a political impact.

The affectionate nature of this relationship is reflected poignantly in one particular experience. It was the encounter between the two men when Wesley learned that he had lost his true love, Grace Murray. Whitefield was with Wesley when the news came that Grace had married John Bennett at the insistent urging of Charles Wesley (John's brother). She did not communicate this to John, who was heartbroken by the news, and he fell into the arms of Whitefield and they sobbed together. While Charles' impulsive and controlling action could have caused an irreparable rift between John and Charles, and the resulting dissolution of Methodism, it is probable that Whitefield's gentleness, support and wisdom averted such a disaster.[6] This occurred in 1749, when Methodism was just gaining momentum and would have been most vulnerable.

In spite of their affection, Whitefield and Wesley did not agree on everything. A major disagreement was over Whitefield's staunch position on predestination. While both Wesley and Whitefield had great evangelical success and considered themselves part of the same evangelical movement, Wesley feared that if Whitefield made the doctrine of predestination a public issue it would split Methodism. Societies were already being split as various leaders took sides on the issue. So, as their influence grew they both desired that the world should see their love and unity of spirit more than their theological differences. Agreeing that the primary message of the gospel was more important than a Calvinist or Arminian interpretation, the two men agreed that they would not emphasize or air their differing views publicly. After a temporary breach of that agreement, peace was restored and they decided to show the world the truth of their love and Christian unity by each committing to preach the funeral sermon of whoever died first. Years later Wesley did preach such a sermon for Whitefield.

The other disagreement between Wesley and Whitefield was over slavery. Both men spent time in Georgia and observed slavery first-hand. While Wesley's attitude toward slavery was consistent — unequivocally opposed — Whitefield's view changed from opposition to support. The contrast between Wesley and Whitefield will be developed later (chapter 3), however, in assessing the role of Methodism in ending slavery, the work of Whitefield must not be overlooked.

The success of Methodism was not due to Wesley alone. Whitefield contributed as well and attracted many converts. He, along with Wesley, was responsible for the evangelical move across England that made the populace fertile ground for antislavery ideals and action. It is even possible that Whitefield's early opposition to slavery (before 1751) was known by and influential among early Methodists, especially the followers of Wesley. Later these same followers took up Wesley's position and loyally supported the cause.[7] It is impossible to confidently attribute such influence to Whitefield, but it would be less than honest to attribute the growth of Methodism, with its attitude of humanitarianism, singularly to Wesley without considering Whitefield's contribution.

Whitefield's work was parallel to Wesley's in promulgating Methodism, and ultimately in creating a social climate that was conducive to widespread support of the moral concern to end slavery. In addition, the combined evangelical influence of Whitefield and Wesley on William Wilberforce, through his Methodist aunt, must be acknowledged.[8] Wesley and Whitefield were the primary factors in the massive evangelical awakening of the eighteenth century in England. That awakening was crucial to the development and success of the antislavery movement.

Commitment, self-awareness and a kindled heart

In addition to the education, compassionate ministries and the relationships mentioned already, three experiences stand out as particularly relevant to Wesley's eventual involvement in the antislavery movement. They include the time surrounding his ordination as a deacon in 1725, his time in Georgia from 1736 to 1738, and his evangelical heart-warming at Aldersgate in 1738.

As Wesley was preparing for ordination as a deacon he read extensively. Two of the sources he explored were Jeremy Taylor's *Rule and Exercises of Holy Living and Dying*, and Thomas a' Kempis' *Imitation of Christ*. Somewhat later (late 1726 to early 1727) he read William Law's *Christian Perfection*. It is impossible to overstate the importance of these sources for Wesley's theology and ministry. After reading these works he committed himself to a radical kind of discipleship and became extremely disciplined in applying his religion to life. Some would term this time his "conversion," or the beginning of his conversion.[9] From the time that he first read them he would refer to the principles he learned in those books. They formed the foundation of his understanding of the full Christian experience — what some would call his doctrine of sanctification. This will be developed in chapter 3 but for now it is sufficient to mention that his grasp of the complete Christian experience embraced the love of and responsibility to others as well as to God, and this thinking was rooted in his reading of these devotional writers. Without this pivotal experience, and the deep commitment of 1725, the well known and celebrated experience of 1738 would not have occurred. He would have had no motive for going to America and subsequently would not have seen the Moravian demonstration of vital faith in the face of death. Nor would he have developed such a bond with the Moravians, which became so influential to his thinking.

America and self-awareness

In 1728 Wesley was ordained a priest.[10] He served in parish ministry until he was called back to Oxford to fulfill his duties as a Fellow in residence. He remained in Oxford until he accepted the call to go to America. That call came through a series of persons and events. Wesley's father was a friend of General James Oglethorpe who was settling the colony of Georgia, where the Society for the Propagation of the Gospel in Foreign Parts (SPG) had established a ministry. Dr. John Burton, a tutor at Corpus Christi College encouraged Wesley to serve with the SPG. While the primary purpose of the SPG was typically ecclesiastical service to displaced Anglicans — not the evangelization of indigenous people — Wesley warmed to the call because it would afford him the opportunity to preach to Native Americans.[11] Officially, he was filling the vacancy left by a Mr. Quincy, whose pastoral responsibilities were with the English settlers. Wesley would go to America accompanied by his brother Charles and other members of the Holy Club.

The time in America proved to be difficult but important for Wesley. On the personal side, he had a disappointing romance and experienced conflict with the local officials. In terms of ministry, he did his best in the ways he was accustomed. He was both diligent and consistent (some would say rigid), and the more independent colonists did not acquiesce to his style or requirements. In terms of new experiences, he was exposed to Native Americans, to slaves and to the cruelties of slavery. This was an important aspect of his time in America and he would never forget these impressions. He also saw firsthand what he later described as the results of human depravity: drunkenness, greed, debauchery and human brutality.

Although his brother Charles returned to England after only six months, John spent nearly two years in Georgia.[12] While his work was not futile, he left America both depressed and discouraged. He had expected great success, but experienced the opposite. On the return voyage he confided in his journal, "I went to America to convert the Indians; but oh, who shall convert me?"[13] Back in London, his closing interviews with the Trustees of Georgia were anything but reassuring; they added salt to the wounds of an injured man. In short, he felt that he had failed, and that he was a failure vocationally and spiritually. Along with his experience of 1725, this would serve as preparation for his discovery in 1738. Like a recurring refrain, without the humiliating experience of America it is highly unlikely that the well known and celebrated experience of 1738 would have followed.

Aldersgate and a kindled heart

Wesley, though in the depths of discouragement, found support and direction from some German Moravians — a group he had encountered on his initial voyage to America. In the Moravians, he witnessed for the first time a devout evangelical faith that embraced personal assurance of salvation and a clear sense of service. Back in London, unsure of both his spiritual condition and his calling, he sought the counsel of his Moravian friend, Peter Böhler. The insightful and encouraging words of Böhler are indicative of the help Wesley received at this crucial time. Wesley had asked if he should cease preaching because he did not feel he had authentic faith. Böhler advised, "Preach faith *till* you have it, and then, because you have it, you *will* preach faith."[14] This counsel would prove to be prophetic.

Böhler and Wesley continued to dialogue. After several months of spiritual and vocational introspection, in May 1738, his spiritual "opening" came. Böhler insisted that it was possible to *experience* a living and dynamic personal faith and be fully assured of God's free pardon of all sins. Wesley wondered if there were living witnesses to such an experience, and Böhler produced three the following day. Wesley was convinced and resolved to seek that assurance until he found it. Within five days his quest was satisfied. He had the spiritual awakening that is so frequently associated with him, and is often termed his "conversion." His journal describes the events of the day beginning with readings from 2 Peter 1:4 and Mark 12:34 ("Thou art not far from the kingdom of God"), followed by an afternoon service at St. Paul's where the anthem (based on Psalm 130:1-4,7-8) spoke to him, and finally attending a gathering of devout Moravian Christians in Nettleton Court, Aldersgate Street.

What happened that evening brought the personal, spiritual awareness he so longed for. At the meeting there was a reading from Luther's preface to his commentary on the Epistle to the Romans. In it Luther describes how *faith* prevents us from being charged with sin and transforms us so we can do what the law requires.[15] It was a concise answer to all Wesley had been wrestling with regarding the penalty and the power of sin. In words that have become familiar, Wesley articulates his experience:

> About a quarter before nine, while he [Luther] was describing the change which God works in the heart through faith in Christ, I felt my heart strangely warmed. I felt I did trust in Christ, Christ alone for salvation, and an assurance was given me that he had taken away *my* sins, even *mine*, and saved *me* from the law of sin and death.[16]

Wesley's italics reveal how deeply personal this moment was.

For many years both Wesley's followers and scholars have debated exactly what this experience was. Many have taken the position that it was conclusively his "conversion," before which Wesley was not really a Christian. This may be somewhat anachronistic, reading a late nineteenth and twentieth century evangelical (even fundamentalist) interpretation into Wesley's experience. A number of facts temper that view. Nehemiah Curnock quotes Wesley in 1772 as saying to Charles regarding the Oxford years, "I did then walk closely with God, and redeemed the time. But what have I gained during these thirty years?"[17] For another example, many years later (1766) Wesley wrote Charles that he did not "love God," "never did," and never "believed in the Christian sense of the word."[18] Such a comment makes clear that different definitions are inferred for the same term at different times in his life. Being a "Christian" could mean being justified by God's grace, which many can claim, or it could mean *completely* living up to all the values Christianity entails, which none can claim. Wesley himself differentiates between his experiences before and after Aldersgate with the terms, "faith of a servant" and "faith of a son," but he acknowledges that he did have faith. He does not qualify that the former is inadequate for salvation, but leaves the role of judge to God, as he does with those who have never heard the gospel.

Perhaps the most telling perspective on this matter is presented by Reginald Ward, who lets Wesley's literary treatment reveal whether or not Aldersgate is the most important aspect of Wesley's life (as a unilateral "evangelical conversion" would imply). Ward states, "By keeping the *Journal* to within a few months of his death ... Wesley reduced the conversion narrative to an insignificant proportion of a huge work running to a million words, of which the principle theme was his service to the Kingdom of God and the gathering of the Methodist people."[19] This statement modestly places Wesley's Aldersgate experience in the larger context of his entire life.

Aldersgate is relevant to this study because it was crucial in Wesley's life and clearly affected his later efforts against slavery. However, caution must be applied to avoid either overemphasizing or undervaluing Wesley's Aldersgate experience. While it was important, it was not so important that it overshadowed the rest of Wesley's life. It was certainly a turning point in his life and ministry but that truth can be maintained without having to conclusively define it.[20] The point is that the importance of Aldersgate is not dependent on how it is defined (conversion, awakening, heart warming), but in the fact that it contextualized former aspects of his journey and energized his ensuing ministry. That obedient ministry was, in Wesley's thinking, the essence of Methodism — and obedience would push him to pursue social issues such as slavery. As Wesley describes, Aldersgate was the warming of his heart to the freeing, transforming gospel, and to an authentic, world-changing ministry that continued for the rest of his life. As such, the experience can stand on its own as a very significant spiritual encounter without having to be proscribed by a definition.

The major events of Wesley's life come into focus when they are seen as parts of a spiritual tapestry. His approach to ordination in 1725 sowed the seeds of his dominant message, the love of God and neighbour (Christian perfection), and brought about the discipline and dogged determination that were so characteristic of him. Later, this was essential when he began to advocate for the slave. The discouragement of his two years in Georgia brought him to the realization that his own resources were limited. In this time he was brought to the end of himself and came face to face with the truth that he needed a greater source of energy than he could generate by himself. This was necessary for him and for the people he wanted to encourage (for example, William Wilberforce) when facing the incredible odds of popular opinion or the powerful West Indian lobby. Aldersgate opened his awareness to the intimate and personal relationship with God that empowered the commitment of 1725 and addressed the loneliness and alienation of the Georgia years. It opened the door to the kind of relationship with God that would give meaning and sustenance to the commitment he had made in 1725. It sustained him in difficult times and levelled him in good times.

These three pivotal experiences brought about a dynamic interaction of commitment, accurate self awareness and spiritual resources. They could well be termed a genuine Wesleyan synthesis — and without any one of them Wesley's work would not have developed as it did. He certainly would not have embraced both the evangelical and social dimensions that made his work effective and relevant to the world of the eighteenth century and that continue to make it relevant in an ever changing world.

Out of the broader spiritual experience that includes his ordination, Georgia experience and Aldersgate, Wesley became sensitized to the generally unacknowledged problem of slavery — and then was able to have a major impact on that problem. In this he stands apart from his contemporaries. He was the first major religious leader, known worldwide, to take a clear stand against slavery and thus have a distinctive influence on the abolition of slavery and the slave trade. The substance and development of that argument form the content of this book.

We turn now to the specific engagement of John Wesley in the issue of slavery, beginning with a chronology of his antislavery journey.

chapter 2

John Wesley's antislavery journey

For much of his life John Wesley was interested in the issue of slavery. At times he merely mentions items or events which caught his interest. At other times he becomes deeply involved. The chronology of his contact with slavery creates a setting from which to explore the development of his thought and the extent of his involvement. The following overview is relatively complete, although not exhaustive.

Wesley's first intellectual exposure to slavery seems to have occurred in 1726, when he was twenty-three years old. The year after his ordination as a deacon he read a play entitled *Oroonoko* by Thomas Southerne. The play was based on Aphra Behn's novel, *Oroonoko*, the story of an African prince who started a slave rebellion after being kidnapped and sold into slavery.[1] Reflective of the time, both the book and the play focus on the unjust treatment of nobility but not on the institution of slavery. Wesley does not comment on the issue or the play, but it is significant that this reading was his introduction to the topic of slavery.

Wesley in America (1736-1738)

Nine years later, in 1735, Wesley went to America under the auspices of the SPG. He was accompanied by Charles and other members of the Holy Club. His assigned task was to replace the Rev. Quincy in ministering to members of the Church of England in the colonies, particularly in Georgia. Although the use of slave labour was against the rules of the Georgia Trustees,[2] a letter from Burton to Wesley mentions the goal of converting the slaves in Purrysburg, South Carolina.[3] Wesley also saw his work to include evangelizing the "heathen," a term that for him included both Native Americans and slaves.

Wesley's two years in America provided his first personal contact with slaves. Firsthand observation of the extreme punishment and murder of slaves confronted him with a reality he would not have known in England and it aroused his unequivocal opposition. He supported General James Oglethorpe who enforced the Georgia policy of not allowing slavery in Georgia.[4] He also opposed the movement to change the law and introduce slavery in Georgia. His conflict with one Dr. Tailfer, a supporter of slavery in the new colony, related to slavery among other issues.[5]

Charles' descriptions of encounters with slavery give a view of their shared experience. As members of the Holy Club, and brothers, the two conferred often even though they were stationed in different towns. Their abhorrent response to slavery is caught in Charles' journal entry for August 2, 1736. They were together in Charleston on the date of this entry.

> I had observed much, and heard more, of the cruelty of masters towards their negroes; but now I received an authentic account of some horrid instances thereof. The giving a child a slave of its own age to tyrannize over, to beat and abuse out of sport, was, I myself saw, a common

practice. Nor is it strange, being thus trained up in cruelty, they should afterwards arrive at so great perfection in it; that Mr. Star, a gentleman I often met at Mr. Lasserre's, should, as he himself informed L., first nail up a negro by the ears, then order him to be whipped in the severest manner, and then to have scalding water thrown over him, so that the poor creature could not stir for four months after. Another much applauded punishment is, drawing their slaves' teeth. One Colonel Lynch is universally known to have cut off a poor negro's legs; and to kill several of them every year by his barbarities.

It were endless to recount all the shocking instances of diabolical cruelty which these men (as they call themselves) daily practise upon their fellow-creatures; and that on the most trivial occasions. I shall only mention one more, related to me by a Swiss gentleman, Mr. Zouberbühler, an eye-witness, of Mr. Hill, a dancing-master in Charleston. He whipped a she-slave so long, that she fell down at his feet for dead. When, by the help of a physician, she was so far recovered as to show signs of life, he repeated the whipping with equal rigour, and concluded with dropping hot sealing-wax upon her flesh. Her crime was overfilling a tea-cup.[6]

Not only was Charles appalled by such inhuman cruelty, he noted with disgust the legal system which countenanced and furthered such treatment:

> These horrid cruelties are the less to be wondered at, because the government itself, in effect, countenances and allows them to kill their slaves, by the ridiculous penalty appointed for it, of about seven pounds sterling, half of which is usually saved by the criminal's informing against himself. This I can look upon as no other than a public act to indemnify murder.[7]

Such a scene and the lack of legal protection would certainly have made a lasting impression on both John and Charles Wesley. How could such a graphic image be erased from one's memory? There is little doubt that this and similar experiences would eventually move John to invest himself in the cause of the slave.

When given the opportunity to teach slaves John responded enthusiastically. The day before Charles' journal entry, John preached at Charleston and took note that there were "several negroes at church." He discovered that one of the women attended church regularly and he began to talk about religion with her. He was disappointed that she was not more knowledgeable about the Christian faith. He laments in his journal, "O God, where are Thy tender mercies? Are they not over all Thy works? When shall the Sun of Righteousness arise on these outcasts of men, with healing in His wings!"[8]

Several weeks later, John Wesley notes in his journal that he read *The Negro's Advocate*. This was probably Morgan Godwyn's 1680 publication, *The Negro's and Indian's Advocate, suing for their admission into the church*.[9] Wesley would certainly be interested in the topic because he was a clergyman with strong desires for evangelism.

Months later, in April 1737, Wesley had more conversations with black persons. Lodging at the home of Rev. Thompson in South Carolina Wesley had a significant conversation with a young female slave. Before coming to America she had lived as a slave in a minister's home in Barbados. She too had attended church regularly, so Wesley was intrigued to discover what she knew of Christianity. Once again he was surprised and disappointed to learn that she knew little or nothing about the Christian faith. He told her some basics of theology and was pleased with her enthusiastic response. He noted, "the attention with which this poor creature listened to instruction is inexpressible." He was impressed that the following day she remembered everything they had discussed.[10]

The horseback journey to and from Thompson's home gave additional opportunity for conversation with one of Thompson's servants, probably a male slave. He escorted Wesley twenty miles to the home and again on his journey away. On that same excursion Wesley met an older black man who had substantial knowledge of Christianity. He then met a young Negro[11] lad who accompanied him to Purrysburg. Such conversations would have been possible in South Carolina, where slavery was legal, but not in Georgia where it was still illegal. So the trips to South Carolina were formative for Wesley's contact with slavery.

From these few days Wesley had an unusual amount of interaction with slaves and seems to have been extremely interested in their experiences. He mentions dialogue about religion with them. He was also encouraged about their interest and ability to learn, but was distraught that Purrysburg had embraced slavery. He registered his disdain: "Alas for those whose lives were here vilely cast away, through oppression, through divers plagues and troubles! O earth! how long wilt thou hide blood? How long wilt thou cover thy slain?"[12]

Such experiences caused Wesley to begin considering ways to educate slaves. He mentally devised a simple method for plantation slaves:

> ...perhaps one of the easiest and shortest ways to instruct the American negroes in Christianity would be, first, to inquire after and find out some of the most serious of the planters. Then, having inquired of them which of their slaves *were best inclined* and understood English, to go to them from plantation to plantation, staying as long as appeared necessary at each.[13]

Wesley's return voyage to England (December 1737 into early 1738) found him teaching two young Negro lads about Christianity.[14] 1738 saw the colonists of Georgia petitioning for slavery to be permitted there — and by 1740 their desire was granted.[15]

Wesley's experience in America marked the beginning of his serious thinking about slavery. There is evidence that he and Charles earned a reputation for speaking and teaching against it in Georgia and Carolina even when the latter had booming slave traffic and labour, and public opinion increasingly supported slavery. Frederica, where both John and Charles worked, carries the distinction of being the site of the first protest against the introduction of slavery in America. This occurred in 1749, some eleven years after John Wesley left, but possibly reflected the influence of his teaching.[16]

Back in England

After his return from America several references to slavery or Negroes occur in Wesley's writing. The *Journal* entry for June 29, 1740 records that Wesley "collected for the Negro school."[17] The school is not specified, but was probably a small, private enterprise associated with a ministry in America. In writing *Explanatory Notes Upon the New Testament*, published some years later, Wesley expounds "man-stealers," as "the worst of all thieves, in comparison of whom Highwaymen and House-breakers are innocent! What then are most Traders in Negroes, Procurers of Servants for America, and all who list Soldiers by Lies, Tricks, or Inticements."[18] It is clear that the slave was still Wesley's concern.

Correspondence with Samuel Davies (a friend, Presbyterian preacher and later president of Princeton) relates this concern. Between 1755 and 1757 Wesley sent Davies books (hymns and psalms) to be given to slaves. It is likely that the money raised for a Negro school, mentioned above, was sent to Davies. As a means of making his preachers aware of his concern for evangelism and teaching among slaves, Wesley published Davies' letters in his *Journal*.[19]

In 1757 an interesting reference occurs in Wesley's treatise on *Original Sin*. He quotes a Dr. Jennings who subscribed to the "curse of Ham" theory of slavery. The theory comes from the story of Noah and his son, Ham, who saw his father in his drunken nakedness. Following this Noah cursed Ham's son, Canaan, to slavery (Gen. 9:24-27). In the eighteenth century this narrative was used as a popular biblical justification for slavery. By contrast, Wesley does not cite this text to justify slavery, but to indicate how it began. It served as an analogy of original sin and how all people "suffer... by the sentence inflicted on our first parents."[20]

In 1758 Wesley preached in Wandsworth at the home of Nathaniel Gilbert and noted the "awakening" of two of Gilbert's "servants." Ten months later Wesley was again in Wandsworth and notes that he "baptized two negroes belonging to Mr. Gilbert."[21] While there is no mention of Wesley raising the slavery issue, it appears that Gilbert was a gentle and very humane slave owner. Back in Antigua he served as chairman of the Antigua Assembly and, because he was known as the friend of slaves, was not honoured by the Assembly when he resigned. Two years after the baptism Gilbert began preaching. The result was that, by his death in 1774, Methodism in Antigua had grown to some 200, including black and white members.[22] As a friend and correspondent of Wesley, as well as Anthony Benezet (a Philadelphia Quaker and antislavery activist), it is likely that Gilbert's interaction with these men influenced his attitude toward slavery and his sensitivity to the spiritual and temporal well-being of his own slaves and the slaves on the island.

Entering the cause (1772)

The landscape of Wesley's antislavery journey was dramatically altered in 1772. Two individuals are of critical importance in this development: Anthony Benezet and Granville Sharp. Benezet was a Quaker schoolteacher in Philadelphia and a man of sensitive social conscience. He had begun to write against slavery in the 1750s and is credited with recruiting Thomas Clarkson, Benjamin Franklin and Benjamin Rush to the cause.[23] Granville Sharp of London was the primary activist in England who worked through the legal system for the rights and freedom of slaves from the late 1760s. He influenced the landmark court decisions which made slavery illegal in England proper. Sharp and Benezet corresponded and republished each other's antislavery writings. They also worked tirelessly to encourage anyone who could help in the fight against slavery.

The influence of these two men reached Wesley in 1772. In February of that year he read a tract that would bring about his commitment to throw his weight decisively against slavery. The tract was the work of Anthony Benezet and provided by Sharp.

The sequence began in early 1772 when Sharp supplied Wesley, at Wesley's request, with a bundle of antislavery material, including Benezet's tract — probably *Some Historical Account of Guinea*, 1771, but possibly an earlier tract such as *A Caution and Warning to Great Britain*, 1766, or even *A Short Account of that Part of Africa Inhabited by the Negroes*, 1762. Because this was such an important event it raises questions about how the process began. Did Wesley initiate with his request to Sharp? Had Sharp made earlier contact with Wesley? If so, had Benezet suggested to Sharp that he contact Wesley? What is known is that Benezet had already written to Sharp in May 1772 of his long-standing desire to be in contact with "such well-disposed persons in England" who "are concerned to prevent [the slave trade's] continuance." That could imply that he had earlier suggested to Sharp that he make contact with the Methodist leader. It is not likely that Benezet contacted Wesley directly as Wesley's first mention of him, after reading his tract, is worded in the unfamiliar term: an "honest Quaker."

Wesley gives no hint about why he made the request to Sharp at that particular time. Speculation can be made on the possibility that something revived his memories of slavery in America, or that an event in the news caused him to want to know more about the slave trade. Perhaps he had been reading about Sharp's work with runaway slaves. It may be that Sharp, while acting on Benezet's desires, contacted Wesley at an earlier date, in a general, introductory fashion. Later on, Sharp's work caught Wesley's attention when it was published in the news. Perhaps several influences occurred in the same period resulting in Wesley's desire to know more of the current state of slavery. Regardless, it is easy to understand why it was Sharp that Wesley contacted. Granville Sharp was known as a strong force in antislavery. The landmark Somerset case of 1772 was already in progress in 1771 and in 1769 Sharp had published his research from the earlier case with Jonathan Strong, *A Representation of the Injustice and Dangerous Tendency of Tolerating Slavery ... in England*. Both men were Anglicans and it is certain that Sharp knew of Wesley and almost certain that Wesley knew of Sharp.

Whatever triggered his request, the fact remains that Wesley requested material from Sharp, Sharp supplied Benezet's tract and Benezet's tract influenced Wesley to take a very active and visible role in the antislavery cause. Wesley's journal entry states:

> Wednesday, [February] 12. In returning, I read a very different book, published by an honest Quaker, on that execrable sum of all villainies, commonly called the 'slave trade.' I read of nothing like it in the heathen world, whether ancient or modern. And it infinitely exceeds, in every instance of barbarity, whatever Christian slaves suffer in Mahometan [Muslim] countries.[24]

After reading the tract in February, not only did Wesley enter the cause of the slave, but a relationship and correspondence between Wesley and Benezet began.

Of particular interest is the speed with which the succeeding events occurred. Once the process was set in motion, the chronological pieces fit together quickly. Only three months after Wesley's reading of Benezet, Benezet wrote Sharp, referring to Wesley as his "friend," who, "promises he will consult with thee about the expediency of some weekly publication…on…the slave trade."[25] In light of the time required for transatlantic mail delivery, the May letter indicates a rapid sequence of events — only twelve weeks from Wesley's reading of Benezet to Benezet's mentioning him as his "friend." The rapidity of Wesley's response and correspondence with Benezet[26] also seems to indicate that Wesley had already been thinking about the slavery issue. Reading the tract was the catalyst that set him in motion to act. It would be less than two years before a draft of John Wesley's own antislavery tract was in Sharp's hands (January 1774).[27]

From 1773 to 1774 Wesley also became acquainted with two Africans, Little Ephraim Robin-John and his nephew, Ancona Robin Robin-John. These two Africans were captured in their homeland — snared on the pretense of helping them negotiate peace between two African groups — and placed in slavery in the West Indies and Virginia. They eventually were taken to Bristol and gained their freedom by a warrant from Lord Mansfield in 1774. (Mansfield had been the judge in the famous James Somerset case that Granville Sharp brought to trial in 1772.) In Bristol, Charles Wesley ministered to them and baptized them. John Wesley also had contact with them and ministered to them. They returned to Africa and began sharing their faith and reading the Bible to their fellow Africans.[28] (A very interesting coincidence is that they were taken to Bristol on the *Greyhound*, the name of the ship John Newton had served on some twenty years before.) Although it is difficult to pinpoint the exact time, if John Wesley's meeting and hearing the heart-rending story of the Robin-Johns occurred in 1773, it may have been what triggered his writing the tract in late 1773.

While definitive cause and effect are difficult to determine, due to the number of gaps which exist in the correspondence that has been preserved from that time, the order of events from letters and journal entries can be established:

- February 12, 1772 — Wesley reads the "book" by an "honest Quaker."
- May 14, 1772 — Benezet writes Sharp and mentions that for a long time he has desired to be in contact with those in England who can affect the slave trade. Later in the letter he refers to Wesley as his "friend," who will consult with Sharp about a weekly publication on the slave trade.
- November 9, 1773 — Sworn deposition by Little Ephraim Robin-John in Bristol. Sometime in that general time period, 1773 or early 1774, the Wesleys came to know them and ministered to them.
- January 7, 1774 — Sharp writes Benezet recalling that "some time ago," probably in early 1772, Wesley had written him of his desire to write against the slave trade after which Sharp "furnished him with a large bundle of Books and

Papers." Then "a few days ago," Sharp receives Wesley's manuscript of *Thoughts Upon Slavery*. This letter seems to survey events of two to three years.

Wesley's "weekly publication, in the newspapers, on the origin, nature, and dreadful effects of the slave trade" that Benezet mentioned to Sharp in May of 1772 took a completely different turn. Instead, Wesley wrote and published a substantive and effective tract, *Thoughts Upon Slavery*, in January or early February 1774.

Further evidence that the tract Wesley read in February of 1772 was *Some Historical Account* is the fact that his *Thoughts Upon Slavery* is heavily dependent on that tract. It is unlikely that Wesley would be so moved by a different tract and then base his own work on *Some Historical Account* without mentioning his acquaintance with it.

Wesley was sixty-eight years old when he first read Benezet's tract. He was seventy when his own tract was released. It is a tribute to his energy, but also a clear indicator of how important he viewed this cause, that once aware of the role he could play he invested himself so actively. For the next nineteen years, until his death, he continued his efforts by preaching, writing and encouraging those in the antislavery cause or by persuading others to join.

Thoughts Upon Slavery: "Light collected in a Focus"

Wesley's tract was his strongest statement and most influential work against slavery. It was the unequivocal mark of casting his lot with those who were committed to end the slave trade and slavery itself. While his other antislavery activities were influential, it was the tract that would serve as a declaration of his position once and for all. From the time of its publication there could be no question of where he stood. His sermons, subsequent writing and correspondence continued the themes, developed tangential ideas and re-emphasized the truths he had articulated in *Thoughts Upon Slavery*. By eighteenth-century norms, it was a modest composition, fifty-three pages in length (twenty pages in today's typescript). Its brevity and initial price of one shilling made it accessible to nearly anyone. He explained his typical brevity, not specifically related to this tract, in a *Journal* comment in 1769 (February 17), "Why do persons who treat the same subjects with me write so much larger books? Of many reasons, is not this the chief? We do not write with the same view. Their principal end is to get money; my only one to do good." The brief tract received favourable reviews in the *Monthly Review* and in the *Gentleman's Magazine*.[29] The tract's accessibility and the public's response to it are seen in the fact that it reached three editions in the first year, was reprinted in Dublin the following year, had a fifth edition produced in 1792, and also had at least thirteen editions published in America within thirty years.[30]

Not only was it accessible, but it was persuasive. After reading it, James Ramsay commented that had he read Wesley's tract before writing his own he would have "written in a more warm and decisive manner."[31] Ramsay, a contemporary of Wesley had been stationed for six years in the West Indies as a Royal Navy surgeon and then stayed on for nineteen more years as a minister until 1781. He wrote several pieces related to slavery and the slave trade and played a role in recruiting the British parliamentarian William Wilberforce to the cause.[32]

Wesley's tract was sent to every Methodist Society in England,[33] as well as to people of prominence such as Dr. Benjamin Rush, America's first Surgeon General (Sharp sent him two copies[34]). Rush was a personal friend of Anthony Benezet, who had recruited him to the antislavery cause. The tract would have been an encouragement and a reinforcement of Rush's antislavery work; the previous year he had commented positively on the clergy bearing testimony against slavery.[35] Although we do not know how it arrived there, Wesley's tract also became a part of George Washington's library, which contained some 354 books.[36]

In spite of its conciseness, the tract was sufficiently thorough and well organized, in typical Wesley fashion. It was divided into five sections, beginning with a description and brief history of slavery, both from antiquity and in the present African form. Section II describes the parts of Africa from which slaves were taken and the positive nature, civilization and government of the Africans in their homeland. Section III elucidates the methods of procuring slaves, how they are transported and eventually treated in slavery. The brutal inhumanity of every stage is clearly described, even to the point of how the law offers no protection: the wanton murder of a slave produces a mere fine of £15. Section IV lays out and demolishes the supposed justifications for slavery, including laws which permit it. Two arguments stand out in this regard: the argument of "natural justice," which relates to the philosophical and historical bases of slavery, and the argument of "necessity," which relates to the economic and nationalistic (glory of a nation) bases of slavery.

In Section V Wesley makes his application personal through a direct appeal to those connected with slavery. He states that because of Parliament's involvement with issues they deem more important, it is more efficient to appeal directly to captains in the slave trade, merchants "engaged in the slave-trade," and all slave holders. His appeal contains reference to the humanity of the slave (they are equally human), and the humanity of the slave trader (they are capable of compassion). He does not shrink from using the threat of eternal judgement. He challenges his readers to "show yourself a man," rather than "more savage than a lion or a bear." This is evident from the laws of nature, not only through revelation, so it applies to all persons, not just Christians. Before quoting a verse from one of Charles' hymns, the tract is brought to a close with a powerful prayer that the God of love, the Father of all would arise and "burst ... all their chains in sunder; more especially the chains of their sins!" and "make them free, that they may be free indeed!"[37]

The role that Anthony Benezet played in Wesley's antislavery writing is made clear by the fact that Wesley's tract was heavily dependent on Benezet's 1771 *Some Historical Account of Guinea*. More than half of *Thoughts Upon Slavery* is taken directly from Benezet: directly quoting, paraphrasing or utilizing the ideas.[38] In some ways the more concise tract that Wesley produced was an improvement on Benezet's work. While Benezet did not organize his material as tightly around easily perceived themes and gave the impression of repetition, Wesley extracted cogent material and kept it focused on his points, which developed into a strong appeal. In fact, Sharp complimented Wesley's treatment, particularly because he had reduced the *corpus* and thereby increased its "power and effect." He described it as "Light collected in a Focus" which may be "felt with a living Flame."[39]

While *Some Historical Account* was foundational to Wesley's tract, he also used a few parts from Benezet's *A Short Account of That Part of Africa Inhabited by the Negroes, 1762*. In his excellent analysis, Frank Baker points out that Wesley also utilized two or three other sources.[40] These included the work of Francis Hargrave, Granville Sharp and possibly William Blackstone. Hargrave was one of five men who served as legal council in the landmark Somerset case of 1772.[41] Sharp's 1769 *Representation of the Injustice and Dangerous Tendency of Tolerating Slavery; or of Admitting the Least Claim of Private Property in the Persons of Men, in England* was his treatise following his legal work on the 1765 case of Jonathan Strong and supplied Wesley's introductory material on the nature of slavery. Blackstone wrote legal commentaries, which Wesley was familiar with (according to Baker), but Wesley may have utilized the extract found in Sharp's work. It is interesting that Wesley cites Hargrave and Blackstone, but not Sharp or Benezet, although he does mention the numerous writers that Benezet collected in his tract.

The antislavery triumvirate: a "living Flame"

The result of Wesley's tract was not only that it thrust him into the antislavery contest, but it also facilitated new relationships and correspondence with Sharp and Benezet, among others. Benezet had long hoped for people of influence to join the cause. He had been disappointed that George Whitefield, with all his prominence, did not add his support.[42] John Wesley joining the ranks was a welcome addition. While Wesley spoke sardonically of the "great triumvirate," Rousseau, Voltaire and Hume,[43] in a real sense Benezet, Sharp and Wesley formed an effective "triumvirate" in the antislavery movement: Benezet, the popularizer of Enlightenment thought with application to slavery was the recruiter and supporter; Sharp, the persistent and methodical mind who worked tirelessly through the maze of legal technicalities and delays on behalf of oppressed individuals had the goal of effecting change in the court system; Wesley, the respected and beloved founder of the renewal movement that was sweeping Britain and America, affected the thousands who read his every word and respected his moral and spiritual leadership.

The members of this triumvirate provided genuine support and encouragement to each other. Their correspondence reveals how they valued each other for the cause and how they welcomed each other to what they considered to be the most significant moral challenge of their world. Through the three of them we, more than two centuries later, sense the "light collected in a focus" which burst into a "living Flame." Their work, especially when considered as parts of a cooperative whole was foundational to the practical success that the succeeding generation experienced. Although they did not live to see the victory they were driven toward, it was their work, and the effect of their combined effort, that kindled the flame that ultimately purified western civilization of the brutality, barbarity, rationalization and egocentricity inherent in slavery.

How did they work together? As seen above, the combined efforts of Sharp and Benezet enlisted Wesley to the cause, supplying him with the material necessary to ignite his imagination and evoke his intention to exert influence against slavery. Once Wesley's draft was prepared, Sharp read it, advised and encouraged him.

> Rev[d] Sir, I have perused, with great satisfaction, your little Tract against Slavery, and am far from thinking any alteration is necessary: You have very judiciously brought together and digested, under proper heads of Evidence against that abominable oppression, some of the principal Facts cited by my Friend Mr. Benezet and others; which you corroborate with some circumstances within your own knowledge; and have very sensibly drawn up the

Sum of the whole argument into a small compass, which infinitely increases the power and effect of it, like Light collected in a Focus; and that it may be as sensibly felt with a living Flame by those who inconsiderately oppose themselves, is the sincere wish of Revd Sir,
Your most obedient and obliged Servant,
  Granville Sharp.

P.S. I apprehend, as the Tract is short, that it will appear to most advantage in 12mo but with respect to the mode of communicating it, I am at a loss to advise. A New Edition of Dr. Rushes little Tract is about to be printed by Dilly in the Poultry, with other Papers relating to the same subject, which collection would be greatly enriched by your Tract: nevertheless the latter will certainly have much more weight with many persons if it be separately printed and published with your name.[44]

It was well that Wesley published separately as Sharp advised because Benjamin Rush's tract was rejected by Dilly due to the low sales of such material. As soon as Wesley's tract was published, Sharp began sending copies to others, including Benjamin Rush.[45]

Benezet was equally responsive and encouraging to Wesley. He received a copy of Wesley's tract sometime after May 9, 1774,[46] no doubt sent either by Wesley or Sharp,[47] and was delighted. So pleased with it was he that he immediately had it republished in Philadelphia and wrote Wesley on May 23:

> The Tract thou has lately published, entitled, *Thoughts on Slavery*, afforded me much satisfaction. I was the more especially glad to see it, as the circumstances of the times made it necessary that something on that most weighty subject, not large, but striking and pathetic, should now be published. Wherefore I immediately agreed with the Printer to have it republished here.[48]

The spirit of the letter is that of an ally in a cause. Benezet shares relevant information probably in hopes of future publications by Wesley. The letter is detailed and painstaking, nearly 1,400 words in length. He discusses the expansion of America west of the Mississippi and his fear that land which could be used as a human refuge would instead extend slavery. He even offers a corrective to a misleading generalization in Wesley's tract regarding the people of one African nation. Benezet seems eager that their team effort be as strong and accurate as possible. Of course, this part of Wesley's tract was taken directly from Benezet's tract, so it was appropriate for him to note the inaccuracy, especially in light of the possibility of future editions. He then mentions the death of their mutual friend, Nathaniel Gilbert and copies two paragraphs from Gilbert's correspondence. The letter continues with examples of the inhumanity of slave treatment, material that Wesley will incorporate in his own, future correspondence. Benezet concludes by copying a paragraph he wrote to others in the cause about the degradation and eternal consequences that slavery works on slave owners. The unmistakable tenor of the letter is mutuality. It breathes collegiality and in offering data, it is apparent that he is giving encouragement for the continued efforts of his new colleague.

The relationship is again reflected in Wesley's letter, undated, but probably written to Benezet in 1774:

> Mr. Oglethorp you know went so far as to begin settling a colony without negroes, but at length the voice of those villains prevailed who sell their country and their God for gold, who laugh at human nature and compassion, and defy all religion, but that of getting money. It is certainly our duty to do all in our power to check this growing evil and something may be done by spreading those tracts which place it in a true light. But I fear it will not be stopped till all the kingdoms of this earth become the kingdoms of our God.[49]

Wesley's reference to new settlements (Georgia) and the difficulty of prevailing against those who value money over compassion and religion indicate that this letter may be his brief response to the Benezet letter (May 23, 1774) he had received.[50]

Their correspondence gives an important and clear picture of the interchange and cooperation these three men experienced. There is no question that they saw themselves linked together in a common and important global cause. They considered it their good fortune, even the work of providence, that they had been brought together.

Wesley and plagiarism

Such interaction and relationship sheds light on another issue, the question of plagiarism. As noted above, Wesley relied heavily on Benezet's work for his own tract, extracting numerous quotations wholesale, paraphrasing other sections and taking key ideas. He did this with no acknowledgement to Benezet, only mentioning the authors Benezet had used. The process is so obvious that one of Wesley's biographers, Stanley Ayling blatantly accuses Wesley of plagiarism.[51] Intensifying the issue, this was not the only time Wesley so utilized the material of others. His *Calm Address to the American Colonies* incorporated much of Samuel Johnson's *Taxation No Tyranny*. Was Wesley a plagiarist? Did he disregard the property of others to pursue his own ends?

In order to answer that question two perspectives should be considered: the response of those whose material was used, in this case Benezet, and the literary conventions of the eighteenth century. Fortunately, we have a clear picture of the response of both Granville Sharp and Anthony Benezet. Their response is crucial to an assessment and it is accessible to us.

Sharp was a person of detail and a man of unbending principle. He never relaxed a principle to achieve an end, but would go to any length to bring about a principle's proper end. Where a person's right was concerned he would leave no stone unturned, as evidenced by his successful work to reclaim the peerage of his supervisor. He knew Benezet's work well, having republished it himself and he read Wesley's draft before publication. Sharp's response to Wesley's tract was completely positive. He recognized the use of Benezet and gave no cautionary word. Rather, he complimented how Wesley organized it so that it was more concise. In brief, he was satisfied with Wesley's work and was "far from thinking any alteration is necessary."

But Benezet was the rightful owner of the copied material. What was his response to Wesley's "plagiarism?" It is equally — or even more — positive than Sharp's. In his words, Wesley's tract "afforded me much satisfaction" and he was "more especially glad to see it."[52] So much so that his first action was to republish the tract in Philadelphia. And it was produced under Wesley's name, even though much of the material was Benezet's! This fact alone should be ample evidence that Benezet had no thought that his property or right had been violated. One who feels defrauded by a plagiarist does not compliment and republish the plagiarized material.

Samuel Johnson wrote a letter to Wesley after seeing Wesley's use of his material. He thanked Wesley and added: "to have gained such a mind as yours may justly confirm me in my own opinions."[53] It has been said that this may have been Johnson's magnanimous way of dealing with an obvious indiscretion, or that it was his satire to call attention to the problem. On the other hand, he could have been pleased that this revered man used his words. Which is more likely may depend on the literary conventions of the day.

It appears that in the eighteenth century the free exchange of information and actual documents was common. We need look no further than the interchange between Sharp and Benezet. In 1772 Benezet abridged Sharp's 1769 *Representation* and then wrote to Sharp: "I should have wrote thee thereon, had I known how to direct; particularly as I had taken the freedom to republish a part of thy acceptable, and I trust serviceable, treatise." The point here is that Benezet wrote Sharp *after* he had done the work. Welcoming similar treatment he mentions that he is enclosing some of his own work: "I doubt not but it may be amended by some more able hand on your side of the water." He then returns to the theme of his treatment of Sharp's work: "I trust thou wilt excuse the freedom we have taken in abridging it, even tho' thou should not quite approve our reasons for so doing."[54]

Sharp's reply leaves no doubt about his feelings, as well as the practice of the day. He wrote:

> You need not have made an apology for having abridged my book. It is sufficient satisfaction to me to find that you thought it capable of doing some service in a cause which we have both of us much at heart.
>
> I not only approve, sir, of the abridgment you have made of my arguments in particular, but of your whole performance. Some copies of it arrived here very opportunely, just before the case of James Somerset came to a hearing in the Court of King's Bench; and, by Dr. Fothergill's kindness, I was enabled immediately to dispose of six. [...]
>
> I had thought indeed of reprinting it, as I did your former tract in 1768, but Mr. Clark, the printer, was luckily beforehand with me; so that I had opportunity of purchasing more copies to distribute.[55]

Two points come through clearly in these letters. There were no hard and fast rules about the use of material. Copyright, as we know it, was not yet a practice,[56] so the charge of plagiarism is something of an anachronism. Added to that is the matter of purpose. Wesley did not write to earn money or to gain literary attention. Rather, he wrote for one purpose: to do good.[57] Of course, Benezet and Sharp had the same purpose, and the result was that they highly valued any legitimate means they could use to spread the word about slavery. If someone else's work could be made to serve that purpose, all who were involved in the line of transmission would be pleased. The originator of material would feel honoured.[58] If the material could be improved in order to more effectively draw others into the cause, so much the better. When the cause was at stake, there was no room for proprietary pride or what they would have considered pettiness.

Was Wesley a plagiarist? Was Benezet or Sharp? Hardly. They were men on a mission. They would use their abilities to the fullest to accomplish that mission and they would avail themselves of whatever resources were known. They would rejoice at every bit of work that contributed to the overthrow of slavery. The lives of thousands of Africans depended on it; the souls of thousands of Europeans and Americans depended on it. In that context the very question of plagiarism slips quietly into a different discussion and a different century.

Wesley's journey continued

Thoughts Upon Slavery was a decisive event in Wesley's antislavery journey and it related in many ways to his other activities in the cause from that point on. We turn now to his activities from the time of the publication of this tract.

In October 1774, the *Monthly Review* published a reader's negative response to the tract. This reader expressed doubt about Wesley's description of the brutal treatment of slaves, citing his own kind behaviour to slaves. In November Wesley replied in the *Monthly Review*, citing more support for his case. He quoted the advertisements for runaway slaves that Benezet had sent him from the *Williamsburg Gazette* in Virginia:

> Run away in Prince George, on the 10th instant, a lusty Negro, named Bob, &c. &c. (describing him)… The said fellow is outlawed, and I will give ten pounds reward for his head severed from his body, and forty shillings if brought alive.

And a North Carolina paper:

> Run away last November from the subscriber, Kent River, a Negro-fellow, named Zeb, aged 36 years. As he is outlawed, I will pay twenty pounds Pch out of what the Act of Assembly allows in such cases, to any person who

shall produce his head severed from his body, and five pounds Pch, if brought home alive. JOHN MOSELY.[59]

Wesley continued to push the slavery issue in his preaching and writing. His treatment of slavery in several publications will be examined in the following chapter but the incidences are briefly mentioned here.

In 1775 Wesley published his *Calm Address to Our American Colonies*. It was a scathing attack on the Americans' cries for freedom from the "slavery" they were subjected to by Britain. Wesley used their protest to expose their hypocrisy. While crying for liberty, they enslaved others.

In 1776 Wesley wrote *A Seasonable Address to The More Serious Part Of The Inhabitants of Great Britain*. Lamenting the war between Britain and the Colonies he warns his readers that great nations are destroyed by evil and one of the greatest evils of Britain is slavery.

> One principal sin of our nation is the blood that we have shed in Asia, Africa, and America. Here I would beg your serious attention, while I observe, that however extensively pursued, and of long continuance, the African trade may be, it is nevertheless iniquitous from first to last. It is the price of blood! It is a trade of blood, and has stained our land with blood! ... What millions have fallen by these means, as well as by artificial famine! O earth, cover not thou their blood! ... O ye Governors of this great nation, would to God that ye had seen this, and timely done your utmost to separate those tares from the wheat of fair and honest trade.[60]

In April 1777 Wesley preached in Liverpool, a strong slave trade port. Because America's War for Independence was in progress the slave trade was suspended. This cessation would have had a dramatic effect on Liverpool because of the volume of slaves that normally came through this port. It is estimated that in one ten year period some 300,000 slaves were shipped from Liverpool.⁶¹ Wesley commented in his journal, "the men-butchers have now nothing to do."⁶²

The following year, 1778, saw the publication of Wesley's *Serious Address To The People of England, With Regard To The State Of The Nation*. It was indeed a "state of the nation" address, and he called attention to the evil and sin throughout the nation, particularly the slave trade. While people complained, "Nay, but we have also lost our Negro trade" (due to the war), Wesley countered that it should never be revived because it was the greatest reproach in England's history.⁶³

Wesley viewed these occasions as prime opportunities for him to expose the truth about slavery and encourage people to address the injustice. He made good use of the opportunities.

The early response of American Methodists to slavery is evident in April 1780. At their meetings in Baltimore they discussed requiring slave-owning preachers to free their slaves within a year — and there was talk of excluding those who did not comply. Because slavery was "contrary to the laws God, man, and nature" not only preachers, but all were encouraged to free their slaves. Wesley's position was known, and his influence felt.⁶⁴

In December 1781 Wesley began publishing poetry extracts of a Negro woman, Phillis Wheatley, in the *Arminian Magazine*.⁶⁵ Although her poems were not about slavery, by publishing her work Wesley indicates both his encouragement of her and his quiet recognition and promulgation of the abilities of black persons. Two years later Wesley corresponded with Richard Williams who had sent him some of his poems on slavery. Wesley commented favourably, but for some reason did not publish them in the *Arminian Magazine*. He sent them on to the *General Post*, which likewise did not publish them.⁶⁶ Why Wesley published one author but not the other cannot be positively answered, but it opens interesting speculation that his motive was to publicly affirm Africans. Williams was not African.

Also in 1783 Wesley's *Arminian Magazine* relates the unusual experience of Little Ephraim Robin-John and his nephew,

Ancona Robin Robin-John. Although John and Charles met these men some ten years earlier, as noted, John published their story (including the sworn deposition from the hearing before Lord Mansfield) at this time.[67]

The minutes of the Methodist Conference in July 1786 refer to: "Antigua, J. Baxter, William Warrender."[68] Wesley had supported the appointment of William Warrender to work with the Negroes of the West Indies. It was the first time the Conference appointed a preacher to serve as a missionary to people who were considered "heathen." Within days Wesley ordained Warrender who, on Christmas, arrived in the West Indies, accompanied by Thomas Coke.[69]

Though now in his eighties, Wesley's antislavery activity intensified in 1787 and 1788. The Society for the Abolition of the Slave Trade was formed on May 22, 1787.[70] Thomas Clarkson informed Wesley that the purpose of the Committee was to bring about an act of Parliament to abolish slavery. Wesley expressed strong support and mentioned his long-standing desire for Negro freedom, referring also to his American friends who had begun emancipating slaves. Indicating that his understanding of the problem and its solution had broadened beyond what individuals could accomplish, he encouraged the Committee and offered his services and endorsement:

> What little I can do to promote this excellent work I shall do with pleasure. I will print a large edition of the tract I wrote some years since, *Thoughts Upon Slavery*, and send it (which I have opportunity of doing once a month) to all my friends in Great Britain and Ireland; adding a few words in favour of your design, which I believe will have some weight with them.[71]

By November 24, only three months later, he had fulfilled his promise.[72]

He kept abreast of the activities of the Committee and wrote a second letter to them, by way of Granville Sharp. He again expressed support stating that he "cannot but do everything in my power to forward the glorious design of your Society." Out of concern for their endeavour, and utilizing his vast experience, he cautioned them in two areas: to realize the pervasive appeal of "interest" over human need, and to be beyond reproach in their "manner of procuring witnesses."[73] He was aware of a report in several places that they were paying witnesses and he was concerned that this would compromise their credibility. When he learned that only expenses were being paid, he wrote again that this was "liable to no objection" and he would take "every opportunity of clearing" their character.[74]

In January 1788 Wesley wrote William Thompson, indicating that he had "dispersed many of Mr. Clarkson's excellent tracts."[75] Two months later, a most unusual event occurred while Wesley was preaching. On Tuesday, March 6, he publicized that he would preach Thursday evening on slavery. (He had read on Monday the Genesis 9:25 passage, "Cursed be Canaan, a slave of slaves.")[76] According to his journal entry, the preaching event was extraordinary:

> ...the House from end to end was filled with high and low, rich and poor. I preached on that ancient prophecy, "God shall enlarge Japhet. And he shall dwell in the tents of Shem; and Canaan shall be his servant." About the middle of the discourse, while there was on every side attention still as night, a vehement noise arose, none could tell why, and shot like lightening through the whole congregation. The terror and confusion were inexpressible. You might have imagined it was a city taken by storm. The people rushed upon each other with the utmost violence; the benches were broke in pieces; and nine-tenths of the congregation appeared to be struck with the same panic. In about six minutes the storm ceased, almost as suddenly as it rose; and, all being calm, I went on without the least interruption.
>
> It was the strangest incident of the kind I ever remember; and I believe none can account for it, without supposing

some preternatural influence. Satan fought, lest his kingdom should be delivered up.[77]

Whatever the cause, whether an earthquake, a violent thunderstorm or a supernatural visitation, the experience impressed Wesley.[78] Regarding his sermon of that day, there seems to be no extant manuscript and it was not published. Rupert Davies suggests that because it was preached near the 1788 reprinting of *Thoughts Upon Slavery*, it is probable that the sermon followed the same lines as the *Thoughts* and did not need to be published.[79] If Wesley was working from the content of the tract, it is interesting to speculate what parts he utilized and what his major emphasis was. It is likely that he addressed the brutality and injustice of slavery with an appeal to God for the compassionate humanity of those involved, because he specified the next day

> as a day of fasting and prayer that God would remember those poor outcasts of men; and (what seems impossible with men, considering the wealth and power of their oppressors) make a way for them to escape and break their chains in sunder.[80]

Wesley repeatedly used the *Arminian Magazine* as a means of broadcasting antislavery information. This was particularly true in 1788. In January he published a letter, "On The Slave Trade," by Thomas Walker. In April and May he published "The Resolutions of the Society for the Purpose of Effecting the Abolition of the Slave Trade." These were from the antislavery meeting held in Manchester. In addition to condemning both slavery and the slave trade, this meeting gave verbal and financial support to the London Antislavery Society.[81] In July and August he printed "A Summary View of the Slave Trade." It appears to be based partly on Benezet's work and his own *Thoughts Upon Slavery*, going beyond both to explore financial implications. This will be expanded on later. In October and November he included poetry on slavery by Hannah More. The October selection includes a reference to Oronooko, the slave prince Wesley read about in 1726 (some sixty-two years earlier!). The November selection condemns slave traders in Africa: "They are not Christians who infest thy shore." An interesting insight into Wesley's perspective on the progress of antislavery is seen in a later stanza. Referring to the Quaker followers of William Penn, More states, "Thy followers only have effaced the shame, Inscribed by slavery on the Christian name." By the word "only," Wesley inserts a footnote: "Not so. Vast multitudes in Great Britain and Ireland are, at present, as great enemies to Slavery as ever the Quakers were."[82] His optimism about the burgeoning antislavery cause is apparent.

In 1790, Wesley was in his final year, a man of eighty-seven, but still determined to use his energies for the cause. He wrote his friend, Henry Moore… "I would do anything that is in my power toward the extirpation of that trade which is a scandal not only to Christianity, but humanity."[83] And one of the methods he could still employ was the magazine. In March he included the story supplied by Benjamin Rush of Thomas Fuller, a slave who could almost instantaneously calculate the number of seconds in any selected number of years. In June he quoted the experience of Samuel Paynter,[84] a slave who was converted under Nathaniel Gilbert, who worked to purchase his own freedom but suffered from the enslavement of his family. In September the lines on slavery by his late brother Charles were included:

On the Slave-Trade

Forc'd from home and all its pleasures,
    Afric's coast I left forlorn;
To increase a stranger's treasures,
    O'er the raging billows borne.
Men from England bought and sold me,
    Paid my price in paltry gold;
But though their's they have enroll'd me,
    Minds are never to be sold.

Still in thought as free as ever,
    What are England's rights, I ask,
Me from my delights to sever,
    Me to torture, me to task?
Fleecy locks and black complexion
    Cannot forfeit nature's claim:
Skins may differ, but affection
    Dwells in white and black the same.

Why did all-creating nature
    Make the plant for which we toil?
Sighs must waft it, tears must water,
    Sweat of our's must dress the soil.
Think, ye masters, iron-hearted,
    Sitting at your jovial boards,
Think, how many backs have smarted,
    For the sweet your cane affords.

Is there, as ye sometimes tell us,
    Is there one who reigns on high?
Has he bid you buy and sell us?
    Speaking from his throne — the sky?
Ask him, if your knotted scourges,
    Fetters, blood-extorting screws,
Are the means which duty urges,
    Agents of his will to use?

Hark, he answers — wild tornadoes,
    Strewing yonder sea with wrecks,
Wasting town, plantations, meadows,
    Is the voice with which he speaks.
He foreseeing what vexations
    Afric's sons would undergo,
Fix'd their tyrants' habitations
    Where his whirlwinds answer "no!"

By our blood in Afric wasted,
    Where our necks receiv'd the chain;
By the miseries which we tasted,
    Crossing in your barks the main:
By our sufferings since ye brought us
    To the man-degrading mart,
All sustain'd by patience, taught us
    Only by a broken heart:

Deem our nations brutes no longer,
    Till some reason ye shall find,
Worthier of regard and stronger,
    Than the colours of your kind;
Slaves of gold, whose sordid dealings
    Tarnish all your boasted pow'rs,
Prove that ye have human feelings
    Ere ye proudly question ours.[85]

In December his diary indicates that he read material by a Mr. Winchester. It is likely that it was the recently published book that addressed the slave trade as one of the "Reigning Abominations" of the time.[86] Wesley's diary entry ("read Mr. Winchester!") indicates an emotive response.

In 1791 he continued to look for something more he could do, something of deep significance. By this time William Wilberforce had emerged as the member of Parliament who championed the slave and year after year doggedly brought resolutions before the House of Commons. Wilberforce worked closely with Clarkson and the Committee, but the results had been terribly discouraging. Wilberforce's first attempts to end the slave trade, in 1789, had support and opposition nearly equal. Debate continued through the night until sunrise, but at the crucial moment the resolution failed. The succeeding years showed less, rather than more, promise of victory. The planter class (slaveholders who owned more than twenty slaves) seemed to be gaining political strength and support. Wesley was almost certainly aware of the political developments, the money being given to oppose the abolition campaign and the effect this was having on the small nucleus of abolition activists. With little time or strength left, he summoned his energy to encourage those who were on the front lines. And so, only days before his death, Wesley wrote a powerful and moving letter to William Wilberforce:

> Dear Sir, Unless the divine power has raised you up to be as *Athanasius contra mundum*, I see not how you can go through your glorious enterprise in opposing that execrable villany, which is the scandal of religion, of England, and of human nature. Unless God has raised you up for this very thing, you will be worn out by the opposition of men and devils. But if God be for you, who can be against you? Are all of them together stronger than God? O be not weary of well doing! Go on, in the name of God and in the power of His might, till even American slavery (the vilest that ever saw the sun) shall vanish away before it.
>
> Reading this morning a tract wrote by a poor African [the life of Gustavus Vassa], I was particularly struck by that circumstance, that a man who has a black skin, being wronged or outraged by a white man, can have no redress; it being a law in all our Colonies that the oath of a black against a white goes for nothing. What villany is this!
>
> That He who has guided you from youth up may continue to strengthen you in this and all things is the prayer of, dear sir,
>
>   Your affectionate servant.[87]

Wesley was a revered and respected figure. His writing was amazingly lucid for a man of eighty-eight and his words would have had a profound effect on Wilberforce and others that read them. Wilberforce had been exposed to Methodism in his youth and was an avowed evangelical, so the encouragement would be deepened not only by Wesley's stature, but by the sense of their being kindred spirits. Adding to the impact is the fact that this was the very last letter Wesley wrote.[88] It becomes the fitting "signature" of Wesley's antislavery travel journal.

Chapter 3

A brief excursion into Wesley's position on slavery and Negro inferiority

It may seem unnecessary to examine Wesley's true position on the institution of slavery because his activities seem so conclusive. However, a number of individuals from the eighteenth century have not been adequately understood. Seeing only their activities and the fact that they wrote for the antislavery cause led to assumptions about their positions, assumptions that would be overturned if their writings were looked at closely. Two cases in point stand out. James Ramsay, mentioned earlier, is often thought of as diametrically opposed to slavery. He was certainly opposed to the slave trade and to the abuses of slavery. However, while in principle he opposed the institution of slavery, it was a conditional opposition. He makes it clear in his 1784 *Essay* that while slavery is wrong, it would be better to continue slavery for a period of time than to manumit slaves before they had adequate preparation for freedom.[1]

The most frequently mislabeled antislavery figure is John Newton (1725–1807), author of the hymn, *Amazing Grace*. He is often referred to as the "converted slave trader" who greatly assisted the cause by writing against slavery. However, two misunderstandings repeatedly attach themselves to the Newton story. One relates to chronology and the other to the nature of his opposition. It is true that he was the captain of a slave ship, but this was only *after* his conversion.[2] In fact, his conversion inspired him with new purpose and the desire to pursue a "respectable" vocation. He found this in the slave trade. As a conscientious Christian he experienced no moral dissonance between his vital faith and his work. Rather, he considered this new career "the appointment Providence had marked out" for him, which explained his safety through numerous storms at sea.[3] He only left the business because of a sudden health crisis (probably a mild stroke) on the eve of his fourth slaving voyage in 1754.

Regarding his opposition to slavery, Newton *never* took a stand against slavery, only against the slave trade. While it may seem to be an insignificant difference, it is in fact crucial. Like most people in the eighteenth century he only opposed the abuses of slavery, not the system itself. His opposition was not voiced until some thirty-four years after he had left the trade.[4]

By contrast, the writings of Sharp and Benezet reveal that they were unequivocally against the whole business, both the slave trade and the institution of slavery. Sharp was so adamant that he pushed the antislavery Committee in the late 1780s to work for the abolition of both. They decided to concentrate their efforts on the more attainable goal of ending the slave trade with the plan of tackling slavery itself next. Sharp understood their reasoning, but still felt it was a compromise. He was suspicious of focusing on the abuses and the supply system without attacking the root. As a result, he parted company with the Committee. On the other side of the Atlantic Benezet was also opposed to the entire system. While James Ramsay would hesitate on the issue of preparation for emancipation, Benezet (as did Sharp) proposed a plan. Benezet's plan involved an immediate end to further slave imports with present slaves continuing only long enough to balance the out-of-pocket expenses of the owner. Thereafter they would be declared free, remain in their respective locales where they would be given tracts of land to work for themselves and where their children would be educated. Such a plan would ultimately produce integration.[5] In 1773 he wrote his friend John Fothergill that the segregating of former slaves

> in a body, by themselves will be found as impossible, and it would be dangerous both to black & whites. [...] The only rational safe & just expedient both natural & religious would, I think, be that they be mixed amongst the whites, & by giving them a property amongst us, make them parties & interested in our welfare & security.[6]

However, he never hid behind a plan or its implementation as a condition for emancipation.[7] From his Christian and Quaker principles, particularly the equality and dignity of all persons, he opposed and worked for the overthrow of anything connected with slavery.

Against this backdrop, what was Wesley's true position? Was he opposed to slavery or merely the abuses? Was it primarily the slave trade he opposed? And what was his view of Negro inferiority or equality? In this section an overview of his true position, as reflected in his various tracts, will be presented.

To begin, Wesley was deeply opposed to the inhuman abuses of both the slave trade and slavery. When dealing with these, his descriptions are laden with emotion, a relatively uncharacteristic trait in Wesley. A perusal of his journal entries and correspondence related to slavery makes this abundantly clear. However, a close examination of his more studied compositions reveals the foundation for his opposition and violent response. He rejected the entire institution of slavery. This was the foundation of his emotional response, his arguments and his activity. His rejection of slavery was based on well reasoned principles.

The most concise presentation of Wesley's mature views on slavery and the slave trade is found in his major tract, *Thoughts Upon Slavery*, although passages in other works support or apply these views. Wesley opposed slavery predominantly on the basis of natural law. He also argued against it from the points of what he termed "necessity" (what we might call pragmatism), economics, religion, and the degradation it effected.

Although Wesley would normally not have been a defender of natural rights and natural law, where slavery was concerned he leaned heavily on the argument from natural rights. In some ways it was the starting point: "I strike at the root of this complicated villany: I absolutely deny all slave-holding to be consistent with any degree of natural justice."[8] He supported this claim with the argument of Judge Blackstone, who had reasoned against Justinian's three justifications for slavery: captivity in war, the selling of oneself and inherited slavery. Wesley applied:

> It cannot be, that either war, or contract, can give any man such a property in another as he has in his sheep and oxen. Much less is it possible, that any child of man should ever be born a slave. Liberty is the right of every human creature ... which he derives from the *law of nature*.[9]

Even civil law, which Wesley staunchly defended, must bow when in conflict with natural law. This demolished the often touted argument that slavery was "legal."

> The grand plea is, "They are authorized by law." But can law, human law, change the nature of things? Can it turn darkness into light, or evil into good? By no means. Notwithstanding ten thousand laws, right is right, and wrong is wrong still. There must still remain an essential difference between justice and injustice, cruelty and mercy. So that I still ask, Who can reconcile this treatment of the Negroes, first and last, with either mercy or justice?[10]

Before attacking slavery, Wesley had written about general liberty and related it to natural rights: "all men in the world desire liberty ... by a natural instinct" and "every man living, as man, has a right to this, as he is a rational creature. The creator gave him this right when he endowed him with understanding."[11]

One aspect of the "liberty" Wesley had in mind in these passages was specifically religious liberty, a "liberty to choose our own religion, to worship God according to our own conscience, according to the best light we have."[12] But he also endorsed a less specific civil liberty, "to enjoy our lives and fortunes in our own way; to use our property, whatever is legally our own, according to our own choice."[13]

A major concern for Wesley was individual accountability which necessitated the freedom to make choices. He stated that "every man must judge for himself, because every man must give an account of himself to God."[14] He called this liberty "indefeasible," or "unalienable" and stated that "God did never give authority to any man, or number of men, to deprive any child of man thereof, under any colour or pretense whatever."[15] The above statements on liberty were not made in the context of slavery, but to fellow Englishmen who were crying for more liberty. Wesley accused them of imposing slavery on those who disagreed with them and spoke against Congress or for the King.[16] He was attempting to explain what liberty was, in order to convince them that they had it in England. However, his statements laid the groundwork for his later comments on slavery, a condition whereby a person had no religious liberty, no civil liberty, nor even the right to one's physical body, which must certainly be considered one's property.

In his 1775 *Calm Address to our American Colonies*, Wesley bluntly indicted those Americans who pleaded for "liberty," insisting that they *already* had full religious and civil liberty.[17] He pointed out the inconsistency of pleading for liberty and calling British policy "slavery," when in fact they had genuine slavery near at hand!

> "Who then is a slave?" Look into America and you may easily see. See that Negro, fainting under the load, bleeding

under the lash! He is a slave. And is there "no difference" between him and his master? Yes; the one is screaming, Murder! Slavery!" the other silently bleeds and dies!

The contrast is obvious:

> "But wherein then consists the difference between liberty and slavery?" Herein: You and I, and the English in general, go where we will, and enjoy the fruit of our labours: This is liberty. The Negro does not: This is slavery.[18]

What Wesley meant by liberty was rather limited. Beyond religious and civil liberty, his view was restricted. He opposed self-government in contrast to government by the laws of the country. In that context an individual had "no right at all to be independent, or governed only by himself; but is in duty bound to be governed by the powers that be, according to the laws of the country."[19] Those powers were contained within a constitutional monarchy, which gave those in authority the responsibility to uphold the law. But even the law was subject to the common understanding of justice, because true law came from higher law, not the people, and would always be consistent with what was right.[20] Thus, Wesley's view of liberty would not be a plank in the platform of self government. Rather, he supported total freedom within the just law, which had a higher source and came through a just form of government, particularly a constitutional monarchy.

As he understood political liberty and natural rights, they were totally inconsistent with Negro slavery. His principles, while not "democratic," left no place for one person to be the property of another or to be completely under the authority of another. In *Thoughts Upon Slavery* all those principles came to bear on the institution of slavery. Natural law meant that slavery was unquestioningly wrong.

Wesley also opposed slavery on the basis of pragmatism, or what he called "necessity." No Machiavellian, for him the end did not justify the means. He was quick to realize, however, how pragmatic thinking could justify slavery in the minds of people and that it could be utilized by the proponents of slavery:

> Here also the slave-holder fixes his foot; here he rests the strength of his cause. "If it is not quite right, yet it must be so; there is an absolute necessity for it. It is necessary we should procure slaves; and when we have procured them, it is necessary to use them with severity...

Without hesitation, he counters:

> You stumble at the threshold; I deny villany is ever necessary. It is impossible that it should ever be necessary for any reasonable creature to violate all the laws of justice, mercy, and truth. No circumstances can make it necessary for a man to burst in sunder all the ties of humanity.[21]

Consistent with his philosophy of money he extends his point. He agreed that slavery could be necessary to riches and then asks: "But how is this necessary? It is very possible you might be both a better and a happier man, if you had not a quarter of it. I deny that your gaining one thousand is necessary either to your present or eternal happiness." The same point was taken in regard to the wealth of the nation: "Wealth is not necessary to the glory of any nation; but wisdom, virtue, justice, mercy, generosity, public spirit, love of our country."[22] Such qualities were in sharp contrast to slavery.

Closely related to pragmatism, Wesley also opposed slavery based on economic reasons. He believed that England's economy would not be hurt if she had nothing to do with "that detestable trade of manstealing" and if "there was not a Negro in all our islands, or in all English America."[23] This position stands in stark contrast to that held by most politicians of the day. Even many of those who had a humanitarian conscience or a religious conviction against slavery were concerned that to end it would mean the economic ruin of all England. The planter class nurtured this fear because their economic survival depended on slavery. However,

Wesley cited his experience in the hot climate of Georgia and asserted that white persons could labour there as well as black persons, so the economy would not be destroyed. On this point Wesley differed with George Whitefield whose opinion was that "Georgia never can or will be a flourishing province without negroes."[24]

Within his economic argument, Wesley returns to his point against pragmatism. Slave labour is not necessary for the health of the economy, but even if it were necessary,

> Better no trade, than trade procured by villany. It is far better to have no wealth, than to gain wealth at the expense of virtue. Better honest poverty, than all the riches bought by the tears, and sweat, and blood, of our fellow-creatures.[25]

And four years later, in 1788, when there was no slave trade due to the war with America, Wesley hoped it would never resume. He expresses this in volatile words:

> I would to God it may never be found more! that we may never more steal and sell our brethren like beasts: never murder them by thousands and tens of thousands! O may this worse than Mahometan, worse than Pagan, abomination, be removed from us forever! Never was anything such a reproach to England since it was a nation, as the having any hand in this execrable traffic.[26]

In the first edition he added a postscript:

> With respect indeed to the Trade of our West-Indian Islands, you may grant, it is greatly decreased. The Planters there cannot carry on their Trade — of buying the Bodies and Souls of Men. God grant, (for the honour of our Country and Religion!) that they may never be able to carry it on more! The total, final destruction of this horrid

Trade, would rejoice every Lover of Mankind: Yea, tho' all our Sugar-Islands (so the inhabitants escaped) were swallowed up in the depth of the sea. Certain it is, that England may not only subsist, but abundantly prosper without them: — may increase in Population, Agriculture, Manufactures, and all the other Articles above-mentioned, tho' we no more suck the blood and devour the flesh of the less barbarous Africans. O Earth, hide not thou their blood, and no more cover the stain![27]

For Wesley there was no justification for slavery on economic or practical, pragmatic grounds.

Even though the economic question was not nearly as important as the moral truth at stake, he realized that it was important to the populace and to the leaders of the country. With that in mind, he reminded the leaders of the Abolition Committee in 1787 that, if they hoped to succeed, they would need to address themselves to the "interest" aspect of slavery. In a letter to Granville Sharp he indicated that those who opposed abolition, "men who are not encumbered with either honour, conscience, or humanity," would do anything to "secure their great goddess, Interest." Thus, he reasoned: the profit aspect of slavery must be challenged because "this has the weight of a thousand arguments with the generality of men." He advised: "After all, I doubt [suspect] the matter will turn upon this, 'Is the Slave Trade for the interest of the nation?'"[28]

Under his leadership, the following year the *Arminian Magazine* argued extensively that slavery worked against the material interests of England, even pointing out how the slave trade increased French commercial competition with the British. Since the British fleet supplied the majority of slaves, Britain was assisting her enemy.[29] Almost twenty years later Wesley proved to be correct. The first major victory of the abolitionists, the ending of the foreign slave trade in 1806, pivoted on this very issue. Abolitionists who had tried to convince on the grounds of humanity, and were failing, adopted a new tactical strategy, namely, profit. Perhaps Wesley's sage advice of 1787 had taken root. The strategy worked[30] and there is evidence that the victory of 1806 effectively paved the way for the major victory the following year, the abolition of the entire British slave trade.

It is interesting that the man who labelled himself *homo unius libri* did not build a scriptural case against slavery. One explanation is that he saw religion in general and Christianity in particular as so obviously opposed to slavery and the slave trade that it would have been superfluous to state that which was so clear. He did not believe that Scripture condoned slavery. We catch a glimpse of his hermeneutic of Scripture related to slavery in his *Explanatory Notes Upon the New Testament*. He does not avoid commenting on passages that could be considered problematic. Regarding the book of Philemon, he suggested that Philemon pardoned and freed Onesimus.[31] To Paul's advice, "Servants obey *your* masters according to the flesh, with fear and trembling, in singleness of heart, as unto the Lord" (Ephesians 6:5), Wesley interprets the phrase, "your masters according to the flesh," "according to the present state of things. Afterward, the servant is free from his master." The Titus 2:9-10 passage where Paul urges "servants to be obedient to their own masters, to please them in all things," Wesley tempers: "In all things — wherein it can be done without sin." In this manner Wesley indicates that there is a higher allegiance than slavery allows.[32] It would be another fourteen years until Raymund Harris, an ex-Jesuit priest would publish his scriptural defense of the slave trade. While there is no record of Wesley's response to Harris, it can be surmised.

Another reason Wesley may not have written a biblical treatment against slavery is that he believed authentic Christians could not possibly be involved in such a gross evil; thus to make a biblical case would be irrelevant. To present a specifically biblical case to non-Christians would be equally irrelevant and thus a waste of time. As a result, his appeal was much broader than "Christian," it was "human." He challenged:

> Are you a man? Then you should have an human heart. But have you indeed? What is your heart made of? Is there no such principle as compassion there? Do you never feel another's pain? Have you no sympathy, no sense of human woe, no pity for the miserable? When you saw the flowing eyes, the heaving breasts, or the bleeding sides and tortured limbs of your fellow-creatures, was you a stone, or a brute? Did you look upon them with the eyes of a tiger?[33]

The superstructure for Wesley's humanitarian appeal and his understanding of natural rights was religion. Integral to any discussion of true religion was the golden rule, which he referred to at the close of *Thoughts Upon Slavery*. Within the principle of the golden rule is the practice of mercy and "slave-holding is utterly inconsistent with mercy."[34] His case was made more sure in his thinking because of the infinite worth of human beings, as God's creation. The degradation of slavery coupled with infinite human worth was a blatant contradiction.[35]

The reality of the degradation caused by slavery was poignant to Wesley. By the time he wrote against slavery the supporters of slavery had justified it on the grounds that Negroes were uncivilized and barbaric. Wesley turned the argument around, demonstrating that any appearance of barbarism among the Negroes was singularly the result of slavery. He proposed that there was a cycle of degradation which perpetuated the system of slavery by degrading the victims and then justifying slavery because they were degraded. He describes the process clearly:

> You first acted the villain in making them slaves, whether you stole them or bought them. You kept them stupid and wicked, by cutting them off from all opportunities of improvement either in knowledge or virtue: And now you assign their want of wisdom or goodness as the reason for using them worse than brute beasts.[36]

Benezet had used a similar argument in his *Short Account* in 1762,[37] and based it on the Deuteronomy 25:2-3 passage, which limits punishment to prevent degradation.

Wesley also recognized the reciprocal nature of degradation. To treat human beings as slavery required was only possible if the slave owner himself became degraded. Thus, not only the slave but the slave owner, by his own choice, became degraded: "It can never be necessary for a rational being to sink himself below a brute. A man can be under no necessity of degrading himself into a wolf."[38] Any system or practice that took the highest beings of God's created order, those of infinite worth, and degraded them to the level of or below brutes was obviously and inherently wrong. For this reason, slavery, more than any other evil, was the "sum of all villanies" and Wesley's opposition to it is irrefutable. It was thorough and integral. In his thinking there could be no justification for it. His own description leaves no room for doubt: "However extensively pursued, and of long continuance, the African trade may be, it is nevertheless iniquitous from first to last. It is the price of blood! It is a trade of blood, and has stained our nation with blood!"[39]

Wesley compared to some contemporaries

It is both interesting and revealing to compare Wesley's views on slavery with the views held by some of his contemporaries. Even among those who had reputations as being against slavery, contrasts can be found as seen above in James Ramsay and in John Newton. They would be representative of many conscientious people of the eighteenth century, appalled by the abuses of the slave trade and abuses within slavery, but not so outspoken, or perhaps decisive, on the actual institution of slavery. For most people of the time slavery was an accepted part of society, particularly where colonization and development were valued. To take a position against the slave trade would have seemed radical. Thus, for Wesley to speak against both the trade and the institution put him in a very small minority.

One of the sharpest contrasts exists between Wesley and George Whitefield. While Whitefield was a friend of Benezet and opposed the abuses of slavery, he was not against slavery itself. In fact, he lobbied for the introduction of slavery in the colony of Georgia and when it was legalized he became the owner of some fifty slaves on the land that housed his orphanage, Bethesda. His sentiments are seen clearly in a letter he wrote to Wesley in 1751.

> Reverend and Very Dear Sir: Thanks be to God that the time for favoring the colony of Georgia seems to be come. Now is the season for us to exert our utmost for the good of the poor Ethiopians. We are told that even they are soon to stretch out their hands to God; and who knows but their being settled in Georgia may be overruled for this great end? As for the lawfulness of keeping slaves, I have no doubt, since I hear of some that were bought with Abraham's money and some that were born in his house. I also cannot help thinking that some of those servants mentioned by the apostles in their epistles were, or had been, slaves. It is plain that the Gibeonites were doomed to perpetual slavery; and, though liberty is a sweet thing to such as are born free, yet to those who never knew the sweets of it slavery, perhaps, may not be so irksome. However this be, it is plain to a demonstration that hot countries cannot be cultivated without Negroes. What a flourishing country might Georgia have been had the use of them been permitted years ago! How many white people have been destroyed for want of them, and how many thousands of pounds spent to no purpose at all! Though it is true that they are brought in a wrong way from their own country, and it is a trade not to be approved of, yet, as it will be carried on whether we will or not, I should think myself highly favoured if I could purchase a good number of them in order to make their lives comfortable, and lay a foundation for breeding up their posterity in the nurture and admonition of the Lord. I had no hand in bringing them into Georgia, though my judgment was for it, and I strongly importuned thereto;

yet I would not have a Negro upon my plantation till the use of them was publicly allowed by the colony. Now this is done, let us diligently improve the present opportunity for their instruction. It rejoiced my soul to hear that one of my poor Negroes in Carolina was made a brother in Christ. How know we but we may have many such instances in Georgia! I trust many of them will be brought to Jesus, and this consideration, as to us, swallows up all temporal inconveniences whatsoever.[40]

Whitefield's position had changed from his earlier opposition to slavery so that now he saw it as necessary for the financial survival of his orphanage and a possible means to the conversion of Africans. He was deeply opposed to the slave trade and abuses within slavery, but felt it could be a workable and beneficial system if handled justly.[41] While no other correspondence exists between Wesley and Whitefield on the slavery issue, it is clear that their positions are diametrically opposed. Wesley called slave owners "the spring that puts all the rest [the slave trade and all the atrocities of slavery] in motion."[42] Whitefield was a slave owner with the intention of helping slaves.

Another contrast can be seen between Wesley and two of his very committed followers, Thomas Coke and Francis Asbury, who were early leaders of American Methodism. While the contrast is less dramatic than Wesley and Whitefield, it demonstrates how concessions toward slavery were gradually accepted resulting in the American Methodist church taking a position Wesley would not have endorsed. This occurred within Wesley's lifetime.

Asbury's journal of 1779 indicates strong opposition to slavery. His clear desire for the emancipation of slaves and his belief that "if the Methodists [did] not yield on this point and emancipate their slaves, God [would] depart from them."[43] Coke, equally opposed to slavery, was a key influence in appointing William Warrender to minister to black persons in the West Indies in 1786. His pamphlet of that year, proposing the raising of subscriptions for sending workers to the West Indies, the Scottish Highlands and Nova Scotia, was instrumental in winning Conference support.[44] The organizational meeting for American Methodism in 1784 (the "Christmas Conference" in Baltimore) explored the slavery issue and the rules in the discipline of the following year which were "aimed at the complete emancipation of Black slaves."[45] The reaction was almost overwhelming. Coke and Asbury were threatened and slave owners would no longer allow ministers access to their slaves, effectively shutting off evangelism and the teaching of the faith. It was a difficult and soul-searching time for Methodist leaders; they were convinced that slavery was wrong, but even more committed to evangelism. It appears that Asbury's fear of God departing from the Methodists was forgotten or at least suspended. Coke explains,

> We thought it prudent to suspend the minute concerning slavery for one year, on account of the great opposition that has been given it, especially in the new circuits, our work being in too infantile a state to push things to extremity... But we agreed to present to the Assembly of Maryland, through our friends, a petition for a general emancipation, signed by as many electors as we can procure.[46]

The leaders of American Methodism also found a way to retain access to slaves and not offend slave owners, perhaps saving their own lives. It was by modifying their message. Coke relates:

> I bore a public testimony against slavery, and have found out a method of delivering it without much offence, or at least without causing a tumult: and that is, by first addressing the negroes in a very pathetic manner on the duty of servants to masters; and then the whites will receive quietly what I have to say to them.[47]

They also found ways to more effectively touch their black hearers. It appears that Asbury took a preaching companion with him on his ministry tours, one "Black Harry." It was sometimes reported that the black preacher was more popular as a speaker than Asbury.[48]

Regardless of intent and motives, the position against slavery had been drastically weakened. In order to protect the infant church and retain slaveholding members, the emphasis in preaching and in discipline shifted from emancipation of all slaves to amelioration of slave conditions and (in some cases) to only obtaining the *promise* of preachers to free their slaves in the future.[49] While at the time it may have seemed to be an innocent way to stave off disaster and buy time, in fact it became simply the acquiescing of the church to the prevailing culture. The fruit of this seed would not be peace and unity, but the eventual split of Methodism in 1843 when the Wesleyan Methodist Church was born.[50] The practical fruit was the attachment of religious justification to brutal behaviour by slaveowners. In his 1845 *Narrative*, Frederick Douglass describes the end result of this compromised Methodist position:

> In August, 1832, my master attended a Methodist camp-meeting held in the Bay-side, Talbot county, and there experienced religion. I indulged a faint hope that his conversion would lead him to emancipate his slaves, and that if he did not do this, it would, at any rate, make him more kind and humane. I was disappointed in both these respects... If it had any effect on his character, it made him more cruel and hateful in all his ways; for I believe him to have been a much worse man after his conversion than before.

Douglass reasons that "he found religious sanction and support for his slaveholding cruelty."[51] Douglass later reflects a most damning assessment:

> Were I to be again reduced to the chains of slavery, next to that enslavement, I should regard being the slave of a religious master the greatest calamity that could befall me. For of all slaveholders with whom I have ever met, religious slaveholders are the worst.[52]

History proved that Asbury's earlier instincts and convictions were correct.[53]

A test case?

Wesley was not in America in the 1780s, and the fledgling colonial church was establishing its own autonomy. Likewise, the slavery situation in America was quite different from that in England, where the plantations with their large numbers of slaves were an ocean away and hostile slave owners were not threatening Methodist Society. But how would Wesley have handled the dilemma had he been in Asbury's place? He had seen slavery firsthand in South Carolina, and had been outspoken against it there, at the risk of his safety. While there is no extant correspondence between him and Coke or Asbury in response to the Christmas Conference and subsequent decisions, we can speculate about what his response would have been. Several factors provide guidance. First of all, Wesley was a strong, authoritarian leader, never yielding to public pressure, and seldom to the pressure of his own preachers. He had learned not to yield on matters of principle. Secondly, the threat of bodily danger never seemed to alter his message. The *Journal* is replete with his accounts of facing mobs, being attacked or ridiculed. He sometimes softened the hostility, but never by compromising his message. Thirdly, he was not swayed by the pragmatic evaluation of an issue, especially when a moral principle was at stake. As seen in his *Thoughts Upon Slavery* and his subsequent articles in the *Arminian Magazine*, "necessity" was never an adequate justification. He would not have tolerated a weakened position against slavery even if it cost him members or preachers. Presented with the choice, he would have opted for a smaller, but purer Society.

More evidence for this position is seen in 1789, just two years before his death. He continued to embrace the value of discipline for his people and he preached it strongly. Deeply concerned about his followers who were not giving generously to those in need, he accepted the responsibility: "I many times doubt [suspect] whether we Preachers are not, in some measure, partakers in their sin."⁵⁴ He considered it

> ...a great sin to keep them in our society. May it not hurt their souls, by encouraging them to persevere in walking contrary to the Bible? And may it not, in some measure, intercept the salutary influences of the blessed Spirit upon the whole community?⁵⁵

He believed discipline should have been maintained, even at the expense of smaller numbers:

> I might have said peremptorily and expressly, "Here I am: I and my Bible. I will not, I dare not, vary from this Book, either in great things or small. I have no power to dispense with one jot or tittle of what is contained therein. I am determined to be a Bible Christian, not almost, but altogether. Who will meet me on this ground? Join me on this, or not at all."⁵⁶

His words are strong, and interestingly, they were spoken in the context of how Christians dressed! He believed he should have been as firm in discipline as the Quakers and said, "If you join us, you are to dress as we do; but you need not join us, unless you please."⁵⁷

It is not stretching the point or the application to reason that if Wesley felt this strongly about something as innocuous as attire, sins of extravagance in dress and less than generous giving, he would have been even more adamant about members and preachers who were directly involved in and perpetuated the "sum of all villainies." In 1774 he had written, "Better no trade than trade procured by villany!" He never retracted statements such as this, but continued the theme in his publications and through his support of the Abolition Committee. It is safe to project that he would have responded to Asbury's concessions with, "better no Methodist growth than growth procured by compromise with men butchers, men stealers and slave owners, the spring that puts all the rest in motion."

In comparing him with his contemporaries it is helpful to consider categories of people in terms of their responses to slavery. The smallest group would be comprised of radical activists such as Benezet, Sharp, and Clarkson, those who gave their primary energy to effect abolition. The next group would contain those who became sensitized to the evils of slavery and at that point became involved in the cause, giving energy to it along with other pursuits. These people are responders to the influence of those in the first group and their influence could be either minor or extensive. The third category would contain the large numbers of common folk whose consciences effected their behavioural change but did not thrust them into leadership. These people did what they were able, abstaining from goods produced by slave labour, like cotton and sugar. They supported leaders through the vote or contributions. Many Quakers and evangelicals in this group played important roles through group influence, especially to help the cause gain momentum. A fourth category includes the largest group (at least early on in the movement) of the population, those who had no awareness of the social evil of slavery within their culture. They simply accepted the culture as it was and believed it was what it should be. The final category is the counter to the first. It contains another minority, but at the opposite end of the continuum, those who were actively involved promoting slavery because of their self interest. This would have been the planter class and people directly involved in the economic benefit of slavery or the trade. They formed the lobby that restrained the success of the Abolition Committee for nearly twenty years.

John Wesley fits into the second category. He stood apart from his culture. Even though he did not become actively involved in the antislavery cause until 1772, he had never endorsed slavery. His actions increased with his growing awareness of the problem of slavery. Responding to Benezet's influence, he consistently gave support, leadership and energy to the antislavery cause. While it was not his only endeavour, he shaped his actions and made use of his position to exert significant influence. Both his attitude about slavery and his actions to bring it to an end place him apart from the vast majority of his contemporaries. His perspective placed him apart from the predominant culture. His vision encompassed the good of humankind, beyond the accepted mores. His hermeneutic transcended the typical prooftexting that used Scripture to justify the status quo. His personal integrity and strength gave him the ability to remain firm in the face of opposition, even from fellow Christians.

Wesley and Negro inferiority or equality

A correlative issue to Wesley's position on slavery is his attitude toward black persons. What were his views on human equality or inequality related to race? The question of Negro inferiority requires a separate study in its own right, but it is appropriate to introduce the topic here and summarize Wesley's view.

In the eighteenth century, those who held that Africans were inherently inferior to Europeans needed little justification for slavery. Such a belief in inferiority could have been long held, or it may have been a new idea, reflecting the success of proslavery propaganda. From twentieth and twenty-first century perspectives the issue appears to be rather clear cut. It seems obvious that people in the eighteenth century viewed Negroes as either subhuman or inferior — otherwise they would not have enslaved them. However, there is good evidence that the idea of Negro inferiority did not precede, but rather followed the development of slavery. Only after slavery came under attack did its supporters begin to push the concept that Africans were inherently inferior. This served as a justification for enslaving and consequently even using slavery for a "benevolent" purpose, to expose these inferior beings to "civilization" that could improve them and bring them to the light of the gospel.

Racism was not yet part of the English or American culture when Wesley was first exposed to slavery and was only just developing by the end of his life. By the late eighteenth century, physical characteristics of people began to be associated with their way of life and their culture, a sort of "culture prejudice." It was a relatively short step to reduce that to identifying culture with colour.[58]

It would be the writing of Edward Long in 1774 (*The History of Jamaica*) and others like him that took this to the next step and posited actual Negro inferiority. It is fascinating that nearly a hundred years before, Morgan Godwyn had foreseen the process when he stated it "was in the interest of the planters and traders to propagate the belief that Africans were not really men."[59] The writings of Wesley, Benezet, Clarkson and Wilberforce, which describe the cycle of degradation perpetuating the notion of Negro inferiority, give evidence that racist writing had begun and they were attempting to refute it.

The nineteenth century saw the full development of racism with a thoroughly developed racial theory appearing in Robert Knox's book, *The Races of Man* (1846). Knox believed that "race is everything: literature, science, art — in a word, civilization depends on it."[60] However, Wesley and his contemporaries lived in what can be termed a "pre-racial" period; while attitudes could be prejudicial, they were *cultural* assumptions and prejudices, not based exclusively on race or on a preconceived racial theory. From about the 1840s, the beginning of the "racial period," assumptions began to be based primarily on race. Of course the attitudes of individuals do not always strictly follow timelines and those such as Edward Long thought in racial terms even though living in a "pre-racial" period.

Racial attitudes in the nineteenth century influenced mission philosophies and strategies towards Africans. Philip Curtin suggests two distinct attitudes, "conversionism" and "trusteeship." Conversionism held that European civilization, including religion (Christianity), was superior and attainable by all people. Therefore, the goal and responsibility of Europeans was to "convert" the "heathen" to Christianity, with its assumed European culture. Once this occurred, it was believed they were capable of self-government and could eventually attain to the level of Europeans. This view was predominant from the 1830s until the 1870s. It was followed by "trusteeship," which assumed a lower view of the "heathen." Negroes were seen as innately and unalterably inferior, but the white race was responsible to protect them. Of course, the results were paternalism and imperialism. In conversionism the task of civilizing and facilitating equality was temporary, only until the level was raised. In trusteeship the paternal responsibility was endless; it was the "white man's burden."

This discussion relates to the period nearly a hundred years after Wesley. However, understanding the development allows us to look at Wesley without the preconception that the idea of Negro inferiority has always been present, or was present and prevalent throughout his entire lifetime. And so, back to the question: with all his preaching and writing against slavery, what was his actual attitude toward the Negro race? Did he see black persons as equal? As inferior? Would he have taken what later became a "conversionist" stance, or would he have leaned more toward the paternalism of "trusteeship?"

Wesley did recognize, early on, the practical results of degradation and described, along with Benezet and later Clarkson, the cycle of degradation. Brutal treatment produced the effects of degradation in the eyes of both the slave owner and the slave, with the result of increased acting out of degradation by the slave, and the continued degrading behaviour by the owner. Wesley saw this as a self-perpetuating cycle. However, this was the *result* of slavery, not a reason for it. His view was that Africans were not inferior to other races.

If one reads Wesley selectively the equality in Wesley's thought can be missed. He describes the heathen in general and the Negro in particular differently, depending on his purpose. When discussing human depravity he uses "heathen," particularly Negroes and Native Americans, as evidence of depravity. However, in other essays he also uses Europeans to illustrate the same point. When fighting slavery Wesley paints a very different picture of Africans, that of the "noble savage" and Edenic purity. By contrast he could point out how uncivilized Europeans were. Seeing only some of those passages can distort our understanding of Wesley's real view of the Negro.[61]

Wesley actually held to an equality of all persons. His preaching admonished treating all others with equality, because "the lowest and the worst have a claim to our courtesy."[62] He defined "Christian zeal" as "the flame of love," which was obviously opposed to hatred:

> If zeal be only fervent love, then it stands at the utmost distance from prejudice, jealousy, evil-surmising; seeing "love thinketh no evil." Then bigotry of every sort, and, above all, the spirit of persecution, are totally inconsistent with it. ... All these things are the works of the devil, let them... no longer deceive the unwary children of God.[63]

On occasion he quoted Matthew Prior's *Solomon*, "Love, like death, makes all distinctions void" and indeed, his followers were accused of "perpetually endeavering [sic] to level all ranks and do away with all distinctions."[64]

What was Wesley's specific attitude toward Negroes? Earlier in this chapter, his contact with black people in America and England was traced. He indicates delight in teaching them, notes their ability to learn and supports evangelization and education among them.

An important contrast is evident in Wesley's contact with other non-Europeans. Every personal contact he had with Negroes is recorded as very positive, reflecting their capability or interest. This is not so of his interaction with Native Americans. Before meeting them he held the popular Rousseau view of "noble savage," describing them as "little children, humble, willing to learn, and eager to do the will of God."[65] But after being with them, just prior to leaving America, he recorded, "neither had I as yet, found or heard of any Indians on the continent of America who had the least desire of being instructed."[66] He would later describe the Indians of Georgia:

> They are likewise all, except, perhaps, the Choctaws, gluttons, drunkards, thieves, dissemblers, liars. They are implacable, unmerciful; murderers of fathers, murderers of mothers, murderers of their own children.[67]

By contrast, with increased contact with black persons, Wesley's estimate of them grew higher. The *Journal* for 1780 indicates the presence of a black woman in the "select society," and Wesley's appreciation of her love, her voice and her ability to speak effectively.[68]

Wesley's rejection of the idea of Negro inferiority and his belief in human equality is also seen in his unwavering opposition to slavery. While all individuals or civilizations had not *developed* equally, they were inherently equal and had equal potential. This was a driving force in his antislavery action.

Human equality had a number of bases in Wesley's thinking. These will be developed in the following chapter, but are mentioned here:

1) Since the Fall, an important doctrine to Wesley, all people are equally depraved.
2) All people are equally the recipients of God's grace.
3) Black persons are equally "human," and classed among all people as God's "noblest creatures" with immortal souls. Therefore, in God's sight there is complete equality among all people.[69]
4) While there may be physical differences, these are only in appearance. Wesley's experience in the hot climate of Georgia convinced him of the equal ability of Europeans and Africans to perform strenuous physical labour.

His own answer to the question of equality is uncompromising: "Certainly the African is in no respect inferior to the European."[70]

In support of his view of equality, it is helpful to compare Wesley's attitude of mission with the later conversionism and trusteeship views. From the previous it is clear that he would have rejected trusteeship because of his view of inherent equality. But what about his high opinion of European, and especially English, civilization and government? Would he have been a candidate for the conversionist school of thought? The answer again is no. He did not see conversion as a societal goal. He observed that all too often where it was, as in "Christian England," the people became at best "nominally Christians," and were actually *more* evil than non-Christian heathen. He asks and answers the question himself: "Are [nominal] Christians any better than other men?... To say the truth it is well if they were not worse... In many respects they are abundantly worse."[71]

Wesley believed that individual Christians had a responsibility of love to share the gospel with others, but this did not translate into the idea that so-called Christian nations were responsible for heathen nations in a conversionist sense. In a passage that opposes both conversionism and trusteeship he satirized,

> A crew are driven by storm they know not where; at length they make the land and go ashore; they are entertained with kindness. They give the country a new name; set up a stone or rotten plank for a memorial; murder a dozen of the natives, and bring away a couple by force. Here commences a new right of domination; Ships are sent and the natives driven out and destroyed. And this is done to civilise and convert a barbarous and idolatrous people.[72]

In *Thoughts Upon Slavery* he contrasts Africans in their own land before and after Europeans contacted them. The results are decidedly negative, the opposite of a so-called civilizing effect.[73] Societal conversion had no part in his thinking, nor did imposing European culture or civilization on other peoples. What he did support was the authentic evangelization and teaching of all people, including Africans, Highlanders and Nova Scotians.[74] This was based on his understanding of human equality and his desire to spread the positive influence of the Christian gospel, not a "Christian culture."

His view of the evangelization of heathen nations gives important insight into his genuine posture of equality. Sometimes one's perspective of evangelization masks a subtle or covert assumption of inequality. One's particular form of religion is seen as the exclusively correct form. Cultural and religious biases are confused with "truth," and one's "superiority" is confused with the obligation to bring others to the only salvific light. Wesley seems to avoid such typical misunderstandings.

He rejected the customary belief that heathens are totally dependent on European Christians for salvation. In statements that seem to be surprisingly universalist he says, no more "will be expected of them [who have not heard the gospel], than the living up to the light they had."[75] God alone would be their judge:

> ...we are not required to determine any thing touching their final state. How it will please God, the judge of all, to deal with them, we may leave to God himself. But this we know, that he is not the God of the Christians only, but the God of the heathens also; that he is 'rich in mercy to all that call upon him,' according to the light they have; and that 'in every nation, he that feareth God and worketh righteousness is accepted of him.'"[76]

In a sermon entitled "On Living Without God" he states:

> ...nor do I conceive that any man living has a right to sentence all the heathen and Mahometan world to damnation. It is far better to leave them to him that made them, and who is "the Father of all flesh;" who is the God of the Heathens as well as the Christians, and who hateth nothing that he hath made.[77]

After reading Marcus Antoninus he wrote in his journal, "what a strange heathen!" "I make no doubt, but this is one of those 'many,' who shall come from the east and the west, and sit down with Abraham, Isaac and Jacob, while 'the children of the kingdom' nominal Christians, are 'shut out'."[78]

The point being made here is that he saw the grace of God and the justice of God as adequate for all human conditions and situations. The deleterious effects of spreading European civilization could not be justified by the idea that, without such "Christianizing," those who never "heard" the gospel would be unquestionably lost. For an eighteenth-century evangelical this is an amazing position, and one that transcends the exclusiveness (and cultural bias) of late twentieth, early twenty-first century Christian fundamentalism. It can be explained by Wesley's belief in human equality, both in terms of depravity and the availability of God's grace.

John Wesley totally rejected the idea of Negro inferiority. Where slaves appeared to be inferior, he laid such appearance at the feet of the slave owners who degraded them and prevented their learning. Where the need for evangelism was used as a subtle mask for supporting inferiority, he preached that God's grace was equally available to those who had never heard the gospel. Transcending his culture and his own evangelicalism, Wesley stood for and practiced an egalitarianism that would not be lived up to by many in succeeding generations, even those in the tradition he began.

chapter 4

The relationship between Wesley's theology and his position on slavery

In the preceding chapter we saw that John Wesley's position on slavery was unequivocal. There was never a time in his life when he supported slavery or the slave trade. The only aspect of his connection with slavery that showed development was his level of activity. It dramatically increased from the early 1770s as he became aware of the circumstances and of what he could do to effect change. It was also shown that Wesley's rejection of slavery was based on well-reasoned principles. We come now to the theological base which informed those principles. In this chapter we shall examine both the theological distinctives that set him apart from orthodox Christianity and the tenets he held in common with it. With each facet of his theology we shall look for implications for slavery. The intention is to survey the aspects of his theology which most relate to the issue at hand, not to do an exhaustive study of Wesley's complete theology. Such studies have been adequately done by numerous others.[1]

The Dignity of Human Nature

Years ago, while doing doctoral research, I spent a month at the John Rylands University Library, Manchester, engulfed in the wonderful Wesley collection. Early in the month I discovered a tract written by Wesley entitled, *The Dignity of Human Nature*.[2] Because of my interest in personality theory and theological views of human nature, the title caught my attention and I was eager to read the tract. I thought I had discovered something by Wesley that proposed a lofty view of human nature, something Carl Rogers (theory of Client-Centered Therapy with an emphasis on human potential) could relate to. The title was promising. I put the tract aside, all sixty-six pages, as a Saturday morning "reward" for the end of my month of work.

When the day came, I began reading enthusiastically. As I read, I found it interesting that the first chapter did not portray human dignity; Wesley must be setting up his case for contrast. I read on. Slowly it became clear to me. The tract was consistent. The last section, even the final page, did not paint a different picture, a positive view. The negative view of human nature had not been a foil against which to contrast a positive view. The bottom line of Wesley's tract on the *dignity* of human nature was that there was none.

However, in the larger corpus of Wesley's writing there *are* contrasts. One is between humankind as originally created, in God's image — yes, with dignity — and present humanity, dominated by sin and without dignity. A second contrast emerges, between present fallen humanity and humanity touched by the grace of God, thereby restored to and even superseding the original dignity. But in the tract I read that Saturday morning, the whole scope was not developed. In spite of the title, the focus was exclusively narrowed to the human situation after the Fall and apart from grace. In this case, Wesley believed there is no inherent dignity. All three views of humankind — before the Fall, fallen humanity, and humanity restored by grace — are relevant to the problem of slavery. We shall examine each of them.

Wesley's portrayal of original man and woman, within his doctrine of creation, is infinitely high. Humankind completely reflected the image of God:

> In the image of God was man made, holy as he that created him is holy; merciful as the Author of all is merciful; perfect as his Father in heaven is perfect. As God is love, so man, dwelling in love, dwelt in an incorruptible picture of the God of glory. He was accordingly pure, as God is pure, from every spot of sin. He knew not evil of any kind or degree, but was inwardly sinless and undefiled.[3]

The qualities of such a being included perfect understanding, perfect will and perfect liberty, which functioned together to ensure indescribable happiness.[4]

Wesley developed his concept of the image of God in humankind to include three aspects: the natural, the political, and the moral. The natural meant that humans were spiritual and immortal beings with understanding, freedom and a variety of affections. The political aspect reflected God's governance of the universe with human beings given dominion over the earth. The moral reflected God's character, including righteousness and true holiness. In this understanding of the *Imago Dei* humankind had every possible advantage with nearly unlimited capacities. Human life was genuinely idyllic and filled with pure pleasure. Wesley not only accepts a very high view of original humankind, but describes it in terms that are specific, authentically human and winsome. His description resonates with what it means to be human, connecting it with present experience, but creating a vivid awareness of what was lost. It is as though he touches not only human feelings but the deep-seated psychic memory of what we once were. Only against this backdrop of creation and humankind in original perfection can the rest of Wesley's theology be brought into focus.

Of course, the original righteousness was not only natural and universal, it was "mutable."[5] This opened the way for the loss of original righteousness. For Wesley, the doctrine of human depravity, inseparable from his doctrine of creation, was foundational to the rest of his theology. He believed in total depravity and conceded that on this doctrine he was "within a hair's breadth" of Calvinism.[6] Had he and his fellow traveller to Northampton (mentioned at the beginning of this study) talked about depravity rather than predestination, there would have been no disagreement (and we would be deprived of a humorous story!). He maintained that biblically and sociologically the doctrine of total depravity was irrefutable and that he "always did ... clearly assert the total fall of man, and his utter inability to do any good of himself."[7]

How the Fall occurred was explained by Adam's necessary trial: the prohibition of eating from the tree of knowledge. When Adam failed this test the image of God in humans was partially lost and greatly distorted. Wesley explains the nature of the loss by describing the change in the three aspects of the image of God. The natural and political images are still present, but distorted. Wesley states,

> the "image of God" which remained after the fall, and remains in all men to this day, is the natural image of God, namely, the spiritual nature and immortality of the soul; not excluding the political image of God, or a degree of dominion over the creatures still remaining.[8]

The moral image, however, was not merely distorted, but destroyed. Wesley states that "the moral image of God is lost and defaced."[9]

The observable outcome of the change in the natural image could be seen in intellect, will, love and freedom. Understanding became clouded; it now "mistook falsehood for truth, and truth for falsehood."[10] Whereas the human will had been perfectly free before the Fall, now it was besieged as "grief and anger and hatred and fear and shame at once rushed upon it." It was torn in pieces as "the whole train of earthly, sensual and devilish passions fastened on [it]." And for love, it "became a torment." And what of the great human benefit, freedom? "Liberty went away with virtue. Instead of an indulgent master, it was under a merciless tyrant. The subject of virtue became the slave of vice."

The outcome of the loss of the political image was a chaos in relationships and in nature. Wesley even attributes the idea of female inferiority, with its attendant treatment of women, to the Fall. He warns women against this and encourages them to acknowledge and live up to their potential.[11] Regarding animals, whereas humans would have exercised loving dominion and caretaking before the Fall, they now selfishly and cruelly dominate, use and abuse animals and they even destroy nature. In fact, all of nature experiences the effects of the Fall. Wesley maintains that prior to the Fall animals were not predators and lovingly obeyed humans. But they, like humans, suffered a loss of intelligence.[12] In these two areas, the natural and political image, Wesley suggests that a remnant of the original, pristine ability is retained, but it is distorted and no longer complete or whole. The result is frustration and a negative shadow of the original quality. We are held in bondage by the same thing we desire to be master over, and were formerly capable of being so. It is as though the sense of "ought" enslaves and paralyzes us, when it would have motivated us. The loss of the natural and political image plays out in all relationships between people, as well as the human relationship to animals and the physical world.

But the greatest tragedy was the loss of the moral image, no mere distortion, but a complete loss. Man and woman lost all righteousness and holiness, the only basis on which they could relate to God. The result was total and eternal separation from God. Without God's intervention there was not even a remnant of the moral image necessary to produce a desire to return. Yet, still spiritual and immortal beings (natural image), their living outside of relationship with God meant they would live an eternal death. Wesley believed that the first couple became totally depraved. He also believed that this condition was passed from parent to child, although he acknowledged that he did not understand the process.[13]

Total depravity meant there was no mixture of good and evil in humankind. In his words, there was no "light intermixed with darkness. No; none at all."[14] Even when he admonished doing good, he made it clear that it was only God that could do good, or facilitate it in people. He explained, "otherwise, we might have had some room for boasting, as if it were our own desert, some goodness in us, or some good thing done by us."[15] For Wesley, boasting of good or spiritual ability was evidence of wrong motives, a further example of depravity.

Depravity affected both the nature and the actions of a person. Evil actions were not isolated, but the product of an evil nature with its well-known and universal by-products: death, pain and sickness. Wesley acknowledged that the innocent suffer, as in the cases of animals, infants and Jesus. He reasoned that it is still due to sin, but not necessarily the sin of the sufferers. It was due to what he termed "imputed sin" — that which all beings suffer from as a result of being part of the fallen order.[16]

So important was the doctrine of depravity to Wesley, that he considered it a theological watershed, dividing true and false religion. He saw the essence of true religion as God initiating and reaching out to humans who were helpless to change their own condition. If depravity were not total, there would be some hope of persons changing themselves, and the work of Christ would be superfluous, especially for infants. In Wesley's mind this stood in stark opposition to the long established orthodox Christian tradition and he cited authorities such as Athanasius and Augustine for support.[17] He states conclusively that the doctrine of depravity (original sin)

> is the first grand distinguishing point between Heathenism and Christianity. The one acknowledges that many men are infected with many vices, and even born with a proneness to them; but supposes withal, that in some the natural good much over-balances the evil: The other declares that all men are "conceived in sin," and

"shapen in wickedness;"...

Hence ... all who deny this, call it original sin, or by any other title, are but Heathens still in the fundamental point which differences Heathenism from Christianity.[18]

The reason for such an adamant position was that the whole of Christian doctrine, Christology, the atonement and soteriology was inseparably connected to a necessary cause: the human condition. Were that condition not radically in need and incapable of its own cure, the absolute necessity of all the rest would be compromised.

Wesley did not doubt the efficaciousness of God's work of grace. Grace was God's response to the human need, the desperate condition of God's hurting children.[19] However, the broader consideration, as implied earlier, is that Wesley's doctrine of depravity is not free-standing. He always saw it in context, juxtaposed between humans as originally created in God's image and humans redeemed with the image restored. The restoration Wesley envisioned was not only imputed righteousness, but "renewal in the whole image of God, in all righteousness and true holiness."[20] While righteousness and holiness, the moral image, suffered the most in the Fall (completely lost), this aspect is most wholly renewed in redemption. While the natural and political aspects of the image were not totally ruined in the Fall, only defaced, neither are they reinstated to their former state. Thus, humankind carry some permanent scars in this life. These are mainly in intellectual understanding, but not in the permanent loss of relationship with God, nor in the ability to relate lovingly to fellow human beings.[21]

In the midst of the pessimism of the human condition, Wesley exudes an optimism about the outcome. He would never concede that the Fall was part of God's plan, but God's infinite grace is capable of making humankind even better off than if there had been no Fall. He preached "we may gain infinitely more than we have lost." As well as "higher degrees of holiness," the relational aspect is enhanced because without the Fall "we might have loved

God the Creator, God the Preserver, God the Governor; but there would have been no place for love to God the Redeemer."²²

To conclude this section, it was the totality of human depravity that made grace so necessary; it is the completeness of the Fall that makes the work of grace so dramatically beautiful.

Human nature and slavery

Because Wesley placed so much importance on the doctrine of depravity, or indwelling sin, it is helpful to sift out the implications on slavery. The first implication relates to the fact that he assumed the original equality of all persons. While some of Wesley's contemporaries subscribed to the idea of "polygenesis," or the separate creations of different races, Wesley held to "monogenesis." In the late eighteenth century polygenesis was used as a justification for slavery because Africans could be considered a different species or a subspecies of humans. Being lower on the "chain of being," explained the apparent inferiority, supposed anatomical differences, and even allowed a divine purpose for them. Charles de Montesquieu satirized this theme in his famous *Spirit of Laws*, writing that "it is hardly to be believed that God, who is a wise being, should place a soul, especially a good soul, in such a black, ugly body" and again, "it is impossible for us to suppose these creatures to be men, because allowing them to be men, a suspicion would follow that we ourselves are not Christians."²³ Those who subscribed to polygenesis often missed the satire and saw these words as a support for slavery. Not so Wesley, who saw one act of creation producing all races with inherent equality. No second class stratum had been designed for the purpose of servitude. That was the role of the supralapsarian animal kingdom. As noted earlier (chapter 2, note 20) he saw the Genesis "curse of Ham" as a possible explanation of why slavery existed, but not as a justification for it. But even that would be the result of a curse, not original creation.

If all were originally perfect and equal in their perfection from creation, the second implication stems from the Fall. Wesley did not believe in various levels of fallenness. All were now equally depraved. His position asserts that no one since the Fall was "good," and there is no mixture of good and evil in anyone. Human beings are *totally* depraved and there is an equality in totality. Superlatives are not distributed across the continuum in degrees as comparatives might be; they are at the far end. Almost humorously Wesley reflects this after visiting the House of Lords: "I had frequently heard that this was the most venerable assembly in England. But how was I disappointed! What is a Lord, but a sinner, born to die!"[24] When preaching on depravity he levelled social classes. In 1743 he mentions that some of the rich and great were in his audience and finally one of the Lords left early saying, "Tis hot! Tis very hot."[25] Levelling is not something the privileged class desires, but it was the unavoidable conclusion of Wesley's view of depravity.

So equal was the depravity, that Wesley believed democracy could never work. Every individual was an enemy to the good of the community because of selfishness."[26] A constitutional monarchy was the only guarantee of community welfare, not because the king was less depraved, but because he was held in check by a constitution and his role was to enforce laws that were above him — laws based on God's laws.[27] The king prevented anarchy and the law prevented tyranny.[28] The implication for slavery is obvious. If Wesley opposed democracy or "self government" because of unilateral depravity (selfishness), there could be no justification of a system in which one depraved individual, a slave owner, wielded complete governing authority over another. Even aside from the fact that slavery was contrary to all the precepts of the Bible, the additional fact of the equality and extent of depravity made the practice of one person usurping the total authority and control of another out of the question. It could only result in the debasing and degrading of both. Wesley clearly saw this in slavery, which removed the constraints of law and allowed unrestrained expression of depravity. If one held a less extensive view of depravity, the consequences would not be as great. But Wesley's view of the extent of human depravity required the restraints that slavery abolished.

For Wesley, the corruption of depravity was not the last word. Depravity was always seen as a reality between the more positive realities of original humankind and restored humankind. With this dawns a persistent and penetrating optimism, even within the discussion of depravity. While depravity is total, it is never final. Significantly then, throughout Wesley's view of humanity runs the thread of persons' infinite worth due to grace. Although a human being is tiny when compared to the universe and human life is of short duration when compared to eternity, in God's sight the human soul is of inestimable worth, as evidenced by the offering of God's very Son to salvage such souls.[29]

The doctrine of total depravity had been used by some in Wesley's time to justify slavery. It was argued that since human beings were totally depraved, they could not be held responsible for their actions. This applied to the slave trader and the slave owner. It "explained" the horrors of capture and the middle passage as well as the brutal treatment for the rest of the slave's short life. What else could be expected from depraved Europeans? More often it applied to the slave. What else *should* be expected *for* depraved Africans? Their lack of learning, lack of true religion, debased morals and even appearance were evidence of their not being of the elect, and thus deserving of such treatment.

Such justification could not be supported by Wesley's view of depravity. If the doctrine could stand alone, it might explain and justify slavery. But as Wesley viewed it — a doctrine held in tension between the doctrines of original creation and restored creation — it could not justify slavery or any unkind treatment of others. He would have seen such reasoning as a further example of the fallen intellect which "mistook falsehood for truth, and truth for falsehood," a distortion of the natural image of God. And if Wesley saw the idea of female inferiority as the result of diminished rational abilities he would also see the idea of Negro inferiority in a similar way: a misunderstanding due to the Fall, but with the more blatantly brutal consequences of slavery. No doubt, he likewise would have seen the boasting of slave owners about evangelism among their slaves, while refusing to free them, as spiritual pride and confused thinking.

Slavery, with its rationale and abuses, was a perfect example for Wesley of depravity. The distortion of the political image turned dominion into abusive domination and destroyed wholesome human relationships. But never should depravity be used to justify slavery. Surrounding the issue of depravity was the principle of equality. All people were equally depraved. Therefore, no one had any ability or right to maintain unilateral control over another because no one was sufficiently insulated from the effects of depravity. Wesley's understanding of human depravity both informed and energized his opposition to slavery. Slavery was the unmistakable picture of how devoid of dignity humankind — all humankind — had become.

The grace that comes before

If total depravity means that persons have no inherent ability, or desire to be in relationship with God, how can there be any hope for them? One solution is to reduce the actual effects of the Fall so there is residual human ability to choose the good, to desire God and even move toward God. Another solution is to retain the totality of depravity and have God unilaterally effect change in a person's life. This is predestination. Wesley rejected both. He maintained that the Fall is so serious, persons have no ability or even desire to initiate a relationship with God. He also maintained that God does not irresistibly cause a person to repent. How could Wesley hold to both total depravity and human responsibility? Logically, the ideas of total depravity and responsibility seem to exclude each other.

The answer is found in his concept of prevenient grace. It is pivotal to his understanding of humanity and soteriology and it allows him to hold apparent contradictions in tension. While totally depraved, people still have a conscience. While God's sovereignty is unchallenged, people have a degree of freedom. While salvation is solely dependent on God's grace and totally divorced from human effort people have some responsibility in the process. In this doctrine emerges a balance between the "pessimism of nature" and the "optimism of grace."[30]

The term Wesley most frequently used was "preventing" grace. The meaning of the term is more foundational than the normal English usage of "prevent:" to stop something. Rather it derives from the two Latin words meaning "before" and "to come." Thus, something is prevented because something else comes *before* to stop or cure it. Prevenient grace is the grace that comes before: before human response, before the Fall, even before time. But it is the grace that facilitates all that we can experience of God.

Although Wesley saw himself to be within the theological tradition of Arminius, he believed that the doctrine of prevenient grace came from the larger Christian tradition. At least as far back as Augustine it was used to support the belief in divine initiative in salvation, especially in refuting Pelagianism.[31] However, Wesley found his official source in the Thirty-Nine Articles of the Church of England:

> The condition of man after the fall of Adam is such that he cannot turn and prepare himself, by his own natural strength and good works, to faith and calling upon God; Wherefore we have no power to do good works, pleasant and acceptable to God, without the grace of God preventing us, that we may have a good will, and working with us, when we have that good will.[32]

The doctrine was held firmly in the tradition in which Wesley was nurtured. While he learned from his tradition, his concept of the nature and function of prevenient grace went beyond Anglican doctrine, comprising one of his major contributions to Protestant thought.[33]

Wesley's understanding of prevenient grace changed after 1738. Prior to his Aldersgate experience he believed it was given in regeneration at baptism, thereafter making it possible for a person to be responsible, through obedience, for his or her salvation. In that sense it was grace empowering human effort, but following baptism.[34] After 1738 he saw prevenient grace as more universal; it was God's gift through Christ to every person, even before baptism, preparing the way for regeneration.

Nowhere does Wesley give a theological definition of this doctrine, but he does describe its characteristics. He typically states that it is God's grace going before, or "preventing," and as such is the "power of Christ," without which "we should be devils the next moment."[35] Although it is the result of Christ's atonement, it is not limited to chronological time but affects all persons since the Fall. Thus, it was not only timeless, but universal, withheld from none: "there is no man, unless he has quenched the Spirit, that is wholly void of the grace of God." The initial giving of it is irresistible as it "waiteth not for the call of man."[36] On this point Wesley departs from Arminius who believed that individuals have the power to reject it. Wesley believes that every person in the world experiences this grace, but subsequent to receiving it can respond in ways that increase or diminish it.[37]

According to Wesley, prevenient grace operates in relation to reason, moral law and conscience. As indicated above, when the natural component of the image of God was defaced in the Fall, human intellectual capacity was diminished. This was particularly true regarding knowledge about God. But the grace of Christ partly removes that impediment through God's Spirit "opening the eyes of [their] understanding."[38] Because of prevenient grace, all people of all periods of history know more about God. This was an important beginning, what he termed the "foundation" or "superstructure" of religion, but even divinely-assisted reason did not produce faith, hope and love.[39]

Prevenient grace also operates in the realm of human awareness of moral law. Whereas totally depraved individuals on their own would have no inherent sense of law and justice, through prevenient grace God "re-inscribes" the law on their hearts. All persons have some knowledge of the law, even if they have not heard the commandments, because it is now "written in their hearts by the same hand which wrote the commandments on the tables of stone."[40] Therefore, everyone can recognize good and evil; no one can claim ignorance of the law as an excuse.

The greatest benefit of prevenient grace, however — and this is not unrelated to an inner awareness of moral law — is that every human being has a conscience. Wesley defines the word, from its Latin and Greek roots "with" and "knowledge," as the concurrent knowledge of two different things: one's actions and the quality of those actions. He explains that it is conscience that makes us "at once conscious of our own thoughts, words, and actions; and of their merit or demerit." One produces a sense of pleasure, the other, uneasiness. Significantly, as a result of universal prevenient grace, this gift is also universal:

> Can it be denied that something of this is found in every man born into the world? And does it not appear as soon as understanding opens, as soon as reason begins to dawn? Does not every one then begin to know that there is a difference between good and evil...?[41]

Regardless of religion or culture or nationality Wesley believed that every person has an innate sense of right and wrong, justice and mercy. Every person is aware when he or she conforms to those principles and feels pricked when they do not conform. This experience is so common people think it is "natural." Wesley disagrees. He believes it transcends natural human endowments and attributes it to the supernatural.[42] So important was the concept of conscience in Wesley's doctrine of prevenient grace that in one respect he made the two synonymous: "No man living is entirely destitute of what is vulgarly called *natural conscience*... It is more properly termed, *preventing grace*."[43] In Wesley's thought it was prevenient grace, more than any another doctrine, that began to restore the debilitation of the Fall.

The predominant role of prevenient grace, through reason, awareness of the moral law, and conscience, is to bring people to repentance.[44] But, *how* does prevenient grace facilitate repentance? This has fostered a long-standing disagreement among Wesley scholars. As indicated at the beginning of this section, the challenge for Wesley was to hold two seemingly contradictory positions in tension: the utter inability of fallen humanity to initiate a relationship with God; the necessity of all people having the ability to respond to God (to counter the lack of human responsibility and predestination).

Proposed interpretations lean either toward prevenient grace removing the disabilities of the Fall so persons are free of their own initiative to choose God, or they lean toward prevenient grace sensitizing the conscience and bringing such despair that God's action is singular and decisive, with no human participation. Of course, there are positions between these extremes. The various interpretations are summarized very helpfully by Randy L. Maddox.[45] He goes beyond the previous interpretations to focus on the relationship between God and a person that is effected by prevenient grace. It is God's presence that sensitizes awareness of need and invites response, which allows even greater responsiveness to God's working in one's life.[46] However, for the present study related to slavery it is sufficient to note *what* prevenient grace restores, rather than *how* it brings repentance and justification. Touched by God's grace, debilitated human faculties (reason, awareness of moral law, conscience) are rehabilitated by God's empowering presence. These factors have important implications for slavery.

Prevenient grace and slavery

Wesley's understanding of prevenient grace touches slavery from several vantage points. It relates to the nature of the slave and the slave owner. Regarding the slave, all persons are of infinite worth because all receive prevenient grace through the universal atonement. This Wesleyan assumption brings one of the greatest indictments against slavery. How can that which is of infinite worth be treated with such distain so that it is used, abused and discarded as if it were not even human? Wesley asks rhetorically, "Did the Creator intend that the noblest creatures in the visible world should live such a life as this? Are these thy glorious work, Parent of Good?"[47] The enslaving of human beings, especially when it is permanent, is based on the assumption of inequality of worth.

Beyond the issue of worth is the fact that individuals possess rational abilities and even "rational-spiritual" abilities. The latter especially enhance a person's knowledge about God and are preparatory to repentance. As such, they speak not only to the worth of persons but also to the fact that individuals are capable of living in meaningful relationship with God.

The major significance of this doctrine regarding slavery is what it implied about the slave owner. That all human beings have the moral law "re-inscribed" on their hearts draws attention to their accountability. Prevenient grace, guaranteeing that everyone has a conscience, places the slave owner and slave trader (anyone connected with slavery) in a far more responsible light. This would have given Wesley a stronger sense of mission and hope when he preached at Bristol or Liverpool, centres of slave trade activity. This doctrine must also have encouraged him to focus his comments directly to those involved in the slave trade when he wrote his tract.

Wesley concurred with Francis Hutcheson who asserted that conscience could contain both a "public sense" and a "moral sense." This became a more specific way of understanding how conscience functioned relative to others' pain and especially to the human response of relieving or inflicting pain. One's public conscience empathizes or shares in the misery of others, whereas the moral sense passes judgement; it "approves of benevolence and disapproves of cruelty."[48] As a result, the great evil of slavery (which, in Wesley's view, caused more pain, heartache, injury and death than anything in history) could not be dismissed on the grounds that people are ignorant of right and wrong, or that they were devoid of feelings. Neither Christian nor non-Christian could claim such an excuse.

Based on this principle Wesley reminded his readers in *Thoughts Upon Slavery* that slavery could not "be reconciled (setting the Bible out of the question) with any degree of either justice or mercy."[49] It had to do with the fact that every person on earth, through universal prevenient grace (not organized religion or

Scripture), possesses a conscience and a sense of mercy and justice. No one could feign blindness to so graphic a need for benevolence. This was the same position that fueled Anthony Benezet's clear sense that there was no need to substantiate how evil slavery was because it was so obvious. It was this conviction that caused Wesley to plead with those involved in slavery: "Whether Christian or no, show yourself a man!"[50] Throughout *Thoughts Upon Slavery* Wesley appealed mostly to the benevolent in his reader. By contrast, some of his contemporaries appealed more to fear of retribution.[51] In Wesley's thinking human benevolence and the ability to empathize were rooted in prevenient grace.[52]

Another implication for slavery which grows out of prevenient grace relates to the universality of the atonement. This implication would apply to Christians who were involved with slavery. Because he believed the atonement is universal, it follows that all persons are potentially recipients of God's saving grace. Wesley was convinced that the most effective way of communicating God's love was through doing good works for one's neighbour. This is seen clearly in his sermon, "Free Grace," in which he stated that the doctrine of predestination (and limited atonement) destroys a major motive for doing good to others. He explains,

> This uncomfortable doctrine directly tends to destroy our zeal for good works. And this it does, first, as it naturally tends ... to destroy our love to the greater part of mankind, namely, the evil and unthankful. For whatever lessens our love, must so far lessen our desire to do them good. This it does, secondly, as it cuts off one of the strongest motives to all acts of bodily mercy, such as feeding the hungry, clothing the naked, and the like, viz., the hope of saving their souls from death. For what avails it to relieve their temporal wants, who are just dropping into eternal fire?[53]

While George Whitefield disagreed with Wesley and felt that the doctrine of election was his most powerful motivation for doing good works, Wesley was not persuaded. Whitefield even felt that preaching could have a restraining effect on the evil of the non-elect. But again, Wesley's position was that the greater restraint would be universal prevenient grace and the effect that conversion, available to all, would have on restraining evil.[54] Wesley was convinced that, in spite of Whitefield's experience, the practical result of teaching predestination would be to deter good works among the masses. He would have been aware of Oliver Cromwell's theological justification of his massacre at Drogheda, Ireland.[55] Because the garrison was comprised of Roman Catholics, considered "heathen" by Cromwell, they were exterminated. Wesley realized that if grace were not seen as universal (given equally) not only could Drogheda be justified, but also the enslaving of the non-elect, because their worth was questionable.

The focal point for Wesley was that every slave was a potential believer and doing good for them as neighbours, acting in love, would be the most effective means of persuading them of God's love. This clearly flies in the face of the evangelizing approach of others, such as Whitefield and the SPG, who believed that slavery, in spite of its brutality and cruelty, facilitated evangelism by exposing Africans to Christianity. There is no question that this aspect of Wesley's theology influenced his position. From his own actions on behalf of the slave, it is clear that the good works he envisioned as a means of evangelizing the slave included: helping the destitute slave, and especially removing the chains of slavery.

Wesley's doctrine of prevenient grace helped lay a foundation for antislavery thought, his own and that of his followers, by addressing the nature of the slave (capable of experiencing a relationship with God), the nature of the slave owner and slave trader (they knew right from wrong and had a capacity for benevolence), and the nature of Christianity, which seeks to bring all to the awareness of God's love and grace by doing good to them.

Free indeed? The question of free will

Many years ago, when our daughter was approaching two years of age, we were enjoying a nice meal in the Campbell House

Restaurant in Lexington, Kentucky. At one point in the meal I noticed that she was eyeing a wedge of lemon that was within her reach. Before long she caught hold of it in her small fist. Of course, like anything in a small child's hand, it went immediately to her mouth — unsweetened lemon. She frowned, squeezed her eyes shut and took her hand away from her mouth. But the lemon remained in her grasp, so before long, it was back in her mouth with a repeat of the pained expression and rejection. Still, the lemon stayed firmly in her hand. Several times in the next few minutes the cycle recurred. It seemed that even though she didn't like it, she could not keep from putting the lemon in her mouth. As long as it was in her hand the motion was repeated. I finally took it from her and ended both her displeasure and our entertainment. She was very pleased to let me have it, although she had not been able to release it herself. Was she free? Augustine said we are free to do evil and that is what we will do, repeatedly. In our bent condition we are incapable of doing good. We are slaves to our defaced will.

Wesley's view of human depravity indicated that persons had relinquished their freedom. Not only were their rational faculties diminished and their sense of morality distorted, but their wills became enslaved by sin. However, as seen in the previous section, Wesley believed that prevenient grace restored some of what was lost, especially the rational ability to know about God and the restoration of a healthy conscience. We are not in a cloud of unknowing, but are fully cognizant of the quality of our thoughts and actions.

So, where does that leave us? Are we still under the control of sin, with our wills bound? Or are we once again free moral agents, able not only to discern good from evil, but capable of choosing and doing the good? Throughout Wesley's works, statements that seem to reject free will can be found:

> Such is the freedom of his will; free only to do evil; free to "drink in iniquity like water;" to wander farther and farther from the living God, and do more "despite [injury] to the Spirit of grace!"

and,

> But, indeed, both Mr. F[letcher] and Mr. W[esley] absolutely deny natural free will. We both steadily assert that the will of man is by nature free only to evil.[56]

Then, in apparent support of free will he writes,

> For he made you free agents; having an inward power of self-determination, which is essential to your nature. And he deals with you as free agents from first to last.[57]

and,

> We cannot impute too much to divine Providence, unless we make it interfere with our free agency.[58]

The problem in accepting either approach at face value is that neither fully correlates with the rest of Wesley's theology. If human beings are totally depraved, with their freedom completely destroyed, those after Adam and Eve can only follow the course of sin which was irreversibly programmed by the choice in the garden. The injustice of that position is that we would be condemned for the sin of our first parents. Wesley did not accept this, but believed people would only be condemned for their own sinful activity.[59] On the other hand Wesley was not willing to believe that people are simply free to choose God and avoid sin. This position nullifies the gravity and influence of human depravity. Wesley held unwaveringly to human moral inability due to depravity.[60]

Wesley's true theology does not align with either extreme position. To understand the true meaning of the earlier quotations and how they can coexist without contradiction they must be seen in the context of his overall perspective of free will. It must be viewed in relation to the human creature before the Fall, in the depths of depravity, under prevenient grace, and then fully regenerated.

According to Wesley, before the Fall the human will was completely free. Choice could be made for either good or evil and actions would congruently follow the choice. He termed the freedom to perform actions as "liberty," distinguished from merely willing. Such complete liberty was part of human capacity from being created in the moral image of God.[61] After the Fall, however, the moral image was lost, and with it freedom; "we have no power to do good works."[62] By "good works," in this context, Wesley was referring to what was pleasing, or of merit to God, as reflected in the moral image of God.

In the physical or non-moral realm Wesley held a different opinion of the freedom of even depraved humankind. He strongly opposed the idea of a mechanistic universe. In spite of the Fall, persons were not determined in all things, but retained some of the natural image of God. They maintained a "degree of liberty; of self-moving, yea, and self-governing power (otherwise we were mere machines; stocks and stones.)"[63] He did not hesitate to disagree with the new theories that human actions were merely responses to sensory stimuli and therefore part of an unchangeable chain of events. Such a view made God the source of all the evil in the world. He also took issue with Jonathan Edwards, stating that actions cannot be described as free unless the will is also free, which Edwards denied.[64] Wesley believed that both the will and actions were free in terms of physical, non-moral actions. He refused to believe "the noblest creature in the visible world to be only a fine piece of clock-work."[65] The fact that people *feel* they have some self-determining power was not illusory for him, but rooted in truth.[66]

Wesley's argument against determinism was in the context of his battle against predestination, which he believed removed responsibility from human activity. But beyond actions, we are completely helpless to "merit" anything "good" that leads to salvation. Wesley's strongest statements against free will occur in that context. He maintained unequivocally that "since the fall, no child of man has a natural power to choose anything that is truly good."[67] That would be taking free will too far; "Natural free will [in moral things], in the present state of mankind, I do not understand."[68] In sum, speaking of "things of an indifferent nature;"[69] in practical, non-theological terms Wesley allowed human freedom, but when speaking soteriologically, he believed depraved persons have no freedom to do good. Seen in this light, the opening quotations are compatible. Wesley rejected the concept of natural free will in moral, salvific issues, but not in the generality of physical movement.

How then could individuals incapacitated by depravity be held responsible? At this point it is helpful to consider a paradigm of Wesley's view of human freedom as consisting of three levels. The lowest level, that of bodily movement and "things of an indifferent nature," are part of the existing remnant of being created in the natural image of God. Everyone experiences this kind of freedom. It is natural and has no connection with prevenient grace or salvation.

The second, or intermediate, level has to do with moral choices, including human interaction (not to be confused with salvific choices) and relates to human accountability. This level was lost in the Fall but has been universally restored by prevenient grace. While it is not "natural," in that it cannot be experienced apart from God's grace, it is a part of every person's life because the atonement is universal. Wesley explains, "there is a *measure* of free-will supernaturally restored to every man, together with that supernatural light which 'enlightens every man that cometh into the world.'"[70]

The third level of freedom is only possible for those who have been regenerated; those who have exercised their moral freedom (intermediate level, through prevenient grace) and responded through God's empowering presence to the experience of sanctification. They are now free to work with God and continue to allow God to work "good" in their lives, not for the purpose of merit or salvation (that is accomplished), but for the working of God's will in the world.

To summarize, before the Fall, all three of these levels were present in Adam and Eve. After the Fall the lowest level is present by nature, the intermediate level is present by prevenient grace, and the highest level is possible in salvation.

Using this paradigm we can explore how Wesley's understanding of human freedom relates to the process of justification. There is a very significant relationship between prevenient grace and free will. Prevenient grace restores the middle level of freedom, giving awareness of our need (conscience): "It is undeniable, that [God] has fixed in man, in every man, his umpire, conscience; an inward judge, which passes sentence both on his passions and actions, either approving or condemning."[71] However, that awareness does not remove the impediment so we can overtly choose God. The problem of depravity is not simply solved by conscience, which plays an essential role, but "has not power to remove what it condemns." Indeed, as Wesley said, "it shows the evil which it cannot cure."[72] In addition to awareness of the problem, prevenient grace brings awareness of God's adequacy and willingness to help: "But the God of power can cure it [that which conscience condemned]; and the God of love will, if we choose he should."[73] In this passage we see the intricate working of prevenient grace with its fruits of conscience and freedom. When the individual becomes aware of the need and his or her inability to rectify it, there also comes the awareness of God's adequacy and love. The role of freedom at this point is the ability to acknowledge God's presence, which contains the power to cure what only God can cure. Wesley's use of the word "choose" in this statement reflects the fine balance between the human inability to initiate faith and the responsibility of responding. His wording indicates that we choose for God to act in our lives rather than acting ourselves. It is the *relinquishing* of control so God can act. It is a negation of the self as opposed to overtly choosing faith, or spiritually moving on one's own behalf.[74] If sin is the radically egocentric elevation of self, then the assumption that a person can do something to solve it on their own by initiating, is simply a further expression of such egocentricity. Paradoxically, the intermediate level of freedom enables a relinquishment of control, allowing God to be active (in control) rather than self.[75] The result is acknowledging God's presence and action. This is contrasted to the highest level of freedom, in pre-Fall persons, which would permit the overt move to God.

To return to the analogy of my daughter and the lemon, she had a kind of freedom. She could freely grasp the lemon, and freely move her hand to her mouth. She was also free to take her hand away from her mouth, but she did not seem to be free to stop repeating the motion toward her mouth, or to discard the sour tasting lemon. By some kind of reflex, what was in her hand had to go to her mouth. Finally she became aware of me, and with her pained facial expression acknowledged her difficulty. She didn't seem to be able to solve her problem alone, but I was able to replace the lemon in her hand with something more pleasing.

In some ways my daughter's "freedom" is analogous to how Wesley saw humanity in its depraved condition. There is an element of freedom, but there is also a proclivity to something not ultimately good or pleasing. Her rational ability was not adequate to solve the problem, although she was clearly aware of it. Depraved individuals cannot even initiate a move toward God, but by prevenient grace can become aware of God's loving presence and can respond to God's initiative.[76]

The process that Wesley described ("the God of love will, if we choose he should") is consistent with the soteriological process he described elsewhere. In the context of the "means of grace" he speaks of works of piety (prayer, scripture reading, worship) and works of mercy (loving acts to others). These are never understood by Wesley as salvific, the means of gaining God's approval; that would be "works righteousness." On the contrary, they are the ways we respond to our awareness of spiritual inadequacy, acknowledging our need and waiting for God's touch and presence. Significantly, they are called the works of "repentance," not the works of faith and they are done while waiting, not in place of waiting. The statement which introduces them begins, "we wait ... in universal obedience."[77] To choose to do them is not tantamount to choosing the "Good," but choosing in humility to allow God to do the work of good in a person's life. In this process again, the middle level of freedom is appropriated, whereby the person is free to be in a position of response to God, to acknowledge the need and desire for God's presence.

With this understanding, human responsibility (by prevenient grace) is maintained, but not at the expense of God's sovereignty.[78] In his sermon "On Working Out Our Own Salvation," Wesley gives his clearest explanation of the process:

> Every one has, sooner or later, good desires; although the generality of men stifle them before they can strike deep root, or produce any considerable fruit. Every one has some measure of that light, some faint glimmering ray, which, sooner or later, more or less, enlightens every man that cometh into the world. And every one, unless he be one of the small number whose conscience is seared as with a hot iron, feels more or less uneasy when he acts contrary to the light of his own conscience. So that no man sins because he has not grace, but because he does not use the grace which he hath.
>
> Therefore, inasmuch as God works in you, you are now able to work out your own salvation.[79]

In the final sentence Wesley states the interaction of God's initiative and human response and responsibility. That interplay has to do with the freedom which results from prevenient grace and it reaches beyond the individual's justification. To "work out your own salvation" involved doing the works of repentance which included works of mercy to one's neighbour. In a very sophisticated use of "freedom," Wesley avoids works righteousness, but maintains accountability and responsibility for one's treatment of fellow human beings.[80] He says this in the context of justification, revealing an amazingly inclusive perspective considering the context of eighteenth evangelicalism.

However, once a person is justified and regeneration has begun, with no need for gaining God's approval because it has been granted through Christ, the highest level of freedom is approached, whereby persons can initiate authentic good for others. Wesley associates this kind of freedom with regeneration when he says, "A man is not free till he is regenerated by baptism, which repairs the ruins of his decayed nature, and once more leaves him at his own liberty [the ability to act] in the hands of his own counsel."[81] While this sermon reflects baptismal regeneration, Wesley's understanding before 1738, the results of regeneration remain consistent in his thought. The strength and liberty that come from regeneration help "so that when afterward we hear arguments for our duty, they pierce deeper into our mind, than it was possible they should while there was such a thick film of corruption about our hearts."[82] Thus, it is freedom through prevenient grace that facilitates justification and regeneration, which then make possible the highest level of freedom, allowing an unselfish and loving response to others. The acting in love in relationship to others will be taken up in the following section on Christian perfection.

In summary it can be said that Wesley really did posit a kind of free will, but to be seen in a stewardship rather than a possessive sense. We experience sufficient freedom by prevenient grace to have access to greater freedom. The first opens the way to God's presence, working renewal *in* the individual, while the latter to God's working *through* the individual.

Freedom and slavery

Beyond question, Wesley's position on human freedom maintained that all individuals are fully accountable for their spiritual state. That fact has direct implications for slavery. The system of black slavery in the eighteenth century made one person the property and the responsibility of another. A slave owner could and did control not only the resources for the slaves' physical needs, but for their educational and spiritual development as well. This could work for or against the welfare of the slaves. They could be nurtured or kept in the worst conditions and deprived of all educational and spiritual exposure. Where slave owners were Christians, they often saw such responsibility as the opportunity for evangelism. Their role was perceived as mediating between the slave and God.[83] But the point here is that slavery, in effect, removed the responsibility of the slave. The system made slaves totally dependent on their masters. They were responsible to another human being rather than to God. The form of predestination that Wesley opposed could take a softer position on slavery because, in the context of theological determinism, a system that removed human responsibility to God was irrelevant; God would work salvation in the elect regardless of circumstances.

By contrast, Wesley's idea of freedom, even though limited to the first steps toward acknowledging God, meant that all persons were responsible for themselves. Another could not justly usurp that authority. If persons were fully responsible to God, they must be allowed the external freedom to do what their internal freedom directed. Any system that destroyed such freedom must not be tolerated. It was from the vantage point that persons must have the right to obey God and conscience that Wesley defended English political freedom.[84] Any system that blurred awareness of responsibility to God, or hindered acting on that responsibility, was antithetical to the principles of Christianity. Slavery was undeniably such a system.[85]

Another implication derives directly from Wesley's concept of liberty blended with his view of prevenient grace. While prevenient grace facilitates conscience (no one could take part in such an evil as slavery and not be conscious of the wrong), the measure of freedom people experience enables them to proactively do good in opposition to evil. Undoubtedly this implication fueled Wesley's very direct words to those involved with slavery. Had Whitefield survived beyond 1770 there would likely have been interesting dialogue between the two, because Whitefield used slave labour to support his orphanage in Georgia. Although Benezet honoured Whitefield's integrity of conscience,[86] one wonders if Wesley would have been less accepting in light of his highly developed theology of conscience and liberty. As noted above, Wesley believed all persons could initiate works of mercy toward their neighbours, but Christians were enabled to cooperate with God in doing an even higher good. Thus, *all* people were capable of doing some degree of good for the rest of humankind and in fact, were responsible to do so. There was no justification to remain idle in the face of injustice. Ability implied responsibility and Wesley preached that the works of mercy done for or withheld from the hungry, thirsty, and naked were actually done for or withheld from Christ.[87] He knew of no one more hungry, thirsty or naked than the slave.

Wesley's doctrine of free will carries direct implications for slavery in the light of both the nature of the slave (everyone is accountable to God and must be left free to live responsibly), and the nature of those in a position to remove such oppression (all have sufficient "liberty" to act in benevolence). All people, especially Christians, have sufficient freedom to oppose evil.

The triumph of grace: Christian perfection

Wesley saw the teaching of Christian perfection as God's definitive calling for him and his followers. In the last year of his life he spoke of it as "the grand depositum which God [had] lodged with the people called Methodists."[88] It has accurately been called his "most distinctive doctrinal emphasis,"[89] but it was much more than a doctrine among doctrines for Wesley. It was integral to and inseparable from the body of Christian truth. The entire corpus of salvation by faith contained two branches: justification and sanctification. Justification received much emphasis in teaching, preaching, and writing by Wesley's contemporaries. Wesley saw his mission to bring awareness to the balance, the complete story of God's power as well as his love. It was not just forgiveness; it was the transformed life, and Wesley never relegated this application of God's power to a secondary place. Colin Williams rightly points out that Christian perfection was the "climax" of Wesley's understanding of grace and the place where "his theology comes to focus."[90]

So central was this theme to his theology that Wesley used various terms interchangeably when referring to it. He could speak of "holiness," "perfection," "sanctification," "full salvation," "true religion" or "righteousness" and consistently use the same definition or description. Even the "altogether Christian," contrasted to the "almost Christian" was described by the same characteristics.[91] (In this study, the terms sanctification and Christian perfection will be used interchangeably, although others have specified nuanced differences.)

Because his concern was the central content of Christian perfection (the actual working of God's power in the human life, not the specialized doctrinal terminology), he claimed to have no "particular fondness" for the actual term, and stated that "it seldom occurs either in my preaching or writing."[92] In 1768 and 1772 he and Charles even corresponded about dropping the term.[93] But in reality he did use the term frequently because it was biblical and in his mind it resonated with the truth he so valued. For Wesley, the dynamic truth that the term Christian perfection represented espoused the whole of Christianity and was crucial enough that he believed "one cannot see the Lord" without it.[94]

How did sanctification fit into the schema of God's work of grace? It was initiated at the moment of the new birth: "…at the same time that we are justified, yea, in that very moment, sanctification begins."[95] In his sermon, "On The New Birth," he explained the relationship of justification and the new birth:

> In order of *time*, neither of these is before the other; in the moment we are justified by the grace of God, through the redemption that is in Jesus, we are also "born of the Spirit;" but in order of *thinking*, as it is termed, justification precedes the new birth. We first conceive his wrath to be turned away, and then his Spirit to work in our hearts.[96]

While the two are parts of a whole, they should not be confused as one and the same. They are of a "totally different nature" and sanctification is a "distinct gift from God." The new birth serves as the "gate" to sanctification.[97] While separate and distinct, they are integrally related. In a sermon describing the results or evidence of the new birth, Wesley listed faith, hope and love. It is revealing that the last of this trilogy becomes such an important component of his concept of perfection.[98]

In examining sanctification and justification (the new birth) a number of parallels become apparent. Each is considered a gift of God which comes only through the "condition and instrument" of faith.[99] He specified that "sanctifying as well as justifying faith is the free gift of God."[100] But if a gift, how does one wait for the gift? The process Wesley describes is the same for justification and sanctification. The waiting involves repentance and doing the works of repentance which function as God's appointed means of grace. In a very similar description to that used in the context of justification, he says about sanctification:

> We wait ... in universal obedience; in keeping all the commandments; in denying ourselves, and taking up our cross daily. These are the general means which God hath ordained for our receiving his sanctifying grace. The particular are, — prayer, searching the scripture, communicating, and fasting.[101]

These activities are more fully specified in "The Scripture Way of Salvation," and include not only the ordinances but service to one's fellows:

> But what good works are those, the practice of which you affirm to be necessary to sanctification? First, all works of piety; such as public prayer, family prayer, and praying in our closet; receiving the supper of the Lord; searching the Scriptures, by hearing, reading, meditating; and using such a measure of fasting or abstinence as our bodily health allows.
>
> Secondly, all works of mercy; whether they relate to the bodies or souls of men; such as feeding the hungry, clothing the naked, entertaining the stranger, visiting those that are in prison, or sick, or variously afflicted; such as the endeavouring to instruct the ignorant, to awaken the stupid sinner, to quicken the lukewarm, to confirm the

wavering, to comfort the feebleminded, to succour the tempted, or contribute in any manner to the saving of souls from death. This is the repentance, and these the "fruits meet for repentance" which are necessary to full sanctification. This is the way wherein God hath appointed his children to wait for complete salvation.[102]

The kinds of activities in this passage are classified as either works of piety or works of mercy.

There are two apparent differences in the waiting for the faith of justification and the faith of sanctification. Since justification relates to forgiveness, the repentance *following* justification and preceding sanctification implies no guilt.[103] In addition, the works of repentance following justification, but preceding sanctification, have a greater focus on works of mercy. In light of how Wesley develops the life of the sanctified Christian, this is significant and will be explored later.

Wesley makes it clear that the works of repentance are in no sense to be understood as the earning of a spiritual state. They are simply the way God has chosen to bestow faith. This is again parallel for both justification and sanctification. For justification Wesley explains the relationship of works and faith:

> …both repentance, and fruits meet for repentance, are in some sense, necessary to justification. But they are not necessary in the *same sense* with faith, nor in the *same degree*. Not in the same degree; for those fruits are only necessary *conditionally*; if there be time and opportunity for them. Otherwise a man may be justified without them … but he cannot be justified without faith.[104]

In regard to sanctification he gives the same explanation:

> …both this repentance and its fruits are necessary to full salvation; yet they are not necessary either in the same sense with faith, or in the same degree: — Not in the *same*

degree; for these fruits are only necessary *conditionally*, if there be time and opportunity for them; otherwise a man may be sanctified without them. But he cannot be sanctified without faith.[105]

He further clarifies the delicate balance and the difference between faith and obedience:

Probably the difference ... lies in words chiefly. All who expect to be sanctified at all expect to be sanctified by faith. But meantime they know that faith will not be given but to them that obey. Remotely, therefore, the blessing depends on our works, although immediately on simple faith.[106]

Still, it is not something one earns. Human effort has absolutely no salvific merit because faith is the only condition and faith is God's free gift. However, there must be a human response to God's enabling presence, and that response is experienced in the works of repentance. Thus, Wesley's understanding of the process leading to sanctification involves the beginning of sanctification in the new birth. It then requires repentance subsequent to justification and usually the works of repentance, during which the gift of faith for full salvation is granted.

As indicated above, God's love and power effect not only forgiveness, but a completely transformed life. While the means of sanctification is faith, the result is an actual moral change in the believer. Wesley disparaged the antinomian teaching that completely divorced justification from the resulting behavioural change. He would concur with Quakers who disagreed with those that "preach up sin to the grave," (those who preach that we continue to sin until death), accepting human fallenness as an excuse for lack of moral reform. Authentic salvation includes holiness and he contrasted the result of justification with the result of sanctification by using insightful comparative phrases. While justification produces a "relative" change (one's relationship to God), sanctification produces a "real" change (the person's inner being). Justification is what God does "*for* us, through his Son," and sanctification is what God works "*in* us by his Spirit." Through justification Christ's righteousness "entitles" us to heaven, but his power in bringing personal holiness "qualifies" us for it.[107] In these phrases he is not minimizing justification, but identifying the more complete nature of the full work of grace. He explains that "the title 'holy,' applied to the Spirit of God, does not only denote that he is holy in his own nature, but that he makes us so."[108] The consequences are practical. While justification deals with the guilt of sin, sanctification affects the power of sin in the believer's life.[109]

It should be noted that while some of Wesley's thinking about sanctification changed after Aldersgate (the relationship to the overall process of salvation), the idea of Christian perfection and even his description of it were present before 1738 and remained consistent to the end of his life. His first writing to be published was *The Circumcision of the Heart*, preached at Oxford University in 1733. It contained his description of the characteristics of holiness and in 1777 he commented that he continued to hold that view.[110]

How does Wesley specifically describe holiness, the genuine moral change in the human life? Three perspectives occur frequently in his sermons and other writings and they are presented clearly in *A Plain Account of Christian Perfection* — his most comprehensive treatment of the topic. They include:

a) a reorientation of motivation which he calls purity of intention;
b) the renewed image of God (moral image);
c) the ability to love God and neighbour.

In a passage that underscores the similarity, congruity and integral relationship of the three perspectives he states:

> In one view, it is *purity of intention*, dedicating all the life to God. It is the giving God all our heart; it is one desire and design ruling all our tempers. It is the devoting, not a part, but all our soul, body, and substance to God. In

another view, it is all the mind which was in Christ, enabling us to walk as Christ walked. It is the circumcision of the heart from all filthiness, all inward as well as outward pollution. It is a *renewal of the heart in the whole image of God*, the full likeness of Him that created it. In yet another, it is the *loving God with all our heart, and our neighbour as ourselves*. Now, take it in which of these views you please, (for there is no material difference,) and this is the whole and sole perfection . . . which I have believed and taught for these forty years, from the year 1725 to the year 1765.[111]

As indicated above, sanctification, according to Wesley, was one of two main branches of salvation. The essence of this branch was that the image of God can be restored in persons. For him the greatest tragedy of the Fall was that we completely lost the moral image of God, in which we had been created. The moral dimension of the *Imago Dei*, holiness and true righteousness, was the basis of our relating to God and inseparably connected to our ability to love genuinely. While the natural and political dimensions of the *Imago Dei* are only partly restored by prevenient grace, the moral dimension can be completely restored in "full salvation." It was not by chance that Wesley chose such a term because he believed that at this level of salvation the moral image could be fully restored. And with that restoration we can again experience full relationship with God.

The various perspectives Wesley referred to (purity of intention, the mind which was in Christ, love of God and neighbour) were simply extensions or derivatives of the renewed moral image. In his writings the idea of purity of intention usually occurs in the context of having the mind of Christ, which is the result of the restored image. Certainly the ability to love, especially to love God with the whole heart, mind, soul and strength, was an attribute of unfallen humanity with the image intact.[112] As the image is restored such capacity to love returns. Seen in this light Wesley's understanding of sanctification goes far beyond justification; it appropriates the power of God, not just God's pardon.[113]

If Wesley's doctrine of human depravity reflects his very low view of humankind, without dignity, his view of sanctification reflects the opposite end of the continuum: humankind with nearly unlimited potential. The greatness of human potential lay in the fact that the image of God was able to be restored. In addition to the comparative phrases mentioned above, in later years Wesley spoke of justification restoring us to God's "favour," while sanctification restores us to God's "image."[114] As far back as 1730 he had spoken of the image of God being "reprinted" on the soul.[115] The concept of the restored image was used consistently by Wesley in describing Christian perfection.[116]

Far more than a mere theological tangent or hobby horse, this was nothing less than radical transformation: being made a new person with a different moral foundation and new moral abilities.[117] For Wesley it was much more than a passive theological concept; it was active because it was love. If sanctification was most succinctly described as the renewed image of God, the most accurate and explicit outworking (or expression) of that image was love. The two concepts, image of God and love, are brought together in his statement, "the very image of the invisible God" is love.[118]

Wesley goes to great lengths to identify the sanctified life with love, as represented in the following passages:

> But what is perfection? The word has various senses: Here it means perfect love. It is love excluding sin; love filling the heart, taking up the whole capacity of the soul. It is love "rejoicing evermore, praying without ceasing, in everything giving thanks."

> Entire sanctification, or Christian perfection, is neither more nor less than pure love — love expelling sin and governing both the heart and life of a child of God.

> Indeed, what is it [Christian perfection] more or less than humble, gentle, patient love![119]

He affirmed that Christians should aspire to "nothing more, but more of ... love;" they could go no higher than this.[120]

It must be acknowledged that in many of his statements about love, Wesley was specifying love for God. One example is his noting that love is the essence of all commandments,

> In this is perfection, and glory, and happiness. The royal law of heaven and earth is this, "Thou shalt love the Lord thy God with all thy heart, and with all thy soul, and with all thy mind, and with all thy strength."[121]

However, he saw God's love for us as the foundation of both human happiness and the ability to change morally and conform to holiness.[122] In this we see a hint of the spiritual dynamic for transformation; God's love elicits our response of love to God.

To the point of the full development of the process, however, Wesley does not leave our love for God unspecified or ethereal, because love for God implied something more tangible. He operationalizes the concept by focusing on what people can do to actually express their love for God. Realizing that there is an inseparable connection between loving God and loving one's fellows, he clarified that the practical result of loving God included love for one's neighbour. One could not serve or love God in a vacuum:

> One of the principal rules of religion is, to lose no occasion of serving God. And, since he is invisible to our eyes, we are to serve him in our neighbour; which he receives as if done to himself in person, standing visibly before us.[123]

This was not an optional response but the necessary expression of love for God, and it meant loving all persons, not only fellow believers.[124] He was consistent in this emphasis.

Aware that love of neighbour could possibly be generalized to the point that its practical effect was lost, he specifies exactly what it entailed, using the words of the apostle Paul in Galatians 5: "love, joy, peace, longsuffering, gentleness, goodness, fidelity ... meekness, temperance." Then building toward his point he observes, "What a glorious constellation of graces is here!"[125] Finally, he marshalls these specific and wonderful qualities to his theme: "Now suppose all these things to be knit together in one, to be united together in the soul of a believer, this is Christian perfection."[126] It is an effective homiletical device, used in the service of his driving theological concern.

In other settings Wesley continued to expound the nature and importance of love as the expression of Christian perfection. It was best described in the thirteenth chapter of 1 Corinthians. He advised people to read this chapter if they wanted to understand Christian perfection, because "there is the true picture of Christian Perfection! Let us copy after it with all our might."[127] Such love had a profound effect on whole persons, not just "souls," as it was carried out in the concrete acts of feeding, clothing, visiting, instructing and giving spiritual guidance to those in need.[128] The effect of such loving acts would be so profound that a miracle no less dramatic than that of the first century of Christianity would result. Want would be ended by voluntary distribution and the powerful example would remove the stumbling-block of Christianity. It would be a new day for evangelism.[129] In such rhetoric one again senses that the theme of perfection for Wesley was not an appendage, but the essence of Christianity. Through love it even established a bridge between meeting desperate human need and evangelism.

His confidence and optimism were not rooted in the natural abilities of people, but in the power of God's grace and presence. He was clear that "this love of human kind cannot spring but from the love of God." No one can love others, especially the vast variety of others and those that are so difficult to love "unless that affection flow from a grateful filial love to the common Father of all." This results exclusively from faith.[130] Wesley took issue with those who advocated the love of fellows independent of the love of God. Thinking of Rousseau, Voltaire and Hume, whom he called "the great triumvirate," he contended that apart from the love of God such love was "neither better nor worse than Atheism."[131] Behind his criticism was the conviction that it was impossible to genuinely and disinterestedly love others unless energized by God's grace and power. However, his optimism was rooted in his equally strong conviction that individuals were really given new abilities through grace. The restored *Imago Dei* made it possible to live out the two great commandments: loving God with all one's heart and loving one's neighbour as one's self.

Faith alone or faith and love?

Placing such a high value on love, how did Wesley relate it to faith? Beyond question, he followed the Protestant tradition of giving very high priority to faith. As seen above, it was the *only* condition for both justification and sanctification. God works in the human heart by *sola fide*. It is not some human blend of faith and works that gains God's favour. Faith alone, God's unmerited gift, is the condition. But moving beyond much of Protestantism, Wesley saw the importance of faith not in what it *was*, but in how it *functioned* in God's overall desire for people. Its importance lay not in itself, but what it made possible — love. What was lost in the fall was the divine relationship of love. The entire plan of redemption was to restore that relationship, and faith was merely part, albeit the crucial part, of that process. Wesley described faith as "the handmaid of love." He explains, "as glorious and honorable as [faith] is, it is not the end of the commandment. God hath given this honour to love alone: Love is the end of all the commandments of God."[132] In a very clear description, he develops this theme:

> Faith, then, was originally designed of God to re-establish the law of love. Therefore, in speaking thus, we are not undervaluing it, or robbing it of its due praise; but, on the contrary, showing its real worth, exalting it in its just proportion, and giving it that very place which the

wisdom of God assigned it from the beginning. It is the grand means of restoring that holy love wherein man was originally created. It follows, that although faith is of no value in itself... yet as it leads to that end, the establishing anew the law of love in our hearts; and as, in the present state of things, it is the only means under heaven for effecting it; it is on that account an unspeakable blessing to man, and of unspeakable value before God.[133]

The primacy of love in Wesley's theology of Christian perfection gives it continuity with the basic principles of Scripture, projects broader appeal and prevents it from being reduced to an archaic doctrine. Love cannot be "contained" in a doctrine, but must be experienced and expressed through actions. Only then does it remain alive. Although Wesley modified his position on peripheral details of Christian perfection, he was consistent on the core issue: love.[134] His interpretation of Christian perfection remains timeless and its applications are far reaching.

Christian perfection seen as relationship

Throughout this section I have pursued the idea that, for Wesley, Christian perfection transcended the level of a doctrine. It referred to the nature of humankind after the moral image of God has been restored. In that context it becomes obvious that it is more accurately seen in terms of a *relationship* than a state. Many controversies about "perfection" have been fostered by viewing sanctification as a state or a possession. Long before the recent debates, Wesley saw this danger:

> Does not talking, without proper caution, of a justified or sanctified *state*, tend to mislead men; almost naturally leading them to trust in what was done in one moment? Whereas we are *every moment* pleasing or displeasing God, according to our works; according to the whole of our present inward tempers and outward behaviour.[135]

What would be the "proper caution" for preventing a misunderstanding of the true nature of sanctification? For Wesley, it had to do with seeing it as the empowering for a life of service, rather than a single religious experience that one would always be looking back to as an idol.[136] He had too often heard the verbal claims of people whose lives contradicted their words. (No doubt "Christian slave owners" fit this category in Wesley's mind.) So, if the "state" was divorced from accountability and love, and from the present experience of obedience, it was dangerous. On the other hand, if it were viewed as the controlling centre out of which flowed the actions of love, it would facilitate godly relationships with people and with God.

In seeing perfection as a relationship, a number of difficulties are resolved. An ongoing debate has centered on whether sanctification is instantaneous or gradual. Wesley pondered this issue. At times he leaned toward the gradual and at other times toward the instantaneous. His more extreme positions occurred when he was pushed polemically. Most frequently, however, he asserted that sanctification is both instantaneous and gradual.[137] In the context of relationship, both instantaneous and gradual aspects can be maintained. A relationship has a moment of beginning. It can also have moments of great intensity. However, following and surrounding such moments is the continual process of living and growing. Wesley believed the faith which initiates sanctification is given in a moment, but once that has occurred, a process has been set in motion and is continued gradually.[138] He explains this dynamic in his *Plain Account of Christian Perfection*:

> [Sanctification] is constantly both preceded and followed by a gradual work.
>
> An instantaneous change has been wrought in some believers: None can deny this.
>
> Since that change, they enjoy perfect love; they feel this, and this alone; they "rejoice evermore, pray without ceasing, and in everything give thanks." Now, this is all that I mean by perfection; therefore, these are witnesses

of the perfection which I preach.

"But in some this change was not instantaneous." They did not perceive the instant when it was wrought. It is often difficult to perceive the instant when a man dies; yet there is an instant in which life ceases. And if ever sin ceases, there must be a last moment of its existence, and a first moment of our deliverance from it.[139]

The fact remains that after such instantaneous experiences, whether perceived or not, the ongoing process of relationship is absolutely necessary. Wesley affirms:

> The holiest of men still need Christ, as their Prophet, as "the light of the world." For he does not give them light but from moment to moment: The instant he withdraws, all is darkness. They still need Christ as their King; for God does not give them a stock of holiness. But unless they receive a supply every moment, nothing but unholiness would remain. They still need Christ as their Priest, to make atonement for their holy things. Even perfect holiness is acceptable to God only through Jesus Christ.[140]

His use of the phrases "moment by moment" and "every moment" clearly portrays the nature of the relationship as an ongoing process.[141] Again, because perfection was not an isolated issue but a continuation of the entire redemptive process (restoring relationship with God through the restored image of God), it is most accurate to not limit it to either the instantaneous or the gradual.[142] Maddox describes Wesley's conception as a "progressive journey" and contends that "Wesley's most fundamental concern lay on the theme of gradual growth in holiness." He insightfully describes this process as a "dynamic tension" between celebrating what God's grace has done, while maintaining responsibility to apply that grace to new areas that God reveals.[143] This is an excellent picture of a living and vital relationship.

The sense of process is also conveyed in Wesley's indication that the sanctified believer *can* and *must* continue growing, not only temporarily but through eternity.[144] Because the term "perfect" was used to describe such believers, it was often thought that there was no further possibility of growth or improvement. Wesley countered such a view, completely rejecting the notion of absolute perfection:

> The highest perfection which man can attain, while the soul dwells in the body, does not exclude ignorance, and error, and a thousand other infirmities. Now, from wrong judgments, wrong words and actions will often necessarily flow: And, in some cases, wrong affections also may spring from the same source.[145]

Indeed, not only are we prone to ignorance, error and other infirmities, but we remain below the level of our original parents in the garden.[146] Living in relationship with God, however, allows the believer to receive constant benefit from the atonement and live under the "law of love."[147]

Viewing sanctification as relationship also sheds light on the question of "sinless perfection." The question was not only present among Wesley's followers and detractors, but became a major source of controversy related to holiness groups of the nineteenth and twentieth centuries. Beside the fact that Wesley discouraged the use of the term, the idea of relationship makes it non-applicable.[148] If perfection were a state that must be maintained for God's acceptance, sinlessness would be a crucial condition. However, if it is a relationship of grace whereby God's presence deals with and extinguishes sin, the resulting sinlessness is a by-product rather than a condition. In such a relationship, intent and the desire to maintain relationship become more important than a contractual condition.[149] A relationship of love, even a "perfect relationship," becomes the focus rather than a "perfect Christian."

Perhaps the most important by-product of seeing sanctification as relationship, is the effect it has on evaluating one's spiritual condition. No longer can it be considered on a different scale or in isolation from one's interpersonal dealings. As mentioned earlier, Wesley believed that one's loving actions to the invisible God simply had to be directed to one's visible fellow human beings. Thus, a perfect relationship to God could not be compartmentalized away from one's relationships to other people. The two directions of relationship became synonymous. Simply stated, Wesley equated holiness with doing good to others.[150] To know if one loves God with all one's heart requires only to observe one's interaction with others, especially those in need.

The power of relationship and the dynamic of transformation: commands and promises

Within Wesley's understanding of relationship we glimpse his dynamic for personal transformation. As developed earlier, the two components of salvation involve both forgiveness of sin and restoration of lost abilities. Randy Maddox uses the terms "pardon" and "power" to refer to this completeness.[151] The issue is that God's power, through Christ's atonement, restores human abilities which were lost in the Fall. Those abilities relate to the moral image of God in humankind, specifically the ability to live a life of love for God and others. As lost abilities are restored, directives which were out of reach under the law become attainable under grace and the higher ethic of love is made possible.

The dynamic of *how* this is brought about is one of Wesley's important contributions. With great insight he suggests a subtle, but extremely significant, change within the person. It involves the difference between law and grace (if seen separately), and the difference between aspiring to something beyond one's reach and being empowered to *actually* experience it. Deep within the person comes a shift of perspective. It is a result of God's work, affecting the person at the deepest level of motivation. God's view of the restored person unveils a completely new awareness and brings an awakening within the person. This awakening involves the moral image being restored so that the person has the mind of Christ. God's view becomes the individual's view. A radically new sense of self becomes the starting point of new ability, with the individual's relationship to God (the source of power) providing the energy to act. Wesley's paradigm, simply stated, is that God's commands are *transformed* into promises. Because God is the source of these promises, they are fulfilled. As Wesley asserts, "'Thou shalt love thy neighbour as thyself,' is as express a promise as a command."[152]

Wesley's most explicit treatment of this issue is in his discourse on the Sermon on the Mount. The dynamic of his thought is that what was viewed as a command, possibly a threatening command because of fallen humanity's inability to fulfill it, by grace becomes God's promise of human performance. Rather than the view of a command, "you had better love your neighbour or there will be consequences to pay," the promise is what a person will actually experience and do. "You will really love your neighbour." God's promise makes this reality, not wishful thinking. Wesley has captured an amazing shift in thinking. Those duties which were *commands* under the law (and impossible to fulfill solely by human effort), become *promises* under the gospel:

> ... there is no contrariety at all between the law and the gospel ... there is no need for the law to pass away, in order to the establishing the gospel. Indeed neither of them supersedes the other, but they agree perfectly well together. Yea, the very same words, considered in different respects, are parts both of the law and of the gospel: If they are considered as commandments, they are parts of the law; if as promises, of the gospel. Thus, "Thou shalt love the Lord thy God with all thy heart," when considered as a commandment, is a branch of the law; when regarded as a promise, is an essential part of the gospel; — the gospel being no other than the commands of the law, proposed by way of promise ... On the one hand, the law continually makes way for, and points us to, the gospel; on the other, the gospel continually leads us to a more exact fulfilling of the law. The law, for instance,

requires us to love God, to love our neighbour.... We feel that we are not sufficient for these things, yea, that "with man this is impossible:" But we see a promise of God, to give us that love ... We lay hold of this gospel, of these glad tidings; it is done unto us according to our faith; and "the righteousness of the law is fulfilled in us," through faith which is in Christ Jesus.[153]

Wesley illustrates both the difference between law and grace, and the interfacing of the two. In addition, Wesley makes a profound connection between grace and law, and between the personal and social dimensions of the law. The fact that loving God is inseparable from loving one's neighbour, and the fact that an individual has a restored ability to live such love, means that there are no excuses for not fulfilling the law of love to others. Here, the ethic of realization is brought into focus.[154] It is clear that this teaching carries profound implications to all social interactions.

In his perspective on commands and promises Wesley asserts the possibility of a radical spiritual/psychological transformation. What was unreachable is now within our grasp. What we once perceived as unfulfillable laws are now promises to be claimed and enjoyed. Human ability and perception are drastically altered. This is not merely a psychological ploy or "positive thinking." The difference is the reality of God's presence. The transforming power of God's presence constantly brings awareness of the true self as God created it and sees it. With the awareness and presence come the ability to live accordingly. It is also very different from a moral admonition. Wesley believed that living in such love was simply not possible apart from the energy supplied by God through faith. Only faith could establish "anew the law of love in our hearts;" it was "the only means under heaven for effecting it."[155] But faith could effect such love.

It is singularly important that Wesley used this concept in reference to holiness, which he defined largely in social terms. He rooted social concern in the command to love one's neighbour as oneself, and then asserted this to be possible not by negating the law, but by the gospel fulfilling the law and turning it into promise. Thus, a realized ethic is possible. By grace, through faith, the Christian becomes capable of loving neighbour as self.

To deny the ability to experience this promise (the ability to keep the law of love) was to deny the very power of the gospel. In simple, but colourful terms Wesley stated it was tantamount to giving Christ the kiss of Judas.[156] What could be worse than to acknowledge the presence of Christ while denying his power in one's life? This was the "kiss of Judas."

Full salvation and slavery

Wesley's understanding of Christian perfection contains the most profound implications for slavery. Again, these relate to both the nature of the slave and the nature of the Christian. The first is apparent and is a further extension of the implication from prevenient grace. Not only is God's grace universal and therefore a part of the slave's experience, but sanctification is a part of the earthly completion of the process of redemption and is for every individual in the world. It crosses all lines of division, race, sex, age and status. Beyond the level of prevenient grace, sanctification meant the complete restoring of God's moral image on the human heart. How could one justify enslaving and degrading a person who has the potential of bearing the very image of God? The extremely high view of humankind portrayed in Christian perfection is totally incompatible with any system that allows, or worse forces, a person to become the equivalent of a serving beast, finding value only in being of physical use to "superiors." A theology that fosters the ideal of humanity as capable of the very image of God cannot co-exist with an institution that reduces human beings to the image of a beast. Rather than enslave, the desire would be to teach and nurture everyone with that potential, that is, every human being.

By contrast, the late eighteenth century development of the idea of Negro inferiority spoke to this very fact. Realizing that there would be resistance to treating African persons as less than human, it was decided to preempt the issue by categorizing them as less than human. For Wesley to describe Africans, among all people, as potentially "more" than what we normally envision as human (more spiritually and morally capable than persons in their natural, depraved state), would have a devastating effect on the Christian sensitivity of those who believed in sanctification. It would be impossible for followers of Wesley, who believed his teaching on Christian perfection, to enslave others. To be a true Wesleyan and a slave owner would require cognitive dissonance.

While this theological position would have an influence on Wesley's followers, the point here is how it related to *his* view of slavery. He is the one that articulated this concept of sanctification, with its lofty description of moral potential. The point is unmistakable. It would have had an overwhelming influence on his position on slavery and his motivation to work for its extirpation. Of course, those who accepted Wesley's view of sanctification restoring the image of God would also become sensitized to the incompatibility of enforcing slavery on bearers of the *Imago Dei*.

The second implication is seen in Wesley's prescription of how the Christian lives in anticipation of sanctification. The response to awareness and the desire for full salvation resulted in the "works of repentance," which included works of mercy. Wesley saw these as the loving response to human need. Holding others in the bonds of slavery would be worse than ignoring human need; it would be inflicting human misery. In understatement, slavery would be adverse to works of mercy. With the physical, intellectual and spiritual deprivation inherent in eighteenth century slavery, could one take part in it and make any claim to do the works of mercy? On the contrary, to take seriously the works of mercy would require the believer to minister to the needs of the slave. More significantly, it would require working for the annihilation of the system that perpetuated those needs.

Beyond anticipation of this work of grace, those who genuinely experienced some measure of perfect love for one's neighbour, by which Wesley described Christian perfection, would find it impossible to justify the system or practices of slavery. The two experiences, authentic love for others and participation in slavery, were mutually exclusive. The fact that perfection cannot be experienced apart from relationships meant that, wherever the neighbour was afflicted, where human happiness was being destroyed, the Christian living in perfect love could not be content. He or she would be drawn to those needs. Relational love could not turn a blind eye toward the gross injustices of slavery. Admittedly, there might not be clarity on what action to take, but that is a matter of strategy, not principle. In principle, the kind of love Wesley advocated was antithetical to slavery. It *must* produce loving action to the slave.

Finally, in Wesley's understanding of sanctification is seen the most powerful model of personal and moral transformation. In this teaching the Christian is not only taught truth, but is enabled to live out that truth. Biblical commands do become promises. The power of the gospel goes beyond forgiveness to new abilities. The cognitive understanding of love and service is converted into active love and practical service. Orthodoxy becomes orthopraxis. Wesley believed that right belief without application was proof that the belief was, in fact, not genuinely right or not authentically believed. As a result, there was no excuse for not doing what human need required of love. If human depravity brought loving action to a halt, Christian perfection provided the inertia and momentum to bring in God's kingdom. This may be the explanation for Wesley's dramatic entrance into the slave cause at the age of seventy. His love of fellows provided the concern, and when the awareness and opportunity intersected, he was empowered to do what the moral image required. In the spirit of love the commands of law became the promises of love, and the promises were kept. For Wesley, this was not just novel rhetoric, a good idea or good teaching. It was more than an encouraging talk to his followers. It was the realization of the transformative power of God to live on a new level, a level which he experienced and taught.

Grace and human resources: the theme of stewardship

Many of the theological themes reviewed so far relate to a consistent corollary: the theme of stewardship. While it is not technically a doctrine, it appears throughout Wesley's writings in various contexts, and was an intentional focus of his personal life. In his view, all that any person has, whether material or spiritual, is held only by the grace of God. An individual is never the owner, or possessor, but is considered the trustee. Wesley was explicit: "You are not the proprietor of anything — no, not one shilling in the world, you are only a steward of what another entrusts you with, to be laid out not according to your will, but His."[157] This applied to everything, including spiritual gifts, the measure of free will we experience, justification, sanctification, as well as material wealth and "natural rights." The last two will be discussed in this section.

In regard to wealth Wesley is well known for his advice to "gain all you can, save all you can, and give all you can."[158] Many attribute the increasing social elevation of the first generation of Methodists to this teaching, the essence of which included:

1) being as industrious as possible;
2) saving all one could, not in the sense of hoarding, but conserving and living simply;
3) using the positive results of those principles to give generously to others.

By following Wesley's dictum, the poor reversed the habits of idleness and foolish spending and began to prosper. Their conservative living and retaining no more than the "necessities" of life produced what they considered an excess, which they gave generously to others.

Unquestionably, this was a teaching of social benevolence. Wesley's perspective on material wealth was a simple matter of social concern, governed by love of neighbour and demonstrated by materially helping that neighbour. Gaining and saving all one could became evil when not connected to the goal of giving. Then riches became sinful.[159]

Wesley's teaching on money was inseparable from his comprehensive view of the church. The connection is vividly seen in his sermon, "Causes of the Inefficacy of Christianity." After laying out local presence and the members' discipline as criteria for an effective church, he explains that even when these conditions are met, there is often failure. He identifies the predominant reason: believers are not giving all they can to meet the needs of others. In essence, he attributes the ineffectiveness of the church to a lack of social concern: Christians not feeding and clothing the destitute.[160] His message is clear: the world is influenced by personal social concern and action. If understood clearly, Wesley's explanation of the primary reason for the church's failure would surprise many of his later followers, who *assume* that failure is the result of insufficient evangelizing activity.

Wesley's principle establishes the context from which he preached that Christians should not be involved in certain activities. Many were wrong, not in themselves, but because they prevented, or reduced, demonstrating love to one's neighbour. Examples included buying expensive clothing: "the more you lay out on your own apparel, the less you have left to clothe the naked."[161] Horse racing ("public diversion") was condemned for the same reason.[162] In his sermon, "On Worldly Folly," Wesley discussed the judgement of the man who grew rich and built larger barns to house his wealth (Luke 12:20). Wesley's condemnation is that his foolishness consisted not in being wealthy, but in using his wealth for his own ease rather than helping the poor. It is a strong social comment on all the man could have done to help those in need.[163]

When wealth was viewed as a possession rather than in the context of stewardship, Wesley believed it was destructive both to the "possessor" and to society. Such an individual grew harmfully self-willed (antithetical to the true Christian disposition):

> ...as not only his domestic servants and immediate dependants are governed implicitly by his will, finding

their account therein, but also most of his neighbours and acquaintances study to oblige him in all things: So his will being continually indulged, will of course be continually strengthened; till at length he will be ill able to submit to the will either of God or men.[164]

Society was harmed because the hoarding of wealth produced economic inequities which were perpetuated and increased by continued hoarding.[165]

By contrast, in the context of stewardship, Wesley saw wealth as one of the greatest blessings of life:

> God has entrusted us ... with a portion of worldly goods ... he has committed to our charge that precious talent which contains all the rest, — money: Indeed it is unspeakably precious, if we are wise and faithful stewards of it; if we employ every part of it for such purposes as our blessed Lord has commended us to do.[166]

There was no question about how that money should be used and what it would accomplish:

> In the hands of his children, it is food for the hungry, drink for the thirsty, raiment for the naked: It gives to the traveller and the stranger where to lay his head. By it we may supply the place of an husband to the widow, and of a father to the fatherless. We may be a defence for the oppressed, a means of health to the sick, of ease to them that are in pain; it may be as eyes to the blind, as feet to the lame; yea, a lifter up from the gates of death![167]

Wesley saw all material possessions as a trust from God, to be shared with an open hand. Where he encouraged industriousness, it was for the purpose of helping those in need. Stewardship meant sharing.[168]

Such a view of material and monetary stewardship has direct

implications on slavery. Wesley's advice to "gain all you can" carries the provision that this is to be done without doing any harm to oneself or one's neighbour, his "substance," "body," or "soul."[169] In no way could the system of slavery be rationalized to meet this condition. Under the best conditions, where the slave's body or soul might not be harmed, his or her "substance" was injured because the system negated the slaves' claim to the fruits of their labour. His advice to "save all you can,"[170] avoiding extravagance and living only by necessities, was the opposite of the purpose of slavery. Too often the slaves would not be given necessities in order that the slave owner could maintain a life of luxury.

His third dictum, "give all you can," assumed a lifestyle of perceiving oneself as God's property, supplying the necessities progressively to oneself, one's immediate family, the "household of faith," and finally "all people." Wesley saw material resources in graduated levels: those which supplied "necessities," those which provided "conveniences," and finally, those which added "luxuries." Only after the necessities of "all people" were met could one consider having a convenience for oneself or one's immediate family. And only after conveniences were available to all people could one consider a luxury for oneself or one's family.[171] Again, the system of slavery was a reverse of this philosophy. The slave's purpose was to provide luxury for the slave owner, at the expense of the slave's necessities, even the slave's life. The system systematically robbed the poor in order to oversupply the rich.

Wesley's attitude of stewardship in regard to money applies identically to property. He maintained that the exclusive title to property was held by God alone. Souls, bodies, goods and talents (including time) belonged to no human being, but were merely entrusted to human "stewards."[172] If a person could not even claim ownership of his or her body, but received it as a trust from God, it would be ludicrous to presume that one person could "own" another, as slavery maintained.

It was pointed out in chapter 3 that Wesley was not a consistent proponent of natural rights. Rather, he used the argument selectively, especially when contesting slavery. It is in the context of stewardship that his view of natural rights can be clarified. He believed that what people consider "rights," were in fact received from God through grace, and as such, were dependent on God's sole authority and will. What liberty persons did experience came from prevenient grace.[173] As a result there were no absolute rights, only the rights of stewardship. These must be exercised in regard to the will of God, which always involved serving God and one's fellows. Because the system of slavery was based on the absolute right of one person over another, with no regard to God's will of serving others, it stood in stark opposition to Wesley's stewardship basis of rights. The will of God evoked giving service freely *to* others; slavery demanded being served *by* others. For Wesley, no one could claim such a "right."

Any consideration of personal rights or possessions, in Wesley's thought, must be seen as stewardship. In the early nineteenth century it was argued that Europeans and North Americans had a "stewardship responsibility" for those less capable: the Africans. Congenial slavery was portrayed as a blessing and a means for Christians to fulfill their obligation. However, this argument could not be sustained with any awareness of Wesley's perspective on stewardship or on Africans. He did not consider the Africans to be less capable than Europeans, except as they had been degraded by Europeans. Secondly, as a steward, every person was directly accountable to God. Slavery made persons accountable to other persons, thus nullifying one of Wesley's basic theological tenets.

Wesley's view of stewardship also stood in opposition to slavery with relation to believers. Of all people, they should be aware that they had no absolute rights. They should be even more aware that everything that came to them, material and non-material, was theirs by trust. Acquisition and use were strictly governed by the needs of others. There could be no compatibility between such views and the foundational assumptions of slavery.

The personification of grace and power: Christ

Wesley's understanding of the nature of Christ fell within the traditional teaching of the church, especially as derived from the

Thirty-Nine Articles of the Church of England.[174] He held to the two natures of Christ, fully human and fully divine. The creeds of Christianity, especially Chalcedon from A.D. 451, affirm these two natures but leave the interpretation open to greater emphasis on either the human or the divine nature. Although Wesley believed in the perfect humanity of Christ, he placed far more emphasis on his divinity; Christ existed before the incarnation, but when he became human he took on human limitations while demonstrating the holiness of God in human flesh. Maddox suggests that Wesley saw Christ's human nature created by God, rather than coming from Mary.[175] However, the role of Christ was to embody the grace of God, making it available to all people. As the vehicle of grace, he was also the example of what humankind could become when restored by grace.[176]

The relevance of Wesley's Christology to slavery is apparent. By the full humanity of Christ, the relatedness and commonality of all humankind is established. This fact is assumed throughout Wesley's writings. When referring to the Christian's "brother" or "neighbour," Wesley consistently means *every* human being, not just the "household of faith."[177] Christ's humanity makes him brother to every human being and thus all are brothers and sisters to each other. Rather than the faith separating people as believers and non-believers, the incarnation confirms the equality and commonality of all. There is one source, God as Father of all. There is one goal: the full expression of humanity for all, which is Christlikeness. The only way to reconcile Wesley's Christology with an endorsement for slavery would be to deny the full humanity of the slaves. But Wesley saw Africans as fully human and therefore part of the human family. They were Christ's siblings, and capable of his example. From Wesley's Christological perspective slavery was untenable.

In summary

We began this chapter with Wesley's view of original humankind. It is fitting to come full circle and close the chapter with a comment about his doctrine of creation. His doctrine of humankind in its original condition bears similarity to his doctrine of creation. His view of the original couple in the garden, with the newly created world and all its creatures, is one of pristine beauty and perfection, harmony and precision. All of creation was good. It was the exquisite work of a loving Creator and every detail bore the marks of God's touch. Man and woman were placed in loving governance over the perfect world and enjoyed an unflawed relationship with all of nature, each other and with their Creator. But they were free and the world was mutable. The results of human selfish choice affected every aspect of creation, from the natural order, to complete human alienation from God. Not only was the relationship with God discarded, but human society would never again be the same.

In Wesley's thinking, there was a direct connection of these issues to the problem of slavery. In the paradisical world, governed by love, animals were treated with respect and eagerly brought loving service to humans, as they were created to do. There was no cruelty done toward, or even by, animals. Wesley believed that predatory animal behaviour began after the Fall; before the Fall all animals were herbivores.

Human relationships were mutual and equal, governed by love for God, with attendant love for others, and respect for all creation. In such a world there could be no place for the evil of slavery, which was built on inequality and coerced servitude. Slavery could only be explained by the corruption of the Fall. It served as a perfect example of distorted human relationships, disobedience to God and the preoccupation with oneself at the expense of the good for others. Wesley would have seen the institution and practices of slavery as both the result of fallen humanity and a picture of the unimaginable evil that fallen persons were capable of. In his thinking, it was no accident that the biblical word picture, the "slavery" of sin, was used to capture the worst conditions a human being could experience, the farthest distance persons could remove themselves from God. Slavery was as incompatible with Wesley's doctrine of creation as light is to darkness.

Throughout the traditional and distinctive theological positions held by Wesley, there are numerous implications for the problem of slavery. These implications, contained within his doctrines, form the basis of his antislavery stand. They also supply a sound Christian rationale and impetus to the developing antislavery thought of the late eighteenth century. None of his theological positions provide grounds for any justification for slavery, for either a Christian or a non-Christian. On the contrary, in Wesley's comprehensive theological system, slavery was wrong, and every human being, once exposed to the truth about slavery, would know that. The attributes of God spoke to the entire human situation, universally. God's grace produced awareness. God's love brought forgiveness. God's presence in relationship provided the power for a life of love. Commands were transformed into promises as Christians were empowered to do the work of love to Christ, in the form of the least of humankind. Wesley's theology annihilated any justification for slavery.

Chapter 5

The larger context: Wesley's social ethic and philosophy of social change

The exploration of Wesley's theology and how it relates to implications for slavery is important, but should not be seen in isolation. It is a part of his broader social ethic and is the specific application of it. For that reason it is helpful to briefly peruse the larger context.

A common critique of evangelicals in the eighteenth century was that their emphasis was exclusively other-worldly. It is true that the slave society, having no ability to change their situation, found some release in focusing on heaven. The development and widespread singing of Negro spirituals reflects this. But the critique was levelled at those who did not improve society, but had opportunity to do so. Jean-Jacques Rousseau was of the opinion that Christians in general were too concerned with the future to be socially responsible in the present world. Wesley took issue with this.[1] It was his conviction that Christians were ideal citizens and were a positive influence in the world. It was his desire that Methodism produce the kind of Christians that would fulfill their moral obligation and serve their fellow human beings. For him, the idea of the future world was not a soporific for the miseries of this world, but an incentive to be involved in relieving those miseries and responsibly changing the negative situations of society.[2]

A revealing insight into Wesley's social ethic comes from his treatment of the Sermon on the Mount. It serves as a kind of microcosm of this topic. While this particular text could easily lend itself to a mystical or "inward" focus, Wesley's use goes the opposite direction. Questioning his hermeneutic (how he interpreted this text) reveals his deeper purpose. There is no question about his intent; he uses Jesus' Sermon on the Mount to teach the Christian response to society and its needs. The greater purpose of addressing human need completely coloured his interpretation of various passages. In the thirteen discourses, his overall interpretation of the Sermon on the Mount is consistently conveyed in social terms. His definitions of particular words and his explanations of phrases leave no doubt. Here his social ethics are brought into clear focus, in a relatively concise sermon series. The series also contains various strands of his theology, particularly Christology, atonement and Christian perfection, but with distinctly social applications.

In the first discourse he described "righteousness" as both love for God and "the love of all mankind for his sake."[3] In the same sermon, he defined those that mourn as those who feel conviction for their own sin as well as mourn "for the sins and miseries of mankind."[4] In the second discourse he describes the necessity of social involvement, warning that

> ... the performing our duty to God will not excuse us from our duty to our neighbour: that works of piety, as they are called, will be so far from commending us to God, if we are wanting in charity, that, on the contrary, that want of charity will make all those works an abomination to the Lord.[5]

The trend continued in succeeding sermons. The "merciful" were those "who love their neighbours as themselves," and a "peacemaker" was one that "doeth good to all men." Wesley defined "good" predominantly as physical aid to the needy, as outlined in Matthew 25.[6] In explaining the passage, "take no thought for the morrow," he stated, "the most fatal way of 'taking thought for the morrow'" was to "make the care of future things a pretence for neglecting present duty."

In dealing with God's kingdom (comprised of those renewed in God's image, loving God and all people), he clarified the issue that present duty clearly involved service to others.[7] Wesley's understanding of God's "kingdom" was not seen as a *state* but as a force of Christians *doing* the kind of ministry Jesus did while on earth. This is also revealed in his thinking about the petition, "Thy will be done in earth," which implied deep involvement with the needs of society. His interpretation held that this petition primarily required actively *doing* what God desired, and only secondarily, passively *resigning* to God's will.[8]

In the tenth discourse Wesley spoke of "genuine morality" in terms of the golden rule. Again, it was applied to human need in a manner similar to his teaching about the use of money. He taught that progressive distribution is based on meeting the needs of others before enjoying the luxuries of wealth; "our superfluities" Wesley wrote, "give way to our neighbour's conveniences," then "our conveniences, to our neighbour's necessities; our necessities, to his extremities."[9] Many of Wesley's early followers applied this principle so literally that to outsiders they seemed to be giving recklessly, without regard for their own needs. They were criticized for such behaviour. However, from their perspective, their industry had brought them more than they had ever had and they were gratefully willing to share.[10] The criticisms early Methodists received underscore the point being made: Wesley taught a radical social application of religious truth, not a spirituality that focused primarily on one's self.

Even Jesus' statement, "narrow is the way which leadeth unto life" included social actions for Wesley. He defined that "way" as not only including inner attitudes, but *doing* "all possible good to all men."[11] When such good (the work of charity) was not done, he had an explanation: persons were simply unwilling to deny themselves. Self denial was necessary to genuinely follow Christ and grow spiritually, and charity was the direct correlation.[12] Thus, the topic of self-denial became a platform for social concern.

In the concluding sermon of the series, Wesley reinforced the interaction of faith and works. The two were inseparable, but the order was crucial. The first and foundational step was faith, not works, but the evidence of authentic faith was response to human need. Using the parable of the one who built on unstable ground, Wesley admonished that unless one begins on the inward principle of personal faith, all good works are no more than a foundation of sand. However, to claim faith but not be "zealous of good works" was equally erroneous. Again, good works were defined as feeding and clothing the destitute, visiting the sick and relieving those in prison:

> But "what does it profit, if a man say he hath faith, and have not works"? Can "that faith save him?" O no! That faith which hath not works, which doth not produce both inward and outward holiness, which does not stamp the whole image of God on the heart, and purify us as he is pure; that faith which does not produce the whole of religion described in the foregoing chapters, is not the faith of the gospel, not the Christian faith, not the faith which leads to glory. ... If thou layest stress on this, thou are lost for ever: Thou still buildest thy house upon the sand.[13]

The place where social acts and responsibility were usually addressed was under the topic of works of mercy. Although Wesley sometimes gave his followers specific instructions regarding works of mercy (usually related to the poor), he was more concerned to help the believer establish a basic attitude from which the action appropriate to the situation would result. It was a comprehensive, "Christian" perspective from which to view all of life's responsibilities and relationships. It could be summed up as *the ethic of love* and it comprises the whole of Wesley's social ethic. Social concern and involvement of the believer were essential. By example, Wesley made the application to slavery, which he perceived as the greatest enemy of love for others. The ethic of love, which he often termed "true religion" or "total religion,"[14] involved total commitment even to the extent of relinquishing ownership in favour of stewardship and resulted in the Christian being a distributor of God's bounty. The Christian was the "one for others," and Wesley was committed to teach a style of living that reflected the selfless service of Jesus and the first-century Christians.

It is true that Wesley placed significant emphasis on people's "inward" religious experience. However, he saw clearly that the inner life was the source of — and never a substitute for — the true expression of faith: social relationships in a world of need. The inner life and outward expression worked in tandem, but if there were a choice, the Christian should opt for the latter. He consistently taught his followers to "be more zealous for works of mercy, than even for works of piety." If it had to be either one or the other, Wesley's choice was unequivocal:

> ... works of mercy are to be preferred. Even reading, hearing, prayer, are to be omitted, or to be postponed, "at charity's almighty call," when we are called to relieve the distress of our neighbour, whether in body or soul.[15]

As a result, even in sermons that dealt primarily with inner religion, those of a more pietistic bent, an obvious social dimension was still present. In a sermon dealing exclusively with fasting, Wesley concluded by describing the conditions necessary for that fast to be acceptable to God. The one fasting must "add alms thereto; works of mercy, after our power, both to the bodies and souls of men." He then supported this condition by quoting Isaiah 58:6: "Is this not the fast that I have chosen? to loose the bands of wickedness, to undo the heavy burdens, and to let the oppressed go free, and that ye break every yoke? Is it not to deal thy bread to the hungry?"[16]

It was on the point of inner religion replacing the outer social expression that he disagreed with the mystics and any who physically withdrew from the world. Christians must leave the world in terms of being captive to its values and evil, but must never actually withdraw from the place that so desperately needs their loving influence. He defined this in his sermon, "In What Sense We Are to Leave the World."[17] At another time, in no uncertain terms he condemned the practice of withdrawing from society:

> Directly opposite to this is the Gospel of Christ. Solitary religion is not to be found there. "Holy solitaries" is a phrase no more consistent with the Gospel than holy adulterers. The Gospel of Christ knows of no religion, but social; no holiness but social holiness. "Faith working by love" is the length and breadth and depth and height of Christian perfection. "This commandment have we from Christ, that he who loves God, love his brother also;" and that we manifest our love "by doing good to all men, especially to them that are of the household of faith." And in truth, whosoever loveth his brethren not in word only, but as Christ loved him, cannot but be "zealous of good works." He feels in his soul a burning, restless desire of spending and being spent for them. "My Father," will he say, "worketh hitherto, and I work." And at all possible opportunities he is, like his Master, "going about doing good."[18]

There is perhaps no better refutation of the critique that the emphasis of evangelicals ought to be exclusively other-worldly. Wesley believed the "grand pest" of Christianity was faith without works,[19] and works could not be done in isolation. They were related to human need.

In light of his clear focus on the radical social dimension of true Christianity, it is difficult to perceive how his teachings could be relegated by many of his followers to tame, self-contained and self-serving "doctrines." His theology was expansive and full of application. It was unmistakably directed to meeting the needs of others, and enhancing the good of humankind. He had no tolerance for the kind of Christianity that was egocentrically preoccupied with one's own spiritual state, and therefore blind to the human needs nearby. He understood and tolerated even less a Christianity that acquiesced to or endorsed slavery. That such Christians called themselves his followers or used his name would have deepened the wound!

Wesley's philosophy of social change

Wesley acknowledged that the evils of human society produced tragic consequences for individuals. He opposed those evils. His opposition grew directly out of his theology and was reinforced by his observation and experience. Also, he was convinced from Scripture, reason and experience that sanctified Christians *must* address human needs; Christians were empowered to practice the law of love. There could be no disjunction between true Christianity and the Christian's response to human need. How then could society be changed? We turn now to a brief exploration of Wesley's philosophy of social change.

Wesley firmly believed that all the problems of society stemmed exclusively from the individual. Social difficulties were not due to inherent structural deficiencies or to the community as an entity.[20] They originated in the failure of people, which was traceable to the depraved human will.[21] Unregenerate persons were dominated by the characteristics of depravity, particularly selfishness (or egocentricity), which naturally put them at odds with the best good for the overall community. It was mentioned earlier that Wesley disagreed with Rousseau and Voltaire, who affirmed natural human ability toward benevolence. Here again he disagreed with their optimism about society. He felt they did not grasp or admit the seriousness of human depravity and how it affected society. According to Wesley, the essence of the matter was that human sinfulness prevented peace with God. The byproduct of a broken relationship with God was disharmony among humans, with "every man's sword against his neighbour."[22]

Society's problems were singularly and directly the result of sin, and sin was an individual matter.

It followed for Wesley that if sin was the root cause of society's problem, and a problem within individuals, the solutions to the problems of society also rested in individuals. He did not see social *structures*, but *people* in need of transformation. As sin was dealt with and removed, the problems would be solved, because people would apply their faith to human relationships.[23] For that reason, he saw the gospel as the only cure: "whatever prevents or removes sin does, in the same degree, promote peace, both peace in our own soul, peace with God, and peace with one another."[24] As individuals were renewed, society would reflect the change.

For support of his thesis, Wesley cited how early Christians addressed the problem of poverty, as reflected in the book of Acts. He observed that as individuals were "restored to the image of God," concern for their fellows became "written on their hearts" and they responded by sharing all things in common and distributing to those in need. They did this spontaneously, without being told.[25] He was confident that the intervening centuries had not altered the benefit society would experience when Christians again experienced God's renewal and acted in love. He explicitly made this point in his sermon, "The General Spread of the Gospel," describing the community of believers as choosing to again hold all material goods in common, thus banishing poverty.[26] He believed this could happen.

The benefit was not limited to the Christian community, but spread to all human society. Throughout his writings he clearly indicated that works of mercy begin in the church but extend to all in need. His overall point is that individual conversion results in selfishness being replaced by love and love is the cure for social discord. A clear picture is painted in his sermon, "At the Foundation of City-Road Chapel":

> This love is the great medicine of life; the never-failing remedy for all the evils of a disordered world; for all the miseries and vises of men. Wherever this is, there are

virtue and happiness going hand in hand; there is humbleness of mind, gentleness, long-suffering, the whole image of God; and, at the same time, a "peace that passeth all understanding," with "joy unspeakable and full of glory." This religion of love, and joy, and peace, has its seat in the inmost soul; but is ever showing itself by its fruits, continually springing up, not only in all innocence, (for love worketh no ill to his neighbour,) but, likewise, in every kind of beneficence, — spreading virtue and happiness to all around it.[27]

The crucial factor necessary for Christianity to bring change to society was for Christians to do good to *all*, not a select few.

But specifically, how did individual Christians bring about the improvement of society? In his fourth discourse on the Sermon on the Mount, Wesley related his most concise description of how the social order is modified. Simply stated, it is by infiltration. He explained:

It is your very nature to season whatever is round about you. It is the nature of the divine savour which is in you, to spread to whatsoever you touch; to diffuse itself, on every side, to all those among whom you are. This is the great reason why the providence of God has so mingled you together with other men, that whatever grace you have received of God may through you be communicated to others; that every holy temper and work of yours may have an influence on them also. By this means a check will, in some measure be given to the corruption which is in the world. And a small part, at least, saved from the general infection, and rendered holy and pure before God.[28]

Wesley was not giving a directive, but describing what actually happens when true Christians live in society. Christians will effect change because "they cannot possibly fail to do so as long as [true religion] remains in their own hearts."[29] Loving social acts were the expected level of interaction by Christians and the by-product would be the improvement of society on every level: physical, social, intellectual and spiritual. Within his philosophy, evangelism both resulted from Christians' loving actions in society and perpetuated such loving behaviour by increasing the number of those infiltrating society. To Wesley, evangelism was much more inclusive and comprehensive than an end in itself. He envisioned a dynamic interaction of societal leaven, social change and evangelism. He was convinced that when Christians took the loving lifestyle seriously, the kingdom of God would "silently increase... and spread from heart to heart, from house to house, from town to town, from one kingdom to another."[30] In this context it must be remembered that his understanding of the kingdom of God was not static, but a force of people *doing* acts of love.

Wesley believed that as individuals underwent radical change, so would the social order. The number of changed individuals would continue to grow, resulting in ongoing societal change, even a positive social revolution. A number of social historians have theorized that in some ways Wesley's vision was fulfilled. They hold specifically that Wesley's work, and its transmission through his many followers, constituted a kind of social leaven which contributed to England's not succumbing to a bloody revolution as France did.[31] Indeed, Wesley did intend for his ministry to function as seasoning and preserving salt in a decaying society.

Wesley lived a hundred years before the sociological theories and work of Emile Durkheim,[32] so he and his followers were not aware of the inherent power of social structures and how they perpetuated their influence in spite of individual transformation. It would take time, observation, and trial and error in addressing social issues before Wesley and his contemporaries could become sensitive to the more subtle and complex workings of social systems. Even more significant, Wesley saw evidence of the successful application of his philosophy in three areas: prison reform, the social values of Kingswood and the change in public attitude to the entire Methodist movement.

In the eighteenth century, one of the social institutions that most needed reform was the prison system. Wesley visited prisons frequently and was painfully aware of the problems: rampant drunkenness, prostitution, inadequate food, no sanitation or health care, no rehabilitative effort and no productive activity for the inmates. Those imprisoned for debt had no means of reducing or removing the debt except by family or friends not in prison. If the imprisoned debtor was the family wage earner, the family was reduced to even greater poverty. Wesley graphically relayed his observations:

> Of all the seats of woe this side [of] hell, few, I suppose, exceed or even equal Newgate [in London]. If any region of horror could exceed it a few years ago, Newgate in Bristol did; so great was the filth, the stench, the misery, and wickedness, which shocked all who had a spark of humanity left.[33]

However, it appears that the Bristol jailer, Abel Dagge, had been converted through George Whitefield in 1737 and over the following twenty years completely transformed the Bristol prison. After a visit, Wesley was amazed at the change and made special note of the differences: "Every part of it" was "as clean and sweet as a gentleman's house," there was "no fighting or brawling," grievances were heard and settled by Dagge, drunkenness and prostitution were no longer tolerated, and bribery, which facilitated drinking and prostitution was terminated. Medicine was offered to the prisoners, without charge. A Bible was made available to the prisoners and religious services were conducted. Tools and materials were provided, along with a credit system for those who could work. Wesley was deeply impressed by the dramatic difference. He wrote, "the prison now has a new face: Nothing offends either the eye or ear; and the whole has the appearance of a quiet, serious family."[34]

Such an accomplishment of a Christian prison-keeper was dramatic proof for Wesley that the way to change society was to change individuals. The point is not the accuracy of Wesley's observation or the extent of such reform, but the impression the experience made on Wesley. It reinforced his belief in the power of the transformed individual and would not be quickly forgotten. Some sixteen years later Wesley met John Howard, later credited with bringing about great prison reform. Wesley must have had Dagge's experience in mind when he talked with Howard. Howard later commented, "I was encouraged by him to go on vigorously with my own designs. I saw in him how much a single man might achieve by zeal and perseverance ... and I determined I would pursue my work with more alacrity than ever."[35]

Another experience supporting Wesley's theory of social change came from Kingswood. The coal miners there had a well established reputation for their indifference to God and their hostility to others. Wesley described them as "so ignorant of the things of God that they seemed but one remove from the beasts of that perish." He was not alone in this assessment.[36] However, an undeniable change occurred after Whitefield and Wesley ministered among them. Wesley recorded,

> Kingswood does not now, as a year ago, resound with cursing and blasphemy. It is no more filled with drunkenness and uncleanness, and the idle diversions that naturally lead thereto. It is no longer full of wars and fightings, or clamour and bitterness, or wrath and envyings. Peace and love are there. Great numbers of the people are mild, gentle, and easy to be intreated ... hardly is their "voice heard in the streets" ... unless when they are at their usual evening diversion, singing praise unto God their Saviour.[37]

Such a change had nothing to do with wage and labour settlements, or any subtle issues connected with the mining industry. It simply had to do with an entire community of brutish persons being humanized. In Wesley's thinking, this was the foundational change necessary for addressing other issues related to fairness, working conditions and management. The new spirit and reasonableness of the men were miracles that would facilitate the solving of other problems, and it was the result of individual conversion. He believed a genuine Christian society was beginning to be achieved.

On a scale larger than a single prison or town, Wesley had seen first-hand the influence of his work (and that of his followers) on national public opinion regarding the reputation of the Methodists. Within a short span of years, they had moved from being considered religious outcasts, enthusiasts and even Jacobites, to a respected religious group. Wesley himself was the beneficiary of such change in public opinion. From being the target of mob violence, he had moved to a position of respect and even veneration. It was more evidence that society was able to be changed through the influence of individuals.

In light of these experiences, it is little wonder that Wesley believed individual Christians could significantly address and resolve social problems, even the well-established and profitable institution of slavery. Individual transformation with its attendant social influence were not only possible, but more effective than a more political method. This was Wesley's early position when he felt that neither "the public at large" nor the "English Nation in general," would accomplish the goal; Parliament was too busy and therefore "not likely to attend to this." A top down, or bureaucratic, approach did not hold much promise in his thinking. Wesley's early attitude toward the legislative process was also influenced by the fact that he came from a social/political group which had been defeated in both church and state. It therefore did not feel empowered to utilize legislative process and "made a virtue of restricting the powers of the state."[38] The greatest hope for success, therefore, lay with individuals, "those who are more immediately concerned ... captains, merchants, or planters," and most directly the slave owners, whom he considered "the spring that puts all the rest in motion."[39] As a result, Wesley addressed the common citizens, not the lawmakers. He realized that the entire system would end if the individuals connected with slavery simply acknowledged its injustice and refused to purchase or own slaves. In contrast to this hopeful approach, which was consonant with his other experiences, the arduous process of legislative change seemed unnecessary, even superfluous.

Although Wesley believed the individual was the most effective means to achieve lasting social improvement, he was not opposed to other tactics. On occasion, he encouraged individuals to band together and organize in order to have greater impact against social evils. One such group was the Society for the Reformation of Manners. Wesley's strongest statement in support of organized action occurred in his sermon to this Society in 1763. He praised their past successes, encouraged their continued efforts, and advised regarding their membership selection and motives.[40]

A very interesting insight into Wesley's attitude to group action is seen in his response to two incidents, separated by twenty-one years. The responses seem uncharacteristic of his normal approach and therefore give us broader insight into his perspective. While he typically believed that social justice was the responsibility of the legal authorities, on at least two occasions he made no disparaging or critical remarks when groups took matters into their own hands to ensure justice. In 1758, a load of corn was placed on a ship for export to a more profitable buyer. The loading was done in the presence of starving local inhabitants. The mob intervened, unloaded the corn, and sold it to those in need at the fair market price. Wesley recorded the incident in his journal with no comment about the law or mob interference.[41] The second incident occurred when Wesley was unable to reach his appointed place of preaching because a huge group demonstration was blocking access to the town of Truro. It seems that underpaid tinners had gathered to demand a wage increase which they felt was necessary for their survival. In reading Wesley's account, there is no mention of his inconvenience, just that he found a new preaching site. Rather than disapproval, one senses his sympathy for the labourers.[42] Such sympathy would not necessarily be unusual, but consistent with a general "country" attitude. The two incidents indicate that Wesley was at least open-minded to group action for either protesting injustice or bringing about change.

Adjustment of policy

Regarding slavery, it was noted that initially Wesley felt the individual slave owner was the key to the problem. This was clearly his position in 1773, when he wrote *Thoughts Upon Slavery*. The passing of time, however, seems to have tempered his optimism about individual action becoming collective and he expanded his repertoire of approaches. In 1787 he wrote the Abolition Committee and mentioned that his friends in America had freed several hundred slaves. He then praised the work of Thomas Clarkson and the Committee in attempting to persuade Parliament to legislate against slavery and the trade. In a telling contrast he stated that the individual freeing of slaves only made "a little stand" against slavery, while what the Committee was doing "strikes at the root of it."[43] The following year, as editor of the *Arminian Magazine*, he published a letter requesting readers to petition Parliament against the slave trade.[44] Clearly, he was in favour of attacking the problem by changing the law — a new direction for Wesley.

The reason for Wesley's change of approach can only be surmised. It may be that his early confidence about readers who were involved with slavery was eroded by their lack of decisive response. He may have overestimated how commitedly his followers would apply the principle of love to all of life's relationships. The fact that the second generation of Methodists (within Wesley's lifetime), had not faced the opposition of their predecessors may have weakened their sense of the uniqueness of their identity. They probably would not have realized how radical Wesley's teachings were in their original setting and how revolutionary their effect could be on the overwhelming problem of slavery. Regardless, by the late 1780s, he moved beyond an exclusively individualistic approach. He supported legislative and collective means of ending slavery, a clear modification of his earlier approach.

H. Richard Niebuhr's statement that "the hope of a thoroughgoing social reconstruction was almost entirely absent"[45] in Wesley, is wide of the mark and somewhat anachronistic. Wesley did envision a complete social reconstruction, albeit emanating from the smallest societal unit, the individual, rather than through a reformation of structures themselves. He saw the dynamics of human interaction as the core of social structure, and for these dynamics he proposed mutual respect, trust and care (his word was love), as the means of restructuring. He was not unconcerned about social structures, but idealistic and naïve about how they function. In terms of strategy for social change, he was a man of his times; in terms of values and the equality of human worth he was far beyond his time.

Opposite to the values of love, respect, and care, Wesley believed that sin involved selfishness with attendant greed and oppression. He was explicit on this point, especially when explicating slavery. Individual sin became social when experienced by the masses. Again, Niebuhr's statement that Wesley "envisaged sin as individual vice and laxity, not as greed, oppression, or social maladjustment"[46] misses the heart of Wesley's perspective. He did at times preach against vice and laxity, but because they were the results of the deeper core of sin: selfishness. If he did not speak out against social relationship problems and corporate greed, as brought on by the Industrial Revolution, it was because he still saw such things as individual wrongs, multiplied by large numbers of individuals. They were of the same genre and motivated by greed.

If Wesley overestimated the ability of individuals to redeem social problems, he underestimated the strength of social structures to perpetuate themselves and co-opt unsuspecting individuals in furthering abuse. But within the last few years of his life, he realized that a small minority could keep a structure alive, and a structure utilized the participation of the masses, who sometimes unknowingly extended the evil. The best example of this awakening is his description of the problem to William Wilberforce and to the Abolition Committee. He compared

Wilberforce in his campaign against the pro-slavery lobby as "Athanasius against the world,"[47] and refers to the difficulty of his task due to the "opposition of man and devils." This phrase implies the overwhelming momentum of the institution of slavery. He warned the Committee that the slave holders were "a numerous, a wealthy, and consequently a very powerful body" who would give "rough and violent opposition," raising "all their forces against you."[48] Wesley had begun to come to terms with the power of an institution.

A more balanced assessment of Wesley's approach to social change may be expressed in terms of a developing synthesis. He never relinquished his hope for the influence the individual could exert, but he expanded his view to include specific applications for individuals and additional means beyond general individual activity. My idea of the synthesis grows out of the belief that Wesley's emphasis on the individual was needed in the eighteenth century. His focusing on the sensuality and intemperance was initially necessary for the poverty-stricken of England because they perceived their only escape to be in alcohol and sexual indulgence.[49] Such escape, however, was a continuing threat to their human dignity and Wesley confronted this behaviour. As they heeded his message, a new sense of self-respect began to develop; this was essential for the kind of social action and influence they would exert in later years. The moral strength of the individual would prove indispensable both to sustain the effort and to attract additional supporters.

Although Wesley did not normally relate his social ethic to the structures of society, as time went on the persons he influenced did. The second and third generations of Methodist leaders were more effective in carrying his message to the nerve centres of policy formation, where they would have far reaching sociological effects. The masses were encouraged to lend support through petitions and boycotts.[50] In the late-eighteenth and early-nineteenth centuries, legislative reform was influenced by the evangelical revival and produced reforms such as the temperance movement, organizations to prevent cruelty to children and animals, and even the more fully developed antislavery movement.[51] But even within his lifetime, Wesley began to embrace the newer strategy of social change. It appears that he grew increasingly aware that the reformation of individuals would not automatically reform social structures and institutions. Without direct modification of social structures, the efforts of individuals would be frustrated and perhaps futile.

In general, eighteenth-century thinking focused on the individual as the starting point for altering society. Wesley fits that generalization. Collectivism came later and posed that only as society is changed could change occur within the individual.[52] It could be argued that neither position in isolation is correct. The changed individual is inspired to address the social structure. Such individuals then inspire support to carry through social reform, which increases the likelihood of change within individuals. In this way, it can be seen both as a synthesis and a progressive process. Near the end of his life, Wesley was approaching such a synthesis. He never lost sight of the importance of the individual's integral role in society, but he did come to grips with the real power of structures. As in other areas of his life, Wesley continued to learn from and respond to the contexts and developments of his time. His philosophy of social change reflects that insight and flexibility.

Chapter 6

The significance of John Wesley's antislavery influence

As indicated in the introduction, John Wesley has frequently been cited as a major influence in the antislavery cause. Representative of such citations is Maldwyn Edwards' statement, "when Wilberforce, Clarkson, and Granville Sharp are mentioned, the name of John Wesley must also be included." He asserts, "there is hardly any name more important, hardly any person whose influence was so considerable."[1] Unfortunately, such claims have been made either as broad generalizations or blind assumptions, with no attempt offered to substantiate them.

We come now to the point of trying to assess Wesley's actual significance for the cause. While hagiography does not serve the true cause of history, there is a place for looking at both the clearly documented results and those which are highly probable. My intent is to treat the matter objectively and avoid either assuming that any influence that might have come from Wesley actually did, because of his status, or assuming that no influence could actually be attributed to him, unless it can be conclusively proven and documented. In finding a balance between those extremes Wesley should be given his full due without subjectively making him the lone hero of the cause. In this chapter we shall consider his direct influence on individuals, his indirect influence and the role he played in creating a climate that was conducive to ending slavery. With these considerations, we shall also look at the role of Methodists in the two generations after Wesley and consider in particular some of the demographics which relate to petitions and popular support for the antislavery cause.

The most easily identifiable examples of Wesley's direct influence are the people within his organization, who took up the cause of slavery. Some of these were influenced by their personal relationship with Wesley, the man, others by his authority and example as the leader, and still others by a combination of those and other factors. Thomas Coke and Francis Asbury were at the heart of Methodism and clearly articulated early American Methodist opposition to slavery. They were both deeply committed to Wesley and in complete harmony with his leadership, theology and his views on slavery. The depth of their conviction against slavery can be seen in the threats and persecution they were willing to sustain early on. Although American Methodist opposition to slavery was later softened, the initial position most accurately reflects Wesley's influence. The later softening reveals the development of the American scene rather than Wesley's influence.

Another clear example of Wesley's influence is Thomas Rankin, one of the first Methodist preachers Wesley sent to America. He adopted Wesley's position on slavery and is credited with preaching the earliest recorded antislavery sermon (July, 1775) by an American Methodist. Rankin arrived in America in 1773 and would have had access to the first American edition of Wesley's tract which appeared in Philadelphia in 1774. He also addressed the Continental Congress, pointing out the hypocrisy of contending for liberty while keeping hundreds of thousands of slaves in bondage.[2] This was one of Wesley's themes in his 1775, *Calm Address to our American Colonies*.[3]

Samuel Bradburn was also touched by Wesley's warmth as well as his leadership and responded by following Wesley's example. Bradburn was one of Wesley's preachers and close friends. Wesley had helped "Sammy" financially and enjoyed a fatherly relationship with him and his wife Betsy. When their son died, Wesley wrote Betsy a touching letter of comfort. Later, after Betsy's death, Wesley supported Samuel as counsellor and friend and eventually encouraged him to remarry.[4] On the slavery issue, Bradburn utilized Wesley's methodology and produced his own tract in 1792, *An Address to the People Called Methodists; Concerning the Wickedness of Encouraging Slavery*. He also supported the Manchester boycott by giving up West Indian products, particularly sugar and rum.[5] Wesley's example and personal mentoring touched hundreds of others as well as Samuel Bradburn.

Wesley's clear position, framed in religious/moral terms, also influenced those who were separated from him by distance or time. His "preachers," both ordained and lay, followed his example and added their voice to the cause. One of those, Jacob Gruber, had the distinction of being the first person arrested in America for speaking against slavery. He was preaching at a camp meeting in Maryland, August 1818, where a number of slave owners were present. Defended by Roger B. Taney, who later became the Chief Justice of the United States Supreme Court and author of the Dred-Scott Decision, Gruber was acquitted.[6]

In the West Indies, Wesley's influence is seen in Nathaniel Gilbert, chairman of the Antigua Assembly. As mentioned in chapter 2, Wesley preached in Gilbert's London home (Wandsworth) and baptized two of his slaves. Gilbert later became a Methodist preacher in the West Indies. He died in 1774 before he could read Wesley's tract, so there is no certainty of how his actual position would have developed had he lived longer and had more interaction with Wesley. However, he did improve slave conditions during his administration and later was also committed to the evangelization of slaves, bringing many into Methodism. Because of his respect for Wesley and because he served under Wesley as a preacher, it is reasonable to assume that once Wesley's tract was published and Gilbert learned of Wesley's stand, he would have eventually become a strong advocate of the antislavery cause. The actions he pursued reflected Wesley's influence, and predicted the direction he would have followed, given more time. His strong ties with Benezet, and Benezet's great respect for him, support this assumption.[7] It is also interesting to note that numerous Gilbert descendants ministered both in Antigua and England. Gilbert's own son, also named Nathaniel Gilbert, became the first chaplain of Sierra Leone in 1792.[8] This, no doubt, reflects Wesley's direct and indirect influence.

Another Methodist preacher following Wesley's trend was Richard Watson. Preaching to the Wesleyan Methodist Missionary Society in 1824, he defended racial equality and made a strong case for providing religious instruction to West Indian slaves.[9] As stated in chapter 3, Wesley was uncompromising in his view of human equality. His conviction that slaves were not inferior gave increased motivation for those such as Watson to speak out and added momentum to the antislavery movement. As this attitude toward slaves spread, the effort on their behalf increased and the time of emancipation was hastened.[10] Years later, in 1830, it was Watson who encouraged voters to only support Parliamentary candidates who promised to support the antislavery cause.[11] The importance of this political effort will be explained later.

Jabez Bunting clearly showed Wesley's influence and carried on his legacy. As the dominant Methodist leader for the first half of the nineteenth century (dubbed the "Methodist Pope"), he was actively involved in the Antislavery Committee. Other Methodists played similar roles, such as the respected barrister Richard Matthews who served as secretary of the Anti-Slavery Society.[12] While it would be too cumbersome to continue to trace first and second generation Methodists that demonstrated Wesley's influence in carrying on his antislavery work, those mentioned serve as a representative sample.

The influence of Wesley's antislavery tract

One of the most direct and lasting means of spreading Wesley's antislavery influence was his tract, *Thoughts Upon Slavery*. It not only articulated Wesley's position but exemplified an effective method of broadcasting the view and extending the influence. Some hold that Wesley's tract was singularly responsible for the overt condemnation of slavery by American Methodism in 1790.[13] It certainly made Wesley's position on slavery clear and well known. For those who saw him as their guide it provided a solid resource with a logical base. For many it provided a place to stand on the issue.

The tract was also widely read beyond the Methodists. Up to this time only a small number of relatively unknown persons had published against slavery. The unique fact about Wesley's tract was that it marked the first time a well-known religious leader took such a clear stand and identified himself with the cause.[14] His weight, thrown in with the relatively unknown protesters, was significant and therefore greatly valued by other antislavery figures. Granville Sharp commended Wesley's tract highly and distributed it. Anthony Benezet was so convinced of its potential influence that he republished and distributed it in America, just after it was released in England. This was the edition Thomas Rankin procured.

As noted in chapter 2, the extent of its circulation is indicated by the fact that it reached thirteen editions in thirty years, with a copy finding its way into George Washington's library. The longevity of Wesley's influence through the tract is reflected by the fact that it continued to be used into the mid-nineteenth century. In 1835 and 1856, some sixty-one and eighty-two years after it first appeared, it was again republished in the United States. When American Methodists gave serious attention to plantation slavery in the 1840s, disagreeing among themselves, Wesley's tract was quoted by *Zion's Watchman* in 1842 and *Zion's Herald* in 1844.[15] In 1855 Methodist historian Charles Elliott wrote, "perhaps no publication ever did more against slavery and the slave trade than this tract."[16] Certainly Wesley's position, as stated in his tract, was an important factor in the American Methodist controversy on slavery, which led to the division of the church in 1844. Those who opposed slavery claimed alliance with and the authority of the founder of Methodism. His influence remained alive through his writing.

Beyond Methodism

Individuals not directly connected to Methodism but nevertheless touched by Wesley, form an important part of the tapestry of Wesley's influence. Some of these are worth mentioning, in the form of a representative sample.

John Newton, well known for his unusual story and importance to Wilberforce's journey, also had contact with Wesley. After his conversion Newton sought ordination, but encountered resistance from the Church of England. Wesley tried to assist and even attempted to persuade Newton to become one of his itinerant preachers.[17] Although he did not accept Wesley's invitation, he was particularly sympathetic to the Methodists and was even labelled a Methodist during his early years of ministry. His evangelicalism had been fostered by Methodists, especially George Whitefield, and cordial correspondence occurred between Newton and Wesley on theological topics. The point of influence here is that without Newton's association and sympathy with evangelicals, it is unlikely that he would have been approached by Wilberforce in the latter's spiritual struggle. It is also unlikely that in the following years he would have been sought by or responsive to the evangelicals, when they asked him to write against the slave trade. John Newton had been involved in the slave trade as first mate and then captain of a slave ship, so his perspective would have been significant. The result is that he did write against the slave trade in 1788. The fact that Newton had been out of the slave trade some thirty-four years before he wrote against it also implies a coalescing of events that brought about his writing. It is highly probable that his friendship with Wesley and Wesley's having written an antislavery tract, fourteen years earlier, were among the factors prompting Newton to write.

Henry Venn, curate of Holy Trinity Church, London, is known for his role among the Clapham Sect. This was the small group of evangelicals, Wilberforce among them, who banded together to strategize, pray and encourage each other in the Parliamentary fight against social evils — particularly slavery and the trade.[18] Their work was crucial to the eventual antislavery victory. It is not well known that in his early years of ministry Venn felt a spiritual kinship with Wesley and requested a personal commission as he approached a new parish ministry.[19] Although not technically a follower of Wesley, he acknowledged having been helped by Wesley's writing and preaching. The entire Clapham Sect became beneficiaries of the evangelical spirit (in no small way connected to Wesley) which was gaining momentum across England. It is interesting that the new parish Venn was going to when he made his request of Wesley was Clapham. Had Wesley lived to see the effort and success of this group he would have felt not only kinship but delight for having been loosely connected through his encouragement of Venn.

There are also lines of influence from Wesley to Wilberforce, some direct and verifiable, some subtle or not verifiable. As a boy of nine Wilberforce lived with a Methodist aunt who was an admirer of Whitefield. By the time he was twelve he professed conversion to an evangelical faith. This worried his mother enough that she whisked him away from the aunt's influence to the non-Methodist safety of Hull. It appears that he remained steadfast in his new Methodist faith until he was fifteen years old, but by the end of that year his faith lapsed.[20] The close relationship between Wilberforce and his aunt and uncle, also named William Wilberforce, seems to have grown cool in the following years, but was eventually restored. At their deaths, they bequeathed their Wimbledon villa to him. He lived in the house during part of his Parliamentary career and William Pitt's conversation with Wilberforce about taking up the slavery cause probably happened in that yard.[21]

Wilberforce's true conversion began when he was twenty-six years old, in 1785. On a continental tour with Isaac Milner they read together *The Rise and Progress of Religion in the Soul* by Philip Doddridge. By the end of the tour, Wilberforce was deeply moved and sought private counsel with John Newton. He was concerned about his spiritual state, the implications the choice of embracing devout faith would have on his political activity, and whether or not he should remain in politics if he were to become a Christian. Newton advised him spiritually and also encouraged him to remain in politics. As a long time friend of Wilberforce's Methodist aunt and uncle, Newton was also instrumental in renewing that relationship.[22]

It may not be possible to conclusively ferret out all the various strands of influence in a person's life but the interconnectedness and interworking of evangelical forces in Wilberforce's life are obvious. He had heard Henry Venn's preaching in the spring of 1785,[23] and Newton played a key role in his combining his faith and his career. Both men had been touched by the influence of Wesley, who was an integral part of the entire evangelical milieu, and thus, at least a secondary influence on Wilberforce. For political reasons Wilberforce did not want to be associated with the Methodists, but he considered himself at one with them in spirit and faith. In 1786, not long after his conversion, he confided to his diary, "Expect to hear myself now universally given out to be a Methodist: may God grant it may be said with truth."[24] Nearly three years later Wilberforce visited Wesley who commented in his journal: "Mr. W[ilberforce] called upon me and we had an agreeable and useful conversation. What a blessing it is to Mr. P[itt] to have such a friend as this!"[25] Though by this time Wilberforce was merely thirty years old, he was already leading the antislavery campaign in the British Parliament. He would have seen Wesley, who was eighty-six, as a venerable old man, worthy of respect and highly regarded. This is reflected in the annuity he provided for John Wesley's sister-in-law Sarah, the widow of Charles Wesley.

Wesley's influence is again seen in the fact that Wilberforce felt a deep kinship with the kind of religion Wesley professed, and Wilberforce's religion was the driving force of his antislavery work. He would have been aware of Wesley's antislavery tract, now some fifteen years old. With such a background and respectful relationship, Wesley's last letter, written to Wilberforce, would have been a major source of encouragement. It would also document how central this cause was to Wesley even at the end of his life.

The ties between Wilberforce and Wesley continued after Wesley died, through his followers. At the first Wesleyan Conference assembled after Wesley's death Wilberforce appealed for help in petitioning against the trade. He supplied the ministers with copies of the "Evidence" that had been presented before a Select Committee of the House.[26] The fact that Wilberforce appealed to this group is an indication that he was fully aware of and eager to engage Wesley's influence. The success of the appeal is an indication of the directness of Wesley's antislavery influence. The results were dramatic. In 1791, the Methodists secured some 229,426 signatures, compared to 122,978 by all other nonconforming groups combined.[27] This appears to be the first time an attempt was made to use public opinion to influence the House of Commons on the slavery issue. The fact that slave trade agitation was perceived as a religious issue reflects Wesley's influence on the public.[28] For Wesley, the slavery issue was inseparable from true religion. That perspective was spreading.

An additional instance in Wilberforce's political career indicates that he not only felt Wesley's influence but benefited from it. In 1807 the election in England was unexpectedly close. It seems that common folk became aware of the danger of Wilberforce losing the election and thus, his Parliamentary seat at York. They rallied to his support and brought success. Methodists comprised a significant part of the voter bloc.[29] Wilberforce's role in Parliament following 1807 was crucial to the ongoing battle against slavery.

Another strand in the Wesley/Wilberforce connection is more tenuous, but worth mentioning. After his conversion Wilberforce did not immediately see the powerful relationship between his new faith and his political position. In fact, he nearly dropped out of politics altogether, feeling it would be detrimental to his spiritual development. Fortunately, the counsel of those such as Newton convinced him that he could serve God in Parliament, and in fact this may be God's calling for him. Shortly after this his dear friend, Prime Minister William Pitt, suggested that he take up the slavery cause in Parliament. It is likely that Pitt offered this challenge as a means of keeping Wilberforce engaged in Parliament. The connection to Wesley's influence relates to his belief that people are called by God to serve in the world *where they are*. The "world" was Wesley's parish and he persuaded people to serve the world, not withdraw from it. This was the spirit of Wesley's teaching, and it had begun to be felt throughout the church. Therefore, the idea, partly promoted through Newton and partly through the general acceptance by the church, made Wilberforce fertile ground in which this seed could take root. His influence in the cause is incontrovertible; Wesley's direct and indirect influence on him was significant.

The "climate" of England

While it is more difficult to quantify, the attitudinal "climate" of the populace of England was a very important factor in the ending of slavery. It was one thing to have individual abolitionists working to end the trade and slavery. It was quite another for the populace to have the desire and the ability to support the cause. This would have to do with values orientation, attitude and religious sensitivity, as well as sufficient education so they could grapple meaningfully with the issues and respond to the pleas of the abolitionists. One of Wesley's major contributions was the role he played in helping to create that climate. Just as Anthony Benezet played a crucial part in the lives of the front line abolitionists such as Clarkson and Sharp, Wesley, as one of the key leaders of the evangelical revival, helped to effect a dramatic change in the attitudes, abilities and perceived abilities of the people at large. At least four areas are apparent in this social development: education, the spread of the principles of democracy, the popularization of Arminianism and the teaching of Christian social responsibility.

In promoting education, especially among the poor, Wesley was unrivaled.³⁰ His work at Kingswood among the colliers and his founding schools are primary examples. The whole tenor of his approach encouraged thinking and reading. His sermons and writings consistently employed critical thinking, which he also encouraged in his readers. The fact that volumes of his writings were published indicates that he wanted his followers, both the preachers and laity, to read, think and learn. His great effort in editing many important works, both of a theological and general nature, for inclusion in his "Christian Library" was done for the benefit of his people and to encourage their reading and learning. His chief and well-known principles for discovering God's truth included reason, Scripture, tradition and experience. Even in this paradigm (known as the Wesleyan Quadrilateral) reason was essential in the processing and applying of the other three. The point is that Wesley encouraged his followers, and all Christians, to be thinking, informed people — and this required being literate. To facilitate this, he instituted educational systems and provided educational opportunities for those who would not usually have had such options.

The result of this emphasis is that throughout the Wesleyan revival, people, many of whom were poor, began to have new desires and opportunities for education. As this occurred, a large contingent of the population became much more able to think on a different level than mere survival, and became concerned with the broader issues of life and society. This became an important factor when tactics such as petitions and boycotts were used to influence Parliament. The common folk had new desires and abilities and, by their sheer numbers, they would become a kind of groundswell. The fact that the one who had been their mentor and encourager of education was also clearly on the side of antislavery would cement the direction of this influence.

In spite of the fact that Wesley was opposed to what he termed a "democracy" or "republic" (people governing themselves), he was instrumental in the spread of principles which spawned democracy.³¹ He believed a constitutional monarchy was the safest form of government (to counter rampant human selfishness),[32] but he unashamedly believed in and taught liberty, equality and justice, all essential elements of democracy. Regarding liberty, for example, he defended freedom of speech and the press even when that meant promoting evils he strongly opposed. After a situation when the press had been broadcasting "poison" about the king, he queried, "Can anything be done to open the eyes, to restore the senses, of an infatuated nation?" He reasoned that the only way was "by restraining the licentiousness of the press," but he decisively concluded, "Is not this remedy worse than the disease?"[33] He clearly acknowledged the importance of liberty.

Wesley inculcated the principle of equality in his followers. It is inherent in his theology and is seen in his view of the human condition, from the lowest to the highest. There is complete equality of depravity and of grace. This meant showing respect for others, all others, and respect should be expressed through the simple matter of courtesy. Wesley specified, "see that you are courteous toward all men ... whether they are high or low, rich or poor, superior or inferior to you... the lowest and the worst have a claim to our courtesy."[34]

Not just a matter of manners, equality was practiced in how leadership was structured. The early Methodist societies failed to recognize class or wealth as determinants for leadership. As upper class converts were brought in, they were under the teaching and authority of the leaders who were usually from the poorer ranks. Unusual for the time, women were also given positions of service and leadership. They served as class leaders and some even as local preachers. The criterion to become a local preacher was not gender or class, but God's calling.[35] It was honoured equally among women and men.

Wesley's teaching of equality could not but enhance the self-respect of an entire class of people that had previously been denied respect. Self-respect would go a long way in enabling these people to assert their views and become a force to influence politicians and government. It would also play a role in helping individuals realize they could become political leaders and directly influence government policy.

Although Wesley's actual leadership of the Methodists was certainly not democratic, the concept of equality (which he inspired) produced democratic developments. After his death, the "New Connection" of Methodism was formed, predominantly because of the desire for more democratic church government, again, reflecting Wesley's teaching of equality.

The principle of justice is evident in Wesley's journal and writings from the early days of the Holy Club, through his time in Georgia and to the very end of his life. The issue that arrested his censure in his final letter, written to Wilberforce, was the fact that, because a person was black there was no legal recourse to justice in courts of law, when in contest with the testimony of a white person. This was incomprehensible and intolerable to Wesley. Justice was due every individual. He believed this was an obvious fact.

The reality is that Wesley's theological and ethical ideals and his teaching of liberty, equality and justice contributed to the expansion of democratic processes in government at all levels, both ecclesiastical and national. He assisted the process which undermined the old autocratic and authoritarian order. The value of the individual and the good of the many were inherent in his teaching. The paradox is fascinating. As W.J. Warner observed, even though the "labels were conservative," the Wesleyan movement became a "liberal force, because it created the context of liberalism."[36] The paradox is continued in that Wesley, a Tory at heart and opposed to revolution, was instrumental in bringing about a liberal revolution.[37] While he did not live long enough to see the results of the American experiment in government, if he had, his assessment would be interesting because American government was based on many of the values he taught. Indeed, a number of leaders in the democratic movement came from Methodism — where they had gained a sense of right, a love of justice and a faith that motivated them to work for reform.[38]

Not unrelated to instilling democratic ideals, Wesley played a vital role in popularizing Arminianism. He considered himself an

Arminian and titled his chief publication *The Arminian Magazine*. He taught that grace was universal, not particular to a preselected portion of humanity. This was clearly a leveling principle. Such ideas were not unique to Wesley, but the important fact here is that he was more successful than anyone in *spreading* Arminian ideas among the people.[39]

The Calvinism of the eighteenth century had been used to maintain a social and economic status quo. The tenets of predestination and election had often been used to infer a divinely ordered world, where every creature, including people, had a particular "station." Thus, whether servant, freeholder, noble or king, one's position was the result of divine ordination, and not to be tampered with. The authority of religion was a powerful means of justifying those in positions of privilege and wealth, or reconciling to injustice and want those less fortunate.

One result of Wesley's teaching was a general softening of the harsh Calvinism of the time. While English Calvinism had nearly died out earlier in the century, it also experienced a revival and Wesley influenced the second decrease. His rejection of predestination began to destroy the walls which separated the classes. In a view that was very novel, he believed that poverty was not unilaterally the result of inability and certainly not the result of God's plan. It was a result of improper, unjust and unloving distribution of resources. He taught people to take responsibility for their situation, rather than acquiescing to theological fatalism. Resignation could and should be replaced by industry and motivation. Wesley's Arminianism encouraged people to share in the responsibility for their position, both temporal and eternal. His teachings were absorbed by his followers and many did break out of the bonds of poverty and become a strong working class.

With responsibility came inspiration and the desire to bring change. The shifting from an outlook of fatalism to one of productive change had implications far beyond the individual. It meant that the larger, collective problems of injustice and inhumanity need not go unprotested or be accepted as inevitable — or worse, God's will. Such a view would have far reaching consequences on social change. Rather than helpless victims, people could work to alter their own conditions and, even more relevant to social reform, they could work to alter the conditions of their fellows. Roger Anstey states that "it was mainly religious convictions, insight and zeal that made it possible for antislavery feeling to be subsumed in a crusade against the slave trade and slavery."[40] Of course, this is true, but an important specific aspect is that it was Wesley's Arminian perspective that provided the necessary sense of empowerment for the crusade to emerge.

What Wesley taught in this regard was powerful not because it was new, although it was for many, but because he successfully proliferated such ideas. People believed them and began to act on them. The number of people who so responded continued to multiply. The emotional and theological climate of the country began to change. In the early part of the eighteenth century, people tended to accept slavery as a reality of a fallen world and to challenge it theologically would be to doubt God's sovereign purposes. But by the latter part of the century, the views were very different; people viewed slavery as something that needed to be challenged theologically and abolished.[41] Two facts make it reasonable to attribute the change in large part to Wesley: his interpretation (and application) of Arminius is completely consistent with this different way of thinking, and Methodism grew so extensively that his influence was felt throughout Britain and America. At the very least Wesley's work functioned as a kind of "leaven" in society.[42]

The effect was experienced by key individuals who took on causes and by the masses. Persons such as Wilberforce and Clarkson acted in ways that demonstrated their belief that circumstances could be changed. The masses of individuals who would never become known began to live in response to such belief and formed the supporting groundswell for reform. Wesley's Arminianism fostered a fresh understanding of humanity and human ability.

The religious climate

Finally, Wesley's teaching of Christian perfection was also relevant to the religious climate of England during the antislavery struggle there, and to the religious climate in America in her nineteenth century antislavery struggle. It must be remembered that Wesley's promulgation of specific terms such as perfection or sanctification is not of central importance. Many of his contemporaries (as well as those of succeeding generations) rejected such terms.[43] What was important was the essence of Wesley's actual teaching and its relationship to his soteriology and doctrine of humanity. Wesley insisted on the primacy and the ability of loving God and one's neighbour. Further, he insisted that loving God and loving your neighbour were inseparable. By this he shifted piety from an exclusive focus on God to a view that necessitates benevolence. Good works were not merely encouraged, they were indisputably necessary. He rejected the passivity of the Moravians and taught that the major proof of faith is works. As mentioned in chapter 5, he described faith without works as the "grand pest" of Christianity. Further, he taught that benevolence was an essential means of Christian growth.[44] This was such a consistent emphasis that throughout his life Wesley was accused of being a "papist" (i.e. preaching salvation by works). But the result was that within and beyond Wesley's circles evangelicalism in general began putting new moral demands on Christians.[45]

The point here is that what Wesley believed and taught under the general topic of Christian perfection is completely consistent with what could be called "Christian humanitarianism." Even though some like Eric Williams (author of *Capitalism and Slavery*, 1944) believed humanitarianism did not bring down slavery (rather, it ended when it was no longer profitable), the driving motive of men such as Wilberforce, Clarkson, Sharp and Benezet *was* Christian humanitarianism. They opposed slavery on the principle of love of neighbour and it was only a sense of divine calling that sustained their efforts over many years, even when it seemed hopeless. In a word, they attempted to love and serve God by loving and serving their fellows, Wesley's fundamental definition of Christian perfection, even Christianity itself. Wilberforce's statement that "it is the duty of every man to promote the happiness of his fellow-creatures to the utmost of his power," is very similar to Wesley's description of sanctified Christians who "feel as sincere, fervent, constant a desire for the happiness of every man ... as for their own."[46] While it cannot be claimed that the abolitionists acknowledged or were even aware of a connection between their views and Wesley's doctrine, it is clear that their conclusions and motivation were consistent with the line he took. The foundation he laid among the Methodists was congruent with the presuppositions of the abolitionists.

The most graphic example of the relationship between loving God and being involved in the fight against slavery is seen in Granville Sharp's hermeneutic. He interpreted the entire biblical treatment of the question of slavery in light of the commands to love God and one's neighbour.[47] Sharp described the "law of liberty" (James 1:25) as simply loving one's neighbour as oneself. This is remarkably close to the scriptural basis utilized by Wesley throughout his works. Interestingly, the same theme is apparent in the writings of other abolitionists, such as Wilberforce, Clarkson, Ramsay and Benezet, and usually called the "law of love." Wesley's teaching of the same principle occurred from 1725; but from the 1740s, this emphasis gained preeminence in his preaching, long preceding the writings of the abolitionists mentioned. It is conceivable that the core of Wesley's teaching, perhaps disassociated from labels such as Christian perfection, had time to be disseminated among evangelical Christians. At least the fundamental thought — the primacy of loving God and one's neighbour as the essential core of Christianity — had increased visibility because of the growing Methodist movement. There was adequate time for his thought to spread. If calculated from 1725, there were more than fifty years until Sharp's writing; if from the 1740s, more than thirty-five years. Wilberforce did not join the cause until the late 1780s, writing against slavery even later, well after Wesley's concepts had been broadly disseminated.

In terms of the overall theological developments that led to increased antislavery sentiment, Roger Anstey suggested four major themes: salvation understood in terms of redemption, salvation relating to both spiritual and physical bondage, the law of love, unequivocally condemning slavery and the image of physical slavery used to describe a spiritual condition.[48] It is significant that these themes are all apparent in Wesley's theology, with the law of love becoming the hallmark of his view of perfection. It was the completion of his doctrine of salvation. The hymns of John and Charles Wesley accurately reflect their theology and they are replete with images of slavery and freedom.

As the human rights of liberty, benevolence and happiness were elevated, the world began to be prepared intellectually and philosophically for freedom.[49] These values were embedded in Wesley's theology. The source is not as significant as the fact that the ideas were becoming widespread and Wesley's audience was a different segment of society, and were more inclusive of the general public, than that of the philosophers.

The shift of political power

The societal issues just mentioned are extremely important because the role of the people involed in political issues took a decided turn in the second half of the eighteenth century. Prior to that, the power of government resided in a relatively small number of people and families. Little or no influence came from outside Parliament. Robert Fogel notes a particular incident in the early 1760s that marked the beginning of a political era, one in which the new, literate public began to exert political power. John Wilkes, a Member of Parliament and a newspaper editor, was arrested for publishing "libel" against the king. There was such a public outcry through demonstrations that Wilkes was released and restored to Parliament. It was the first time "campaigns mounted outside of Parliament could influence the course of struggles within it."[50] The significance for this study is that in the seventy years following the Wilkes event the issues of the slave trade and slavery were decided. More to the point, they were championed not only within but also outside of Parliament. The fact that the general public were beginning to have a new kind of power makes Wesley's influence on the learning, thinking and attitudes of such a large part of the population very significant.[51]

While it is not the purpose of this study to do an exhaustive statistical analysis, it is revealing to survey the findings of cliometrics for the years following Wesley, as a means of sampling how Wesley's influence filtered down through the population and affected the political workings to end slavery. The collections of Wesley's followers, the Methodist churches, were ideal groups of people, especially lower class people, that could function as a bloc to pressure Parliament. A good example of this force being utilized is the petition campaign of 1791 to 1792. Some 519 petitions, containing 400,000 signatures, came to Parliament from across Britain, with Manchester's 30,000 adults supplying 20,000.[52] It will be remembered that the first mass petition campaign began in Manchester in 1787,[53] and the following year Wesley published the *Resolutions* from the Manchester antislavery meeting in the *Arminian Magazine*, encouraging readers to petition Parliament.[54] His plea was fruitful with most signatures coming from the working and lower middle classes.[55] The fruit of that effort was harvested repeatedly and notably in the successful petition campaign of 1791 to 1792. As mentioned, in the year of Wesley's death, Wilberforce appealed very successfully to Methodists for petition signatures.

In 1814, seven years after England had ended her slave trade, the French agreed to end their slave trade in 1819 but were slow in legislating to that end and did not seem prepared to enforce the position. England's Viscount Castlereagh was willing to ignore France's laxity until English abolitionists launched a nationwide campaign. In just over a month, they secured 750,000 names on 800 petitions. Castlereagh responded and put pressure on France.[56] Methodists played an important role in that petition drive and, over the next twelve years, they "became the main driving force in the campaign for amelioration and emancipation" of slaves.[57] In addition to securing petitions they organized boycotts of West Indian sugar. In 1829 and 1830 it was the Methodists who pushed the antislavery agenda to the forefront after it had been displaced by other pressing issues. Fogel describes their work:

The Methodists launched a series of antislavery activities more militant than ever previously undertaken. The annual Wesleyan Conference of 1830 not only called on its members to support the petition campaign, but also enjoined each congregation to undertake a petition as a religious obligation, thus putting the petition "on a confessional basis." The same conference urged its members to "give their influence and votes" only to those candidates for Parliament "who pledge themselves" to effective measures for the immediate and total abolition of slavery.[58]

Undoubtedly, some of the Methodist intensity was a result of a strong Methodist presence in the West Indies. There had been Methodist missionaries among the West Indian slaves since 1786 when the Conference, under Wesley, sent Warrender to Antigua. By 1823, nearly 15% of the slaves had been converted to Christianity, and 80% of these were Methodist.[59] When persecution of slaves and missionaries followed the Jamaica uprising in 1831, public opinion exploded. It was beyond comprehension that missionaries were being threatened, attacked and terrorized. And when slaves were attacked and killed, with nearly one in eight slaves being Methodist, the Methodists were moved to protect their brothers and sisters in the faith. Describing their response, Zachary Macaulay, part of the Clapham Sect with Wilberforce and Venn, said that the Methodists "have not only caught fire themselves but have succeeded in igniting the whole country."[60]

The dissenting churches, probably led by Methodists, had gained such momentum that by early 1833 one in seven adults were calling for emancipation and a few months earlier candidates for Parliamentary election were even asked to commit to the abolition of slavery. The perceived power of the populace was such that about 200 candidates pledged to support abolition.[61] It is also likely that in addition to responding to the desire of their constituents, many of the candidates were genuinely persuaded of the morality and importance of the issue, another indication of the changed climate in England.

The result was that the government felt the abolitionist pressure and realized the necessity for action. Whereas initiative for the 1807 battle to end the slave trade had come primarily from political evangelicals such as Wilberforce, by the 1833 emancipation struggle popular opinion had become far more influential and the efforts were energized more by nonconformists, especially Wesleyans and Baptists.[62] This again suggests the groundswell of public opinion and its role.

Robert Fogel's analysis is that the voting behaviour of Members of Parliament was influenced by religion, especially among MPs who were members of dissenting churches. Those MPs were most likely to support emancipation. However, this group was too small to sway the outcome on major issues.[63] The more complex factor involved broader political interests and the government's concern to secure the support of a large portion of the voters. Dissenters, with Methodists being the largest segment of this group, comprised about 21% of the electorate by 1832.[64] As stated above, the Methodists were united and politically active in their support of emancipation, so they were considered by Prime Minister Grey's government to be a necessary contingent for the government's success. The Grey government strategized that by supporting emancipation they would win the support of the Methodists and other dissenters, support which was crucial for other issues that they considered more important.[65]

The result was that the government took decisive action and the Emancipation Act was passed, becoming operative August 1, 1834.[66] After 20 million pounds in compensation was paid to slave owners and the transition period or "apprenticeship" was fulfilled, all British slaves were freed in 1838.[67] Fogel's final assessment is that "the government's switch to immediate abolition ... appears to have been a timely response to the roaring demand of the public."[68] Even though it happened indirectly, to secure Methodist support, the point is that Methodists were of one mind in opposition to slavery and they were perceived as important enough to be courted by the government. Having grown to comprise a major portion of the working class, Methodists had become an influential bloc. The strong correlation between evangelical membership and English antislavery activity reaching their height at the same time is significant and not mere coincidence.[69]

METHODIST AND NEW DISSENTING MEMBERSHIP, AND ABOLITIONIST PETITIONS [70]

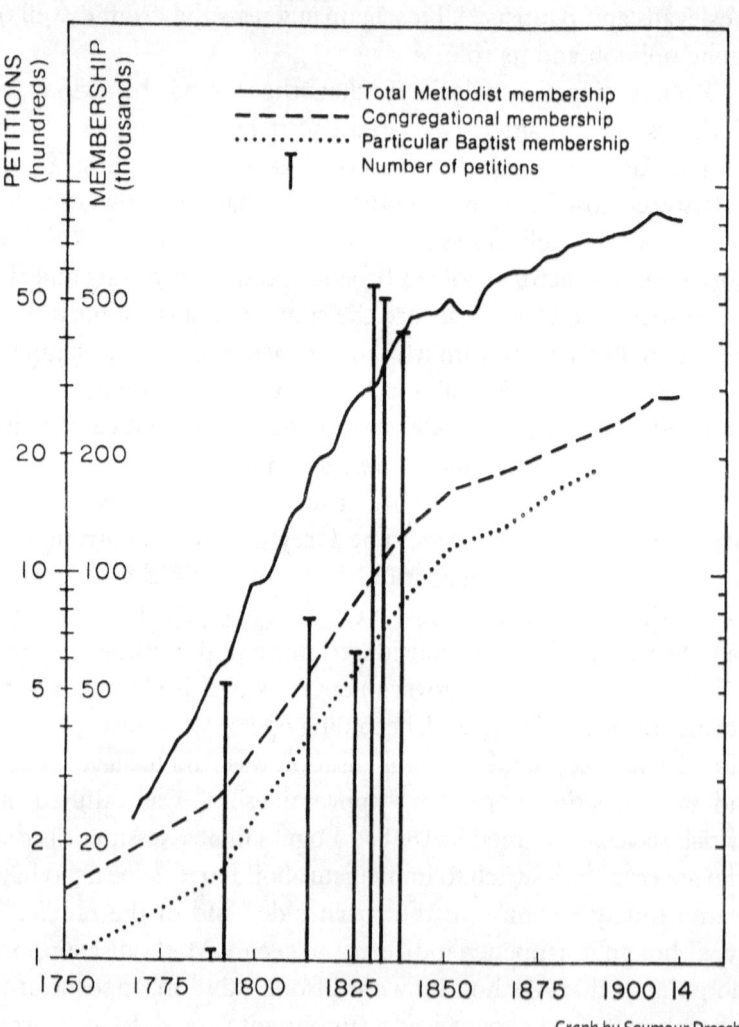

Graph by Seymour Drescher

The role of Methodism within this evangelical and nonconformist pressure is seen in these numbers. During the 1832-1833 petition drive, Methodists (Wesleyan and other Methodists) supplied 236,592 (79.48%) of the total 297,672 signatures, a significant indicator of Methodist strength. By comparison, Baptists supplied 11.64% and Congregationalists, 8.87%. Demonstrating the denominational commitment to Wesley's position, 95.2% of Wesleyan Methodists signed petitions, the highest proportion of any denomination, and more than twice that of their closest rivals, Baptists (39.5% participating).[71] The influence of Wesley is indisputable. His commitment was carried on by his followers. As a brilliant organizer, he also set a precedent of what could be accomplished by cell networks, cooperative effort and organization.

Through his massive organization and cell network, John Wesley spread the principles of authentic Christianity with their deep social implications to a large portion of the population. These principles were conscientiously applied by many in the eighteenth and nineteenth century both within Methodism and outside of it. This was a key factor in establishing a receptive climate for the entire antislavery campaign from 1767 through 1833 (Sharp's early work until complete abolition). That climate affected not only the broader population, but those in government, even those who were initially influential in parliamentary reform.[72] Anstey attributes the success of the campaign partly to "the preparation of the ground by changes in philosophical and theological ideas" and "the slow germination of reform in the bosom of a denominational community."[73] Fogel attributes the "demise" of slavery to the "cumulative impact of the ideological and political ... pressure of the abolitionists."[74] Wesley cannot be separated from these issues but must be credited with having a unique influence. In confronting the great social needs of his time and in altering the social and religious climate, he served as a coworker with those who gave their lives solely to the cause of the slave. Slavery did not die a natural death. It was smothered by a new and vital life, a life which Wesley helped to birth and nurture.

Wesley called upon his followers and upon all Christians to be "citizens of the world" and to "claim a share in the happiness of all the inhabitants of it." He challenged people to be agents of change by being "social, open, active Christians" and to subscribe to the higher ethic of love, the more excellent way.[75] His plea was fulfilled in the lives of all those who took seriously their love for their neighbour as a means of expressing their love to God. It was especially fulfilled in the abolitionists who worked on behalf of the "neighbours" who were helpless to remove their own chains. Through their combined commitment and tireless labour the heartrending prayer of Wesley was finally answered:

> O thou God of love... Father of the spirits of all flesh ...who hast mingled of one blood all the nations upon earth; have compassion upon these outcasts of men ... arise, and help these that have no helper, whose blood is spilt upon the ground like water! O burst thou all their chains in sunder; more especially the chains of their sins! Thou Saviour of all, make them free, that they may be free indeed![76]

epilogue

The end did come. In 1806, fifteen years after Wesley's death, England abolished the foreign slave trade. In 1807, she ended the trade to her own colonies. Wilberforce and Clarkson persevered and in 1833 Parliament passed the legislation that would completely end slavery in all British lands.[1] Within hours of receiving the news, William Wilberforce died at the age of seventy-four. Clarkson continued his efforts against American slavery, "the vilest that ever saw the sun."[2] Although it took years and a civil war, slavery in America was finally abolished.

In one sense, slavery is over. In another, it is not. After a lecture at the University of Edinburgh about eighteenth century slavery,[3] discussion focused on the fact that in parts of Africa (ie. the Sudan) slavery is still going on. This is not metaphorical. It is blatant, overt slavery, the kind this book is about, the kind that most Europeans and Americans think has been abolished for a century and a half. As well, there is increasingly more sex trafficking worldwide, which is also literal slavery.

There are also less obvious forms of slavery. There are sweatshops where wealthy Americans and Europeans increase their profits by the labour and lives of people of the two-thirds world. There are industries that stoop to degrade children to such servitude. There is the slavery of discriminatory policies and attitudes based on race, ethnicity, gender or age.

And there is even more covert, subtle slavery in getting people addicted to products that are profitable to the producer and marketer, but lethal to the buyer. In chattel slavery the slaves are "forced" to give their lives for the wealth of their owners. In the slavery of addiction, the "slaves" are made to desire their chains. It is slavery, just the same.

If forms of slavery continue, does the work of Wesley and his fellow abolitionists provide an example and invite a response? Indeed, if we can see beyond the fact of slavery to the principles which drove it. Indeed, if we can perceive the deeper values which overcame it. With great insight about the role of leadership in liberation, Parker Palmer comments, "the power for authentic leadership … is found not in external arrangements but in the human heart." He continues: "authentic leaders … aim at liberating the heart, their own and others', so that its powers can liberate the world."[4] John Wesley's heart was liberated by his intimate relationship with God and his grasp of the necessity of practical love. Long aware of the existence of slavery, and long convinced of its evil, in later life he was freed to act, to do what he could. Obviously, what he did made a difference in liberating the world.

In considering *how* world transformation is effected, Palmer cites the notion of Vaclav Havel, that

> Material reality … is not the fundamental factor in the movement of human history. Consciousness is. Awareness is. Thought is. Spirit is. These … are the inner Archimedes points from which oppressed people have gained the

leverage to lift immense boulders and release transformative change.⁵

They are also the Archimedes points from which those who are not oppressed (such as Wesley) are moved to liberate their fellow human beings who are. Wesley's inner awareness of the oppression of the slave coupled with his consciousness of his responsibility and ability (the renewed image of God) to make a difference enabled him to influence the world.

A very different view was put forth two generations before Havel by Eric Williams — that material reality is the fundamental reality, and slavery died a natural death for economic reasons.⁶ Havel's description and Wesley's experience take issue with Williams' thesis. What happened in and through Wesley gives witness to the power of an idea, coupled with the motivation emanating out of new inner strength and abilities. Slavery did not die a natural death, but was killed by humanitarian beneficence. Change came through individuals, in spite of what was thought to be economic necessity, or "reality." Such people refused to be prisoners in a world system and became co-creators of a new reality, one of freedom. It is time once again for slavery to be killed by human love.

Therefore, to honour the truth that transformed and drove Wesley, we cannot end this study merely with historical and theological observations. We must ask ourselves the questions: Where does truth once again intersect human need and call *us* to bring change? Will our awareness be heightened, as was Wesley's, so we take seriously human need? How can our lives reflect the truth that God's commands have become fulfilled promises and our God-given abilities match the needs around us? When we internalize Wesley's message that genuine Christianity is love for God and our neighbour, and follow his example of addressing societal evil, we will respond to our fellow human beings wherever they stand in need of justice and love.

At that point John Wesley's prayer, "make them free, that they may be free indeed!"⁷ must again be raised. May we be willing instruments in its being answered.

appendix 1

A sampling of original source material

Extract from the deposition of Little Ephraim Robin-John and Ancona Robin Robin-John [1]

We, Little Ephraim Robin-John, and Ancona Robin Robin-John, believing in One God, the Creator of the world, and that God is a rewarder of them that do well, and an avenger of those that do ill; do swear, that in the year 1767, there being a quarrel between the people of Old and New Town, in Old Calabar, the Masters of some of the English ships there, sent letters to our brother Grandee, Ephraim Robin-John, inviting the chief men of Old Town on board, promising to make up the quarrel: on which the principal inhabitants of Old Town went to them in ten canoes. We, Little Ephraim, Ancona, and our brother Amboe, with twenty-seven more, in our canoe on board the *Indian Queen*. The next morning we all went on board the *Edgar*. From thence we were sent with letters to Capt. Mitchell, Capt. Bevan, and Capt. Parks. We, Little Ephraim and Ancona, with our brother Amboe, (our other people staying in the canoe) went on board the *Duke of York*, and delivered the letter to Capt. Bevan, in the cabin. He went out, and soon came, with several people armed with pistols and cutlasses, threatening us with death, if we made any resistance. The Captain then bade the men on deck "fire away;" and instantly they fired upon our people in the canoe: on which Amboe endeavoured to escape out of the cabin, but was struck and cut by Capt. Bevan and his Officers: when he put his two hands together, and cried out, "O Capt. Bevan, what fashion this, for white men to kill black men so?" We, Little Ephraim, and Ancona, endeavoured to escape out of the cabin-window; but we were knocked down and greatly hurt, and then put in irons. While we were thus confined, we heard a great firing of great guns and small arms from the other ships in the river. Most of the canoes belonging to Old Town were sunk, and many of the people killed, before any from New Town appeared. When the firing was over, Capt. Bevan went on board the *Nancy*, and sent a written order to Mr. Green, his chief Mate, to deliver Amboe to the people of New Town, and to put us, Little Ephraim, and Ancona, in the fore-part of the ship. Mr. Green sent answer, "He would not deliver Amboe to the people of New Town, but that the Captain might come himself." The Captain came, with a canoe of New Town people, and bade his men give Amboe to them. As they were putting him over the ship's side, he put his two hands together, and begged Capt. Bevan, "Not to deliver him to the New Town people to be killed." But the Captain obliged him to go into the canoe, where his head was immediately cut off. We farther swear, that Capt. Bevan brought us away, and sold us to a French Doctor on the Isle of Dominica. We continued there about seven months: when Capt. S. master of a sloop came to Dominica, and hearing our case, promised to carry us to our own country, if we would come down to him at night, which we did.

But instead of carrying us to our own country, he carried us to Virginia, and sold us to Mr. Mitchell, a merchant, with whom we continued five years: where Capt. O'Neile, Commander of the *Greyhound*, from Bristol, arrived. He had on board two black men from Old Calabar, who knew us in our own country, and told the Captain who we were, and how we had been taken away. The Captain sent for me, Little Ephraim, and promised to buy me off Mr. Mitchell, and carry me to my own country; but soon after he said, he had not money to buy me; but if Ancona and I would come to him in the night, he could carry us home. Only we must go to Bristol first; and thence he would carry or send us to Old Calabar. We came down in the night, and he set sail, and brought us to Bristol. We expected he would then put us in some ship bound for Africa, according to his promise; but instead of this, he put us into a ship bound for Virginia, to send us back to Mr. Mitchell. *Sworn, Nov. 9, 1773.*

[This second part seems to be written by John Wesley.]
Mr. Thomas Jones, a merchant of Bristol, being informed of these things, procured a Warrant from Lord Chief Justice Mansfield, whereby both of them were set at liberty. While they were at Bristol, Mr. Charles Wesley was desired to visit them. From that time they came to him every day. He taught them to read, and carefully instructed them in the principles of Christianity. They received the truth with all gladness, appeared to be deeply penetrated therewith: and after some time, desired to be baptized. There is reason to believe, they were then baptized with the Holy Ghost. After they had been in England eight or nine weeks, the people of Bristol furnished them plentifully with every thing they thought might be of use, and they set sail, with a fair wind, and abundance of prayers, for their own country.

I never saw two such Negroes before. They were about five feet, nine inches, well shaped, neither fat nor lean, and exactly proportioned. They were perfectly well bred; all their motions were easy, proper and graceful. Notwithstanding their colour, there was something agreeable in their countenance. But there was a manifest difference both in their look and carriage. Ancona was all Sweetness: Ephraim was all a Prince. No one would have conceived, that he knew what slavery meant.

When they were drawing nigh to their own coast, a storm drove them far away, and stranded the ship on a desert island. They saved their lives, but nothing else. After they had remained there sixteen or seventeen days, and suffered much through hunger, a ship bound for Bristol touched there, and carried them thither once more.

Here they spent eleven or twelve weeks, waiting for another ship. During this time they were more fully instructed in Religion. As also in Reading and Writing, in Gardening, in Agriculture, in making Butter and Cheese, which they never had heard of in their own country. And when they embarked, two of our friends consented to go with them, who were men of a mechanical head, understanding both Wood-work and Iron-work, and carried with them abundance of tools of various sorts. So that there appears to have been an admirable Providence in their return to England.

In the following Spring, Ancona wrote an affectionate Letter to his friends in Bristol: informing them, that they were cordially received at home, and that many of their countrymen, though they wondered and laughed at first, were now glad to sit by, and hear them read the Bible. Here is a good beginning. Who knows what the end may be!

Letter from Anthony Benezet to John Wesley[2]

Philadelphia, the 23d, fifth month, [May] 1774.
Respected Friend,

Having a good opportunity, by means of the bearer, my friend and old pupil, William Dilwyn, a valuable, religiously minded person, who is going a voyage to your country; I make use of it, affectionately to salute thee. The Tract thou has lately published entitled, *Thoughts on Slavery*,[3] afforded me much satisfaction. I was the more especially glad to see it, as the circumstances of the times made it necessary that something on that most weighty subject, not large, but striking and pathetic, should now be published. Wherefore I immediately agreed with the Printer to have it republished here.

The several settlements which are now begun, and will doubtless, vastly increase shortly, on that tract of land which extends some thousands of miles from the mouth of the river Mississipy, to the Northward of the Lake of Canada, instead of being, as I trust the Almighty may intend, a refuge, and affording a comfortable subsistence to thousands, and hundreds of thousands of distressed people, will be occupied, as is much the case of our Southern Provinces, by tyrants and slaves. For in all those places where slavery prevails, a poor industrious white man, cannot procure to himself and family a living, as his labour is rated (except he be some extraordinary workman) no higher than that of a Slave; so that he must, by credit or otherwise, become a Slave-keeper, with all its corrupt effects to himself and family, or lead a poor miserable life, or abandon the country.

I observe that in thy late publication on *Slavery*, in thy mention of the several Negro-Nations who occupy that part of Guinea, situated on, and between the two great rivers of Senegal and Gambia, thou givest a character of the whole nation of Fulys, who are numerous, which from the account given by Moor, &c. is only applicable to a part of that nation, who then resided amongst the Mandigos; having been driven out of their own country. This may be amended in case of a further publication; as it might give an advantage, to the advocate for the trade, to lessen the strength of what is strictly true.

A certain Author, who calls himself an African-Merchant, in a *Treatise* upon the *Trade from Great Britain to Africa*,[4] has endeavoured, though without real ground, to make me appear inconsistent in the account I give of those and other Negro-nations, in my *Historical Account of Guinea*. Indeed the whole of that Author's work is more calculated to shew the iniquity, and dishonesty of the African Traders, even to one another, than to give any grounded answer to what has been written against the Slave-Trade.

Thou wilt probably have heard of the death of my dear friend, Nathaniel Gilbert, of Antigua. The account he gave me in his last letter, wrote two or three months past, was such as afforded me comfort, for the sake of poor Negroes on that Island. I rejoiced that Providence had raised them such a friend, and by his means such an opportunity of comfort in their affliction. But he is gone! It is the Lord, let him do what seemeth Him good. The same hand who raised and removed him, can, and in proper time, will raise more. What he wrote at different times was as follows:

"I can give you but poor account of the progress of religion amongst us. We have a small religious Society here, consisting of about twenty whites, exclusive of my family, and of sixty-four Negroes and Mulattoes. (The word seems to make more impression on some Mulattoes and Negroes, than it does on the white people. There is particularly a Mulattoe woman whom I look upon to be a person endued with great grace.) I have sometimes on Sundays, I believe, no less than eight hundred Negroes, who come to hear the word. They choose to bring their victuals with them, and spend the whole day here.

"I have for several years thought that the Lord had a controversy with the West-Indies, on account of the treatment of our Slaves. Whilst I was a member of the Assembly, I have several times expressed my disapprobation of that act of our Island, which subjects the Negroes to death, for running away from their Masters; but without success. And very little, I conceive, is to be expected in favour of Negroes from a legislature who will not repeal so wicked a law as to the punishment of those who murder Negroes; which is only a fine, and imprisonment till the fine is paid; though every General, who comes to this Government has a particular instruction from the King to use his utmost endeavours to get that Act repealed: so that the crime might remain as it is at common Law, by which every murderer is liable to loss of life."

I understand the Laws of Virginia, and North and South Carolina are much to the same purpose as those in the Islands; tending rather to promote a murderous disposition in the Master towards their poor Slaves; quite abhorrent of that universal brotherhood so strongly enjoined by the Gospel. These worse than Savage-Laws, the Slave-holders apprehend necessary for their safety, and to keep their Slaves in awe. Now can anything more plainly shew the abhorance of the practice of Slave-keeping, with everything that is good and sacred, than the pretended necessity of such detestable Laws? Laws, at which the darkest age would have repunged!

As a farther instance of the inhumanity with which the poor Negroes are treated, even in those Provinces, where they have a less proportion of Slaves, and have not the same plea for keeping them in awe; I will here add the substance of two advertisements, published in the public Prints of the province of Virginia and North-Carolina, viz. From the *Williamsburg Gazette*: "Run away in Prince George, on the 10th instant, a lusty Negro, named Bob, &c. &c. (describing him) The said fellow is outlawed, and I will give ten pounds reward for his head severed from his body, and forty shillings if brought alive."

The other advertisement from one of the North Carolina News Papers is to the following effect, "Run away last November from the subscriber, Kent River, a Negro-fellow, named Zeb, aged 36 years. As he is outlawed, I will pay twenty pounds Pch out of what the Act of Assembly allows in such cases, to any person who shall produce his head severed from his body, and five pounds Pch, if brought home alive." JOHN MOSELY.

I would now leave off writing, particularly in so irregular a manner, and indeed time calls for it, the bearer being upon his departure; but I cannot be easy to do it, without here transcribing, a paragraph of a letter I have just written to your country, viz.[5] "That as dreadful as the slavery now carried on in our Colonies, is to the miserable subject thereof, yet greater, far greater, is its baneful influence on their possessors and their unhappy offspring; these being, thereby, from their childhood nurtured in such scenes and practice, as naturally beget in them habits of idleness, pride, cruelty, and lasciviousness; with a train of other evils, which bear sway; and as age comes on, predominate to the introduction of a much worse kind of barbarism, than that which our

Northern Ancestors were under, before they became acquainted with Christianity. With the poor Negroes the evil of their sufferings will end with this life, and the merciful Father of the family of mankind, will look on their deep affliction, and in his boundless mercy, requite them good for their sufferings; and may favour them with that greatest of blessings, *humble and contrite hearts*. But with respect to their lordly oppressor, the horrible abuse of their fellow-creatures, will extend its baneful influence even in the regions of eternity. For such is the depravity and hardness of heart and mind produced by it, that for many, very many of the subjects of it, it may be feared, Christ will have died in vain."

In the best love I am capable of, and with sincere wishes for thy welfare and prosperity in every thing that is truly good,

I remain thy affectionate Friend,

ANTHONY BENEZET

Letter from John Wesley to Samuel Hoare[6]

Isle of Guernsey, August 18, 1787

Gentlemen, — A week or two ago I was favoured with a letter from Mr. Clarkson, informing me of his truly Christian design, to procure, if possible, an Act of Parliament for the abolition of slavery in our Plantations. I have long wished for the rolling away of this reproach from us, a reproach not only to religion, but to humanity itself. Especially when I read Mr. Benezet's tracts, and what Mr. Sharp has written upon the subject. My friends in America are of the same mind. They have already emancipated several hundred of the poor negroes, and are setting more and more at liberty every day, as fast as they can do it with any tolerable convenience. This is making a little stand against this shocking abomination; but Mr. Clarkson's design strikes at the root of it. And if it can be put in execution will be a lasting honour to the British nation. It is with great satisfaction that I learn so many of you are determined to support him. But without doubt, you [may] expect to meet with rough and violent opposition. For the slave-holders are numerous, a wealthy, and consequently a very powerful body. And when you bring their craft into danger, do you not touch the apple of their eye? Will they not then raise all their forces against you and summon their friends from every side? And will they not employ hireling writers in abundance, who will treat you without either justice or mercy? But, I trust, Gentlemen, you will not be affrighted at this: no, not when some of your Friends turn against you: perhaps some who have made the warmest professions of goodwill, and the strongest promises of assisting you. I trust you will not be discouraged thereby; but rather more resolute and determined. I allow, with men this is impossible; but we know all things are possible with God! What little I can do to promote this excellent work I shall do with pleasure. I will print a large edition of the tract I wrote some years since, *Thoughts Upon Slavery*, and send it (which I have an opportunity of doing once a month) to all my friends in Great Britain and Ireland; adding a few words in favour of your design, which I believe will have some weight with them. I commend you to Him who is able to carry you through all opposition and support you in all discouragements, and am, Gentlemen,

Your hearty well-wisher.

John Wesley

Wesley publishes support for the antislavery petition[7]

Sir,

At the instance of the Subscribers in this place, for the relief of the oppressed Africans, I request your attention to the enormity and impolicy of the African Slave-Trade, as they have been lately held out to the public.

We apprehend that the forcible seizure of the Africans in their native country, (encouraged by the support afforded the traffic by this and other European nations) the miseries attending their transportation to our settlements, the excessive labours and disproportionate punishments to which they are subjected there, and the annual condemnation of so many thousands of innocent persons to unlimited slavery, are evils which demand a full and speedy redress from a free people

And when we add to these Considerations, this undeniable fact, that the *principle* of the Trade cannot be defended on the ground of *common honesty*, we think ourselves entitled to assert that it is the duty of every man, as a Citizen and as a Christian, to signify his detestation of this long-continued abuse.

It is the opinion, not only of the Manchester Subscribers, but of the London Committee, who stand first in this cause, that applications to Parliament, from different parts of the kingdom, representing the nature of the grievance, and praying redress, will prove most effectual in tending to remove the causes of offence.

The intention of the present Address, is to invite you to join with them and us in this measure, which is proposed by the principal inhabitants of the town and neighbourhood of Manchester, and which we are assured will be adopted by several of the most considerable places in the kingdom.

We are also desirous that the petitions to Parliament should be accompanied with instructions to the Members, individually; and in this particular likewise, we request the assistance of your city and neighbourhood.

We trust that the pressure of the occasion, which calls for the immediate and active interference of the just and humane, will excuse the freedom of this Address, as we make no doubt of obtaining the concurrence of all good men, in promoting so desirable an object as the relief of the Africans from this present oppression.

I have the honour to be, Sir
Your most obedient Servant,
Thomas Walker, Chairman.
[Manchester Antislavery Committee]

An extract from a poem on slavery by Hannah More[8]

If heaven has into being deigned to call
Thy light, O Liberty! to shine on all;
Bright intellectual Sun! why does thy ray
To earth distribute only partial day?
While the chill North with thy bright ray is blest,
Why should fell darkness half the South invest?
Was it declared, fair Freedom! at thy birth,
That thou should'st ne'er irradiate *all* the earth?
While Britain basks in thy full blaze of light,
Why lies sad Afric quenched in total night?

O, plaintive Southerne![9] whose impassioned strain
So oft has waked my languid Muse in vain!
Now, when congenial themes her cares engage,
She burns to emulate thy glowing page;
Her failing efforts mock her fond desires,
She shares thy feelings; not partakes thy fires.
Strange power of song! the strain that warms the heart
Seems the same inspiration to impart;
Touched by the kindling energy alone,
We think the flame which melts us is our own;
Deceived, for genius we mistake delight,
Charmed as we read, we fancy we can write.

Though not to me, sweet bard, thy powers belong,
Fair truth, a hallowed guide! inspires my song.
Here Art would weave her gayest flowers in vain,
For Truth the bright invention would disdain.
For no fictitious ills these numbers flow,
But living anguish and substantial woe:
No individual griefs my bosom melt,
For millions feel what Oronoko felt:
Fired by no single wrongs, the countless host
I mourn, by rapine dragged from Afric's coast.

Perish the illiberal thought which would debase
The native genius of the sable race!
Perish the proud philosophy, which sought
to rob them of the powers of equal thought!
Does then the immortal principle within
Change with the casual colour of a skin?
Does matter govern spirit! or is mind
Degraded by the form to which 'tis joined?

No: they have heads to think and hearts to feel,
And souls to act, with firm, though erring zeal;
For they have keen affections, kind desires,
Love strong as death, and active patriot fires;
All the rude energy, the fervid flame,
Of high-souled passion, and ingenuous shame:
Strong, but luxuriant virtues boldly shoot
From the wild vigour of a savage root.

Whene'er to Afric's shores I turn my eyes,
Horrors of deepest, deadliest guilt arise;
I see, by more than Fancy's mirror shown,
The burning village, and the blazing town;
See the dire victim torn from social life,
The shrieking babe, the agonizing wife!
She, wretch forlorn! is dragged by hostile hands;
To distant tyrants sold, in distant lands!
Transmitted miseries, and successive chains,
The sole sad heritage her child obtains!
Even this last wretched boon their foes deny,
To weep together, or together die!
By felon hands, by one relentless stroke,
See the fond links of feeling Nature broke!
The fibres twisting round a parent's heart,
Torn from their grasp, and bleeding as they part.

Hold, murderers, hold! nor aggravate distress;
Repress the passions you yourselves possess;
Even you, of ruffian heart, and ruthless hand,
Love your own offspring, and your native land.
Ah! leave them holy Freedom's cheering smile,
The heaven-taught fondness for the parent soil;
Revere affections mingled with our frame,
In every nature, every clime the same;
In all, these feelings equal sway maintain;
In all the love of Home and Freedom reign:
And Tempe's vale, and parched Angola's sand,
One equal fondness of their sons command.
The unconquered Savage laughs at pain and toil,
Basking in Freedom's beams which gild his native soil.

Does thirst of empire, does desire of fame,
(For these are specious crimes) our rage inflame?
No: sordid lust of gold their fate controls,
The basest appetite of basest souls;
Gold, better gained, by what their ripening sky,
Their fertile fields, their arts[10] and mines supply.

What wrongs, what injuries does Oppression plead
To smooth the horror of the unnatural deed?
What strange offence, what aggravated sin?
They stand convicted — of a darker skin!
Barbarians, hold! the opprobrious commerce spare,
Respect *his* sacred image which they bear:
Though dark and savage, ignorant and blind,
They claim the common privilege of kind;
Let Malice strip them of each other plea,
They still are men, and men should still be free.
Insulted Reason loaths the inverted trade—
Dire change! the agent is the purchase made!
Perplexed, the baffled Muse involves the tale;
Nature confounded, well may language fail!

The outraged goddess with abhorrent eyes
Sees Man the traffic, Souls the merchandize!
...

Plead not, in reason's palpable abuse,
Their sense of feeling callous and obtuse:
From heads to hearts lies Nature's plain appeal,
Tho' few can reason, all mankind can feel.
Tho' polished manners many fresh wants invent,
And nice distinctions nicer souls torment;
Tho' these on finer spirits heavier fall,
Yet natural evils are the same to all.
Tho' wounds there are which reason's force may heal,
There needs no logic sure to make us feel.
The nerve, howe're untutored, can sustain
A sharp, unutterable sense of pain;
As exquisitely fashioned in a slave,
As where unequal fate a sceptre gave.
Sense is as keen where Congo's sons preside,
As where proud Tiber rolls his classic tide.
Rhetoric or verse may point the feeling line,
They do not whet sensation, but define.
Did ever slave less feel the galling chain,
When Zeno proved there was no ill in pain?
Their miseries philosophic quirks deride,
Slaves groan in pangs disowned by Stoic pride.

When the fierce Sun darts vertical his beams,
And thirst and hunger mix their wild extremes;
When the sharp iron wounds his inmost soul,
And his strained eyes in burning anguish roll:
Will the parched negro find, ere he expire,
No pain in hunger, and no heat in fire?

For him, when fate his tortured frame destroys,
What hope of present fame, or future joys?

For *this*, have heroes shortened nature's date;
For *that*, have martyrs gladly met their fate;
But him, forlorn, no hero's pride sustains,
No martyr's blissful visions sooth his pains;
Sullen, he mingles with his kindred dust,
For he has learned to dread the Christian's trust;
To him what mercy can that Power display,
Whose servants murder, and whose sons betray?
Savage! thy venial error I deplore,
They are *not* Christians who infest thy shore.

O thou sad spirit, whose preposterous yoke
The great deliverer Death, at length, has broke!
Released from misery, and escaped from care,
Go meet that mercy that man denied thee here.
In thy dark home, sure refuge of th' oppressed,
The wicked vex not, and the weary rest.
And if some notions, vague and undefined,
Of future terrors have assailed thy mind;
If such thy masters have presumed to teach,
As terrors only they are prone to preach;
(For shou'd they paint eternal Mercy's reign,
Where were the oppressor's rod, the captive's chain?)
If, then, thy troubled soul has learned to dread
The dark unknown thy trembling footsteps tread;
On Him, who made thee what thou art, depend;
He, who withholds the means, accepts the end.
Not *thine* the reckoning dire of Light abused,
Knowledge disgraced, and Liberty misused;
On *thee* no awful judge incensed shall sit
For parts perverted, and dishonoured wit.
Where ignorance will be found the surest plea;
How many learned and wise shall envy *thee*!

And thou White Savage! whether lust of gold,
Or lust of conquest rule thee uncontrolled!

Hero or robber! — by whatever name
Thou plead thy impious claim to wealth or fame;
Whether inferior mischiefs be thy boast,
A petty tyrant rifling Gambia's coast:
Or bolder carnage track thy crimson way,
Kings dispossessed, and Provinces thy prey;
Panting to tame wide earth's remotest bound;
All Cortez murdered, all Columbus found;
O'er plundered realms to reign, detested Lord,
Make millions wretched, and thyself abhorred; —
In Reason's eye, in Wisdom's fair account,
Your sum of glory boasts a like amount;
The means may differ, but the end's the same;
Conquest is pillage with a nobler name.
Who makes the sum of human blessings less,
Or sinks the stock of general happiness,
No solid fame shall grace, no true renown
His life shall blazon, or his memory crown.

Had those advent'rous spirits who explore
Thro' ocean's trackless wastes, the far-fought shore;
Whether of wealth insatiate, or of power,
Conquerors who waste, or ruffians who devour;
Had these possessed, O Cook! thy gentle mind,
Thy love of arts, thy love of humankind;
Had these pursued thy mild and liberal plan,
Discoverers had not been a curse to man!
Then, blessed Philanthropy! thy social hands
Had linked dissevered worlds in brothers bands;
Careless, if colour, or if clime divide;
Then loved and loving, man hath lived, and died.

The purest wreaths which hang on glory's shrine,
For empires founded, as peaceful Penn! are thine;
No blood-stained laurels crowned thy virtuous toil,
No slaughtered natives drenched thy far-earn'd soil.

Still thy meek spirit in thy flock survives,
Consistent still, *their* doctrines rule their lives; ...
Thy followers only[11] have effaced the shame
Inscribed by Slavery on the Christian name.

Shall Britain, where the soul of Freedom reigns,
Forge chains for others she herself disdains?
Forbid it, Heaven! O let the nations know
The liberty she loves she will bestow;
Not to herself the glorious gift confined,
She spreads the blessing wide as humankind;
And, scorning narrow views of time and place,
Bids all be free in earth's extended space.

What page of human annals can record
A deed so bright as human rights restored?
O may that god-like deed, that shining page,
Redeem Our fame, and consecrate Our age!

And see, the cherub Mercy from above,
Descending softly, quits the sphere of love!
On feeling hearts she sheds celestial dew,
And breathes her spirit o'er the enlightened few;
From soul to soul the spreading influence steals,
Till every breast the soft contagion feels.
She bears, exulting to the burning shore
The loveliest office Angel ever bore:
To vindicate the power in Heaven adored,
To still the clank of chains, and sheathe the sword;
To cheer the mourner, and with soothing hands
From bursting hearts unbind the Oppressor's bands;
To raise the lustre of the Christian name,
And clear the foulest blot that dims its fame.

As the mild Spirit hovers o'er the coast,
A fresher hue the withered landscapes boast;

Her healing smiles the ruined scenes repair,
And blasted Nature wears a joyous air.
She spreads her blest commission from above,
Stamped with the sacred characters of love;
She tears the banner stained with blood and tears,
And Liberty! thy shining standard rears!
As the bright ensign's glory she displays,
See pale Oppression faints beneath the blaze!
The giant dies! no more his frown appals,
The chain untouched, drops off; the fetter falls.
Astonished echo tells the vocal shore,
Oppression's fallen, and Slavery is no more!
The dusky myriads crowd the sultry plain,
And hail that mercy long invoked in vain.
Victorious Power! she burst their two-fold bands,
And Faith and Freedom spring from Mercy's hands.

appendix 2

Not only the slave, but wherever Jesus showed his face in the form of human need

BY IRV A. BRENDLINGER [1]

Wesley's teaching of love, his social ethic and philosophy of social change were not abstract theories for him. In his own life he took very seriously and conscientiously applied the principles he taught. His extensive philanthropy and his establishing of programs to relieve social distress speak eloquently to this fact. Although the influence of his theology far outlived his actual philanthropic deeds, it is important and interesting to note what he did because it reflects his spirit and his integrity. Further, it reveals his personal theology in context. He lived in accordance with his judgement that the "grand pest of Christianity" is "faith without works."[2]

A humorous illustration comes from an incident with the excise office. Wesley's commitment to personal stewardship would not let him accumulate wealth while others were in need. When in his seventies, a man of renown and supposed proportionate wealth, he declared a very small amount of silver, the taxable goods of the time. The excise officer challenged him and Wesley wrote back:

> Sir, I have *two* silver teaspoons at *London*, and *two* at *Bristol*. This is all the plate which I have at present; and I shall not buy any more while so many round me want bread. I am, sir, Your most humble servant.[3]

His italics seem to heighten both the subtle humour of the situation and his intensity; humour because the paragon of frugality had been challenged and intensity because within the facts his response conveyed a serious lesson.

Conservative living for the sake of philanthropy had begun during his student days. Wesley describes one of the experiences that evoked his early resolve to live simply in order to give liberally:

> Many years ago, when I was at Oxford, in a cold winter's day, a young maid ... called upon me. I said, "You seem half-starved. Have you nothing to cover you but that thin linen gown?" She said, "Sir, this is all I have!" I put my hand in my pocket; but found I had scarce any money left, having just paid away what I had. It immediately struck me, "Will thy Master say, 'Well done, good and faithful steward?' Thou hast adorned thy walls with the money which might have screened this poor creature from the cold! O justice! O mercy! Are not these pictures the blood of this poor maid?"[4]

For the rest of his life he faithfully kept the resolve he made that day. He records that he and his fellow Holy Club members established the base annual amount they needed to live on. Everything in excess of that amount was given away, regardless of how the income increased. His own circumstances at the beginning of this experiment required twenty-eight pounds, annually, for living expenses. Out of his thirty pound stipend he gave away two pounds. Years later he relayed the results in a sermon, using the third person singular rather than referring to himself.

> The next year receiving sixty pounds, he still lived on twenty-eight, and gave away two-and-thirty. The third year he received ninety pounds, and gave away sixty-two. The fourth year he received a hundred and twenty pounds. Still he lived as before on twenty-eight; and gave to the poor ninety-two.[5]

Such a consistent spending and giving pattern were possible in an age that did not know modern, regular inflation, but it also reveals a concern for others rather than the typical response of increasing one's spending to match one's income.

In later years when he could have been very affluent by the sale of his books and other sources of income, he received only sixty pounds per year from the London Society, and gave some of that away. Henry Moore, Wesley's biographer, estimated that over a fifty year period, Wesley gave away more than £30,000,[6] an incredible sum during an era in which a person could live on thirty to sixty pounds per year. There is no question that Wesley followed his maxim of gaining, saving and giving all he could. He had no interest in keeping what came to him. His attitude is clearly articulated in a letter to his sister: "Money never stays with *me*; it would burn me if it did. I throw it out of my hands as soon as possible lest it should find a way into my heart."[7]

Wesley not only gave money to the poor, but was directly involved with them. He gave personal service and organized his followers to meet the needs of the poor. From his earliest days in the Holy Club he regularly visited the prisons and several local poverty stricken families. He provided needed medicine and gave money for their children's clothing. If there was an opportunity for the children to learn to read that required money, he helped financially and gave a Bible. With all of this he also brought spiritual encouragement. His motive was the biblical injunction to care for the needy and the realization from Matthew 25 that what is done for "the least of these," is done for Christ.[8]

In 1741 Wesley inaugurated a kind of welfare system whereby members of his United Society would contribute spare clothing and a penny per week "to be distributed among those that wanted most."[9] It is estimated that some of the societies provided between £600 and £700 a year.[10] In that same year he organized a system for unemployed women by which they could be paid for their knitting, but receive additional funds for needs beyond what they could earn.[11] An experimental pilot program was tried the previous winter and succeeded. It employed twelve of the poorest women in carding and spinning. Wesley was deeply interested and visited frequently.[12]

Five years later Wesley became aware that a downward economic turn threatened many who owned small businesses. They temporarily lacked capital and money was not available except from the pawnbroker. To bridge the gap he solicited contributions and established a loan fund. It succeeded in assisting some 250 people the first year and continued as a successful venture for many years.[13] It serves as an example of the practical help Wesley envisioned and supported.

Following the dramatic conversions of many coal miners in Kingswood, Wesley, along with Whitefield, realized that one of the great needs of the community was the education of their children. That would be a key to the continued growth begun by their parents' conversion. It appears that Whitefield initiated the idea and Wesley carried it out. The school was successful, continuing into the nineteenth century.[14] Over the years other schools and related ventures were begun including a school at Bristol, a school and "poorhouse" at the Foundry (Wesley's meeting site) in London and an "orphan house" in Newcastle. The Newcastle endeavour was not only for children, but gave assistance to aged and poor widows even more than to children.[15]

Probably from his prison visits, work among the poor and his long-time interest in medical issues, Wesley developed a concern for public health. A number of enterprises were developed to meet community needs. One was a detailed and thoroughly organized system (typical of Wesley) of visiting the sick. He had become aware of the magnitude of the problem of illness among the poor and believed that many died needlessly for lack of money, medicine, food, or basic attention to their needs.

He organized a plan, divided the area into sections, appointed and instructed teams to make systematic visits. Every sick person was to be visited three times a week, encouraged spiritually and given material assistance if needed. Accounts of the visits were to be given to the Stewards of the society. Later the plan adjusted to give this role to class leaders.[16] The program was very successful, particularly with the many instances of less serious illness where the visitors could help prevent increased illness from negligence. It is likely that Wesley's plan contained the seeds of later social case work.[17]

Wesley realized that his program of visitation was not sufficient for instances of greater illness among the poor. To address this need he attempted to get more people admitted to the hospitals, but he was very disappointed with their progress once admitted. They did not seem to receive adequate help even there. As a result he decided to open a Methodist medical dispensary. He describes his thinking and the process:

> For six or seven and twenty years, I had made anatomy and physic the diversion of my leisure hours; though I never properly studied them, unless for a few months when I was going to America, where I imagined I might be of some service to those who had no regular Physician among them. I applied to it again. I took into my assistance an Apothecary, and an experienced Surgeon; resolving, at the same time, not to go out of my depth, but to leave all difficult and complicated cases to such Physicians as the patients should choose.
>
> I gave notice of this to the society; telling them, that all who were ill of chronical distempers (for I did not care to venture upon acute) might, if they pleased, come to me at

such a time, and I would give them the best advice I could, and the best medicine I had.[18]

This appears to have been the very first free medical dispensary in London.[19] It is not surprising that the response of the people was so positive :

> In five months, medicines [costing nearly forty pounds] were occasionally given to above five hundred persons. Several of these I never saw before; nor I did not regard whether they were of the society of not.[20]

Wesley was quite pleased with the success of the venture and reported the results. In the first half year of operation, some 600 persons were treated. More than half of these came two or three times and did not return. More than 200 showed marked improvement and fifty-one were "thoroughly cured." Twenty regular attenders showed no improvement or decline.[21] Probably much of the improvement was due to the strict regimen and moderate living Wesley prescribed. The early success prompted Wesley to establish a similar dispensary in Bristol. The London dispensary continued for six or seven years until it became too much of a financial burden sometime before 1754.[22]

Eager to make the successful remedies of the dispensary more widely available, Wesley published his medical book, *Primitive Physick*, in 1747. With its promise of health (the extended title was *An Easy and Natural Method of Curing Most Diseases*) the book attracted a wide following. It reached twenty-three editions in Wesley's lifetime and thirty-two by 1828.[23] By present day standards some of the remedies appear extreme, perhaps humorous, but by the standards of the day it was sensible and practical. He advocated moderate diet, regular sleep, rigorous exercise and opposed blood letting, the common practice of the day.

Not everyone was supportive of Wesley's encroachment onto medical turf, particularly a physician named William Hawes. In 1776 Hawes published an ad in Lloyd's *Evening Post* describing

Wesley's book as the work of a "dangerous quack." Unruffled, Wesley responded in the *Post* that in the days after Hawes' ad he had "greater demand for [his book] than ever," and he requested Hawes to "publish a few farther remarks."[24] Wesley may not have been an expert in medicine, but his desire to help people with their health needs is another indication of his concern for the well-being of others. He saw a need, most pronounced among the poor, and did what he could to address the problem and alleviate the need. He did it with no other motive than to help his fellow human beings.

Much more could be added about Wesley's personal involvement with the needs of others and his philanthropy, but the examples given convey the fact that he practiced the value system he preached. The true Christian must respond to those in need. He called the Quietist teaching of not doing good "unless our heart be free to do it" the "enthusiastic doctrine of devils."[25] Such a teaching was rationalization for not doing what Scripture clearly instructed. One of the reasons he parted company with the Moravians was their lax attitude regarding benevolence to others, especially non-members.[26]

Wesley considered himself an "evangelist," but his ministry went far beyond what some consider the "spiritual" aspect of evangelism. It reflected his social ethic which embraced people as the receptors of one's love for God. His personal ethic then carried out that belief in every conceivable avenue at every available opportunity. His activities were a conscientious application of what he believed to be the biblical definition of true religion, the loving God with all one's heart, and the loving one's neighbour as oneself. It could mean teaching a child to read, helping a destitute sick person find health, giving money to a distraught business person or liberating a slave from the shackles of slavery. The principle was consistent. The application was as varied as human need and as dogged as the intensity of the need. Wesley's response was not simply *compatible* with his theology; it was the inescapable conclusion and the necessary application of his theology. The slave? Yes. But not only the slave; wherever Jesus showed his face in the form of human need.

An Address to the People called Methodists; Concerning the Wickedness of Encouraging Slavery

BY SAMUEL BRADBURN (1751–1816)[1]

> Hear, I pray you, ye chiefs of Jacob;
> And ye princes of the house of Israel:
> Is it not yours to know what is right?
> Ye that hate good, and love evil:
> Who tear their skin from off them;
> And their flesh from off their bones:
> Who devour the flesh of my people;
> And flay from off them their skin:
> And their bones they dash in pieces;
> And chop them asunder, as morsels for the pot:
> And as flesh thrown into the midst of the cauldron.
> Micah 3:1-3 (Lowth's *Notes on Isaiah*, page 31).

Brethren, a sense of duty, and a desire to serve my suffering fellow-creatures, are the motives which induce me to address you on the subject of the *West India Slave-Trade*. A trade that is manifestly founded in, and supported by a *complete System of Robbery and Murder*. The truth of this assertion is so incontestable, that not one of the persons who are concerned in this odious business, has been able to confute the "Evidence delivered before a select Committee of the House of Commons," concerning their treatment of the Negroes.

By that evidence it appears, that the artless inhabitants of Africa, are stolen from their *lovely* and *beloved* country by the *iron-hearted slave-dealers*, who, without any regard to justice, make use of every species of deception, to get these inoffensive people into their ships. It appears, that by *bribes, lies, intoxicating liquors, threatnings*, and often by *force*, the Captains of the slave-ships, when they could not steal them, have excited the nations to make war on each other, that the prisoners on both sides might be purchased for slaves. This seems to be the most common method of procuring them, and a method that is not pretended to be a secret.

That evidence proves beyond contradiction, that thousands of the Negroes are destroyed, that is, *Murdered*, in attempting to preserve their liberty in their own land. Their towns are burned, their country is laid waste, and the survivors are reduced to the most deplorable situation, and the most horrid tortures that ever were inflicted upon human beings. Thousands of them perish with *hunger, thirst* and *stench*, on board the ships, during the passage from the coast of Africa to the islands. The *distress of their minds*, on account of their being *forced* from their native country, and their dearest relations, with nothing but the gloomy prospect of perpetual Slavery before them, or the apprehension of being eaten by the white people, together with the excruciating pains which they undergo from various causes, have induced some of them *to hang themselves*, others *to leap over board*, others *to refuse taking any food till they have died with hunger*. Several of the witnesses declared, that they left the slave-trade, *because they could not follow it with a good conscience*, being convinced it was an *unnatural, iniquitous, and a villainous trade,* evidently founded on *injustice* and *treachery, manifestly carried on by oppression and cruelty, and not infrequently terminating in murder.*

The same respectable evidence laid open the savage barbarity, with which the negroes are treated *by West-India Planters,* in a detail of the most *deliberate* and *shocking Murders,* that ever were perpetrated by the most *bloody and abandoned Villains.* To say nothing of the manner in which those poor Children of Adversity are exposed to sale, without anything to cover them, without any respect to sex or circumstance; how great must be the anguish of their minds, when *Brothers* and *Sisters, Parents* and *Children,* and *Husbands* and *Wives,* are separated, perhaps to see each other no more, with as little ceremony as a butcher divides the cattle he is about to kill! How moving must the sight be! Rational Creatures, possessed of lively passions, united by the strongest ties of nature, clinging about each other, expressing their mutual attachments in the most pitiable lamentations, 'till the Whipper comes and tears them asunder, and drives them to the plantations of their different owners! Good heavens! To what degree of diabolical insensibility must the heart be reduced, that can witness, with calm indifference, such scenes of human misery.

To pass over the hardness of their work, the badness and scantiness of their food, the wretched huts in which they are lodged, and the consequent diseases to which they are liable, any one of which is sufficiently distressing, and which together, actually destroy thousands of them; what shall we say of the severity with which they are punished, for any thing that their cruel oppressors may deem an offence? To say every thing that ought to be said on the subject, exceeds the power of man; for who can paint in colours sufficiently striking, what is horrid beyond the utmost stretch of human language? One would almost think that the *vilest Reprobate* in *England,* who has not been *hardened by custom,* or *blinded by interest,* on hearing of their cruelties, would sink into the dust with shame and mortification, when he considers himself a being of the same species with a *West-India Slave-Dealer*! What then must be the feelings of a compassionate man, when he hears how those *barbarous Europeans*, guided by *Caprice* or *Passion*, have sacrificed the helpless *African Victims* in the most shocking manner! They have cut off their ears, slit open their nostrils, beat out their teeth, and chopped off their hands and feet, or parts of them! They have shot them through their heads and bodies, and hung, and stabbed them to death! They have whipped the flesh off their bones, and rubbed pepper and salt into the wounds! They have fastened them to the ground, and dropped blazing sealing-wax and boiling lead upon their backs after whipping them 'till their skin was perfectly flayed off; and sometimes they have whipped them to death; They have thrown them into vessels full of boiling cane juice! They have gibbeted them alive, in which state some of them have lived several days! They have burned and even roasted them in the most lingering manner, till the extreme of torture has put a period to their sufferings!

When they have been about to flog a Female slave, and have found her pregnant, that the child might not be killed in the operation, as that would be a loss to them, they have made a hole in the earth large enough to hold her belly, and then laid her on her face and scourged her all over her back and thighs most dreadfully. Some of the women have been delivered of the child at the very time the whipper was scourging them. Some of their ways of torturing the slaves are too obscene and disgusting to be published! And what is still more shocking, to such a degree can the human heart be hardened, that even *Women*, and some women of fortune, are guilty of inflicting punishments not less horrid and indecent than those inflicted by the Men, and that frequently *with their own hands*! They have chained their women-servants to tubs, and made them wash almost naked, *with their thighs and backs in a gore of blood from flogging*! They have torn off their skin and flesh with a cowskin-whip, and dropped blazing wax upon their mangled backs and breasts, and abused them otherwise with *Cayenne Pepper*, in so indecent a manner, that it must not be printed.

Should any one say, these must be only punishments for the most heinous crimes, and inflicted only on a few individuals: The answer is, read the Abstract of the evidence before mentioned.

Therein it appears that the slaves have been punished for *running away* when *wrought, starved*, and *beaten almost to death*; for *lifting a hand against a white person*; or for *breaking a plate*, or *spilling a cup of tea*, or to *extort confession*; others for not coming into the field *in time*, not picking *a sufficient quantity of grass* for the cattle, not appearing willing to work when in fact *sick and not able*, for staying too long on an errand, for not coming *immediately* when called, and for theft, to which they were *often* driven by *hunger*. Under the head of the part which the very Women take in these punishments, female slaves are punished for *being found pregnant*, or for not bringing home the *full wages of prostitution, when hired out by their delicate mistresses*; others, for making a mistake, for *being old and past labour*, and sometimes *in the moments of passion, without even the allegation of a fault. A lady* is represented by Mr. Cook as *having her domestics flogged every Monday morning*. And Lieutenant Davison has often known a mistress send her domestics to be punished *and without telling them for what*! Indeed, the crimes need not be many or great to provoke those blood-thirsty monsters, who manifestly *take pleasure in torturing the defenceless objects of their malicious passions*.

And let none pretend that these accounts may be *false or aggravated*. Where *invincible demonstration* is the proof, the seeming to doubt, *is contemptible affectation*. The witnesses examined, from whose evidence this abstract is taken, were *Gentlemen of Rank and Fortune, Surgeons, Physicians, Captains of the army and navy, Generals and Clergymen*, who testified in the most solemn manner of what they knew to be true, having seen the facts.

That the unconstitutional principles of slavery should be fostered in the bosom of the *British Legislature* in this enlightened age, is a dreadful reflection on the boasted love of liberty for which the English have been so famous, and an utter disgrace to any nation of people, *said to be free*. Yet, the *nation is not altogether to blame*; for, in the year 1788, numerous petitions were sent to Parliament from different towns, cities, and countries for the ABOLITION of the SLAVE-TRADE; in consequence of which, leave was given to bring in a bill for that purpose, in the year 1791.

Mr. Wilberforce, whose character and principles do honour to the British Senate, to Human Nature, and to the Christian Religion, came forward the zealous advocate of the injured Africans. He was well supported by many gentlemen of distinguished merit, who exerted their rare abilities to the utmost in behalf of *suffering humanity*, and made the most vigorous efforts to obtain the object of their benevolent witness. Hence it appears no less *surprising to the reason*, than *shocking to the feelings of an uncorrupted heart*, that means should be found to procure a majority of COMMONS in favour of so detestable and inhuman a traffic, and that the friends of the Abolition should have only the illustrious virtue which prompted their noble minds, for the reward of their God-like endeavours!

But have not several *Regulations* been made by *Parliament in favour of the slaves while on shipboard?* I answer, yes! And, if the depraved hearts of the captains and others concerned, be capable of mirth, they must laugh at such regulations. Opposite page 37, of the "Abstract of the evidence," there is a place representing the manner of stowing the negroes, and annexed there is a regular calculation of the space allowed for each: and I earnestly recommend the reading of that book to every christian who can get it. But as some may not have it in their power either to buy or borrow it, and may therefore be imposed on by persons concerned in the slave-trade, I subjoin part of the note which is at the bottom of page 38. "The situation of the slaves must be dreadful even on the *present regulated plan*; for their bodies not only touch each other, but many of them have not even room to sit upright; for when every deduction has been made, the height above the platform, and below it, is in the *Brooks* but *two feet seven inches*. The average height of nine other vessels measured by Capt. Parrey, was only *five feet two inches*; (which divided by the platform, is the same as above and in the *Venus* and *Kitty*, the slaves had *not two feet* above or below the platform. The slaves immediately under the beams must be in a still more dreadful situation as is seen by the plan." I add what follows, from "A Summary View of the Evidence;" "The room these unhappy beings are allowed *by our Legislature*, appears on a pretty accurate calculation to be about the proportion of 400 persons in a space of 19 feet each way: and is for a grown person, 16 inches each in width, 2 feet 7 inches in height, and 5 feet 11 inches in length, or, as Mr. Falconbridge properly describes it, *not so much room as a man has in his coffin*: and Capt. Knox admits that they sometimes had not room to lie on their backs!" When it is taken into this account, that the slaves lie on the *bare board*, so that their bones are often to be seen through their skin; that they have frequently the flux, owing to the treatment they receive, so that the whole place becomes covered with blood and mucus like a slaughter-house; that in stormy weather they are shut in so close that many of them are suffocated; that when the miserable pittance of water allotted to the slaves, is nearly exhausted or supposed to be so, the negroes are called on deck, and ordered or requested to jump overboard; that the convicts which are transported to *Botany-bay* for *transgressing the laws of the land*, are provided in a manner, every thing considered, *three fourths better* than those *innocent people*; I ask any man what he thinks of the slaves being *favoured* by the *Regulation* of the *Lords Spiritual and Temporal, and Commons in Parliament assembled*? I ask any thinking man, who is not *some way a temporary gainer by the slave-trade*, whether these poor prisoners and captives could have been in a situation much more dreadful and disgusting, if *no notice* had been taken of them *by the Parliament*? And whether it be any thing better than *mocking their misery*, and *tantalizing their grief*, to call any thing *consistent with such treatment* by the name of, *Regulations in their favour*?

Of much the same nature are the laws which are said to be made for the protection of the slaves in the Islands. Let any man judge of the situation of the slaves, prior to such laws, and then consider what sort of protection they derive from them. As I must be as short as possible, I shall only add the following extract: "By the 329th Act, page 135, of the Assembly of Barbadoes, it is enacted, "That if any negro or other slave, under punishment by his master, or his order, for running away, (that is for claiming the right which the God of nature gave him) or any other crime or misdemeanor towards his said master, unfortunately shall suffer in life or member, no person whatsoever shall be liable to a fine; but if any man shall out of *wantonness*, or only of *bloody-mindedness, or cruel intention, wilfully kill a negro, or other slave of his own, he shall* (now mark the dreadful punishment! *he absolutely shall*) *pay into the public treasury fifteen pounds sterling*." And it is the same in most, if not all, of the West-India Islands. And surely there never was a more complete satire on Legislation, nor a greater burlesque on common sense, then impiously to say that *such acts* are intended for the benefit of the slaves: especially where it is considered that *the evidence of a slave is not admissible*; that the bare word of the master is sufficient, if he choose to be at the trouble of accusing his defenceless slave of *some misdemeanor*; that in such a case, he may punish, or order him to be punished *as he pleases*, and if a *limb or life should be lost*, he is not subject to *any fine, being protected by law*. And if a planter be *bloody-minded*, (and how few of them are otherwise?) and should at any time choose to *roast his slave*, or put him to the most *lingering* and *cruel death* that ever the Devil or the Inquisition invented, and that in the face of the sun, what has he to fear? Why, that if any of his *bloody-minded neighbours* happen to owe him a spite, they may *run the law to its utmost rigour*, and oblige him to *pay into the public treasury fifteen pounds*! And trifling as it is, it never need be paid, except the *Murderer please, nor is there any law made in favour of the slaves to this hour, that is of any real advantage to them, either on ship-board or in the Islands*. The planter considers the slave as his *private property*, just as a man in England does his *horses*. The slave has no more power to demand justice than if he were a horse, for *his evidence is not admissible against a white*. Hence, to the great grief of thousands of pious christians, not withstanding the late exertions of the nation, the slave-dealers *by the Authority of the British Legislature* pursue their infamous business with unabating ardour, and the helpless sufferers continue to be treated with unrelenting cruelty: and there is cause to fear, that instead of the petty tyrants being softened towards them, they will, if possible, be more rigorous than ever, and that for reasons too obvious to common sense, to require minute investigation.

"But if the slave-trade could be managed without the degredations and bloodshed, which have hitherto been its inseparable concomitants, would it not be very *impolitic* in government to give it up, considering the advantage it is to the nation?"

I answer, first, the trade in slaves cannot be carried on without depredations and bloodshed. Put together what has been said on the subject, and you will be fully convinced that it cannot, unless it be so reduced as to render it of no value to the traders. But, secondly, suppose it could, it is so far from being any advantage to the nation, that (as the Rev. T. Clarkson has demonstrated,) *it is as impolitic as it is inhuman and unjust.* For the sake of those who have not got his "Essay on the impolicy of the African slave-trade," I insert the following passage from page 132, wherein that inimitable writer collects the substance of what has been said throughout the whole of the work.

"It has appeared, that the slave-trade considered abstractedly by itself, is of *no emolument to the nation*; that it is the *grave of our seamen*, destroying more of them in one year, than all the other trades of Great Britain when put together, destroy in two.

"It has appeared, on the other hand, that the trade which might be substituted for it in the natural productions of Africa, if considered in the same light, would, by affording an inexhaustible mine of wealth to our dyers and artificers in wood, by enabling us to break the monopoly of the Dutch in spices, by repaying us for the loss of America, and by becoming the cheapest market for all sorts of raw materials for our Manufacturers, be of *great national advantage.* —Hence, (page 34) "We may safely say, that whatever argument the *moralist* is able to collect from the *light of reason*, or the *man of humanity* from his *feelings*, the statesman is able to collect others from the source of *policy*, that call equally aloud for the ABOLITION of the SLAVE-TRADE."

But suppose the Africans were used as well as any human beings can be used, and that they had every degree of tenderness showed to them, both by the Captains and Planters; and suppose the trade of the greatest political advantage to the nation, *(which suppositions are totally destitute of any foundation in truth)* yet, as it is in *itself an evil, it ought to be abolished.* Whatever may be the opinions of others, you, Brethren, believe that "God hath made of *one blood all nations of men,* for to dwell on all the face of the earth, and hath determined the times before appointed, and the bounds of their habitation." Who then has any right to go, or to authorize others to go across a vast ocean, to enslave a *free,* and in relation to us, a *harmless people*? None but the Sovereign Ruler of the universe has power to grant such a right. And such is the goodness of his nature, and the harmony of his justice and mercy, that in the severest dispensations of his providence, there is a sufficiency of rational evidence, to justify his conduct from the charge of granting any right like that which the slave-dealers exercise, whether others perceive it or not. But who can, or who does, pretend to derive his right from God? Let such pretenders produce proper credentials of a divine mission, to act as the slave-dealers have done, and as they continue to do, and we will believe them. As they cannot do this, there is nothing plainer, than that the Negroes have as good a right to invade Great Britain, and make slaves of us, as we have to invade Africa and make slaves of them. Hence the very foundation of this detestable commerce is laid in an *unjust seizure* of the *persons* and *property of our fellow creatures.*

Do not then, Brethren, suffer yourselves to be imposed upon by any slave-dealer or his emissaries, who may attempt to dissuade you from endeavouring to obtain the Abolition of this *nefarious trade.* Let those who make no conscience of their actions, proceed to trample upon justice and mercy, and plead a *political propriety* of conduct, till God shall call them to judgment: *you* know better than to act upon such principles, *you* believe the Bible to be the pure word of God; and were there no other reasons for your being in the opposition to the slave-trade, and that dreadful system of slavery derived from it, *this one is sufficient to determine you, it is contrary to the genius and design of the gospel of our Lord Jesus Christ, and irreconcilable to the letter of the New Testament.* Therein, the Apostle to the Gentiles ranks *men-stealers,* that is, *Slave-Dealers of every species,* with the vilest and most atrocious criminals: With the lawless and disobedient, with the ungodly and sinners, with the unholy and profane, with murderers of fathers, murderers of mothers and man-slayers, with whore mongers and sodomites, and with liars and perjured persons. 1 Tim. 1:9,10. Can there be a greater proof of the detestation in which the righteous God held slavery, than his placing *Slave Dealers*[2] in this *infernal group?* then surely it is *equally criminal to countenance the slave trade, as to countenance any of the sins*, which characterize the individuals, in this black list of notorious offenders. And *you* well know what would be deemed *countenancing any of these*. The moment you hear them named, *you feel it your duty* to endeavour by every rational and scriptural method, to put a stop to such works of darkness. Be consistent with yourselves by doing the same, to stop this execrable traffic.

If it be asked what can we do? I answer, (if there be nothing else in your power) you can do the *three following things*, to which I earnestly advise you.

I. Join your neighbours in petitioning the Parliament to *abolish the slave-trade.*
II. Pray earnestly and constantly to God Almighty, that it may be immediately and effectually abolished.
III. Abstain from the use of Rum and Sugar till its abolition be completed, and the slaves emancipated, or till those articles be procured from some other quarter.

I. Join your neighbors in petitioning the Parliament to *abolish the slave-trade*. Or if they refuse, to join with you, petition by *yourselves*. You cannot be engaged in a more laudable undertaking, and you have no sufficient reason to doubt of your being successful, if you act with a zeal becoming the goodness of the cause.

Our society and constant hearers, cannot fairly be estimated at less than *four hundred thousand* in England alone; suppose the half of these to be women, who have no voice at *present* in these matters, there will remain *two hundred thousand* to petition, many of whom are possessed of ample fortunes and very considerable influence. Your petition will certainly therefore have some weight, especially with those who represent towns and counties where your votes are numerous, as it will convince those who oppose the abolition, that they have nothing to hope for from you at future elections; at least it will be bearing an honest testimony against an abominable trade, and the corrupt supporters of it.

I have never conversed on the subject with but one of our people in the nation, who did not avowedly abhor Slavery, and sincerely wish its destruction, and he, I have no doubt, was in his heart against it as much as others, only some part of his worldly gain came from people concerned therein, whom he feared to offend if he discovered his sentiments. Your ministers are to a man decidedly for the abolition. Your late Venerable Pastor faithfully testified against that disgraceful traffic in *human flesh*, near twenty years ago, in one of the best pamphlets which has been published on the occasion, entitled "Thoughts on Slavery." And were he again on earth, I have no doubt but he would exert himself to the uttermost, and employ all his interest in this good work. If your endeavours keep pace with your principles, you may expect great good will ensue. The cause is worthy of the patronage of the greatest *Philosophers, Christians*, and *Divines*, that ever lived. — It is the cause of *Humanity*, of *Religion*, and of *God*! — Show by your exertions in its favour, that it is *your cause* also. In Manchester we signed the Petition in common with our neighbours, deeming it a less pompous way, than sending a distinct petition of our own. Some hundreds signed it in the Chapel at the Communion Table, on the Lord's Day. Nor do I think they could have been better employed; no not in receiving the sacred symbols of the body and blood of the blessed Jesus.

Should our Petitions succeed, what transporting joy shall we feel, when we reflect, that we contributed our part towards attaining so desirable an end! And should they fail, the very attempt to serve our suffering fellow-creatures, will do us honour before assembled worlds, in the great day when God shall judge the secrets of men by Christ Jesus.

I am aware, that a conscientious regard for religion, and a fear of hurting either the cause of God, or your own minds, may subject you to the artifices of designing men, who, to prevent, if possible, your engaging in this labour of love, will strive to persuade you, that, *this is an affair which concerns the State alone*, and that *you ought not to meddle with politics*. But a little consideration, will convince you of the dangerous consequences of yielding to *such fallacious insinuations*.

How does it concern the *State alone*? What is the *State*? If this word have any meaning, as used here, *the State of England is the people of England*. And have you ceased to be a part of the people of England, because you wish to secure the salvation of your souls in a coming world? Or, have you sold your birth-right as Britons, because you dare to think for yourselves on religions subjects, and refuse to be implicitly led into the ditch of perdition, by blind guides, who know neither the Scriptures nor the power of God? If not, then realize yourselves, as a part of the State, by endeavouring to put a stop to an execrable trade, before the displeasure of God against it, be manifested by some dreadful judgments upon its Abettors.

If it be said that, *the State is the Supreme Authority by which the empire is governed*. I answer, the *Supreme Authority* which governs the empire is the LAW. And surely all the subjects of this Supreme Authority, ought to enjoy their proper share of its benign influences! Are not the negroes, while they live in the British dominions, our *fellow-subjects*, and equally entitled with us to the protection of the Laws of the Empire? And is it no concern of ours, that thousands of these are used in a manner, that no man has a right to use tigers or serpents? There is no moral obligation that binds mankind to obey any laws, but such as are designed upon the whole, to promote the *good of the governed*. But those miserable people have no hope of good from their obedience to any law, notwithstanding they are exposed to the Penalties for transgression, in a variety of respects. *Fear* is the only passion that is considered in their nature, and *Pain* the only object to which it is directed. Their rights are violated by the hand of oppression, without any prospect of redress, and the complaints of their grievances are rendered ineffectual, by their being deprived of the power to give legal evidence. And if you, from an unjustifiable attachment to your own present peace, sink into a supine indifference concerning the welfare of those afflicted captives, what proof have you, that the same usurping power which made slaves of them, will not endeavour to enslave you and your posterity?

And as to *not meddling with politics*, it requires some skill, to find out what those who use such language mean. Politics is the *science of government*. And are you not to concern yourselves with the government you live under, and towards the support of which you contribute so large a portion of your property? The British Empire is one *large society*, and the *laws* are the *rules*, by which it is regulated and kept in order. But these rules may be *corrupted*, *transgressed*, or *neglected*, if the members of the society do not meddle, that is, do not care whether they are observed or broken. The British Constitution, like true religion, can suffer nothing from being known. And where the Magistrates, who should be the guardians and executors of the laws, act uprightly, they have nothing to fear from being watched by the people, who are the source of their power, and the support of their dignity. It is only *corruption* that *stands in need of bribery*; and it is *imposture alone* that *affects mystery*. It is therefore so far from being wrong to interfere in such matters, or, as it is artfully called, to *meddle with politics*, that it is your *duty*, as far as you can, for the sake of *yourselves, your posterity* and *your oppressed fellow subjects*, to *acquaint yourselves with the laws of your country, and the administrations of them*: and to exercise, as free citizens of the Empire, your *constitutional right* to *petition*, or *remonstrate*, when the laws are infringed by the extension of unconstitutional power, or the people oppressed by an arbitrary violation of their legal privileges.

But setting aside this part of the subject for the present, and leaving political maneuvers to those, who regard them in preference to the exercise of justice and mercy, still the authority of the Holy Scripture remains inviolable. And while you believe this, your being for the abolition or otherwise, is not so much an *opinion*, or a *point of private judgment*, as *a case of conscience*. *You must most religiously oppose slavery, whatever you may lose by so doing, or you must act the hypocrite*. I therefore, as a Minister of Christ among you, admonish you in the name of God, not to suffer worldly prudence and temporal advantages, to influence you to act contrary to the sacred voice of inspiration, and the clearest convictions of your own mind. The all-seeing eye of your Judge is upon you! Act with simplicity and godly sincerity, and what you could not conscientiously do yourselves, do not, from any motives whatever encourage in others. Exert yourselves with becoming zeal in the use of every legal means, particularly in sending Petitions to the Parliament, from as many places as possible, that the vilest traffic that ever disgraced human nature may be abolished.

And as you believe that a *particular Providence* governs the universe, that God putteth down one, and letteth up another, and that he doeth according to his will in the army of heaven, and among the inhabitants of the earth, you cannot but see the necessity of acknowledging him in all your ways, if you expect your undertakings to prosper, I therefore advice you —

II. To pray earnestly and constantly to God, that the *slave-trade* may be *immediately* and *effectually abolished*; and that the people called slaves in our Islands may be speedily placed in a state of liberty and happiness.

It will not be expected that I should enlarge here upon the nature and efficacy of Prayer; nor is it necessary to *you*, who are so well acquainted with the Oracles of God. In those sacred records, you read of mighty heroes with whole armies, being cut off by the Most High, when pious people have called upon him for help. Therein you are told how Prayer has prevailed, when all other means have proved unsuccessful. — It has subdued kingdoms, raised the dead to life, and shut and opened heaven!

When the Israelitish Slaves were oppressed by the Egyptian Tyrant and his cruel task-masters, they cried to the God of Abraham, Isaac, and Jacob for deliverance, and what could Pharaoh and all his hosts do against them? Their prayers were heard, — Moses was sent to be their deliverer, — and you behold *six hundred thousand men, besides women and children* brought from the most abject state of bondage and affliction, into perfect liberty! God is unchangeable, and his promise stands sure, *Ask and ye shall receive. The effectual fervent prayer of a righteous man quaileth much*; how *much more prevalent* will the prayers of *many thousands be?* There are millions in Britain who sincerely wish the destruction of that infamous business, (many of whom know little of us, or we of them,) and doubtless there are numbers of those, of different denominations, who pray in secret for that desirable event. Add your prayers to theirs, without regarding the scoffs of fools, or the ridicule of infidels. Pray not only in *private*, but in your *families*, and in *all your public meetings*, that the God whose you are, and whom you serve, may make known his power by *removing every hinderance out of the way*, and *accomplish the abolition*, by whatever means he please; and if there be men wicked enough to oppose the Lord of Hosts in this glorious work, *let such look to themselves*; you are in the way of duty, and therefore not accountable for consequences. It is a cause of far greater importance than many of those, in behalf of which the Almighty has so often manifestly interposed. Pray in faith, and fear not but your heavenly Father will answer you in the joy of your souls. – O! what a feast to a humane heart, to behold even in imagination, the arrival of the long wished for period, when the trade in human beings shall be no more! And that period will come! Yea, the blessed time is at hand, when the wicked *Slave-Dealers*, shall cease from troubling, and the weary *Africans* shall have rest. — When, in spite of their proud oppressors, those unhappy people shall change the galling yoke of misery and bondage, for the enjoyments of life and the blessings of liberty! Lord God Almighty, hasten that happy time!

While we thus as christians, take God into our account, we must use every rational and scriptural mean, that may conduce to the end we have in view, otherwise we shall be (what those who knew us not have often called us) ignorant, wild enthusiasts. I therefore solemnly exhort you,

III. To leave off the use of Sugar and Rum till the slave-trade be abolished, and a speedy and effectual plan be established for obtaining the liberty and happiness of those injured people and their unhappy posterity in our Islands; or till these articles can be procured from some other quarter.

Let no silly trifler consider this as a trivial matter, fit only to be laughed at. The importance of most things in human life, is to be estimated by the effects they produce. — The effects produced in Africa and the West Indies, by the Europeans using Rum and Sugar, are of a very alarming nature, and are seriously felt by thousands. The French writer who observed, he could not look upon a piece of sugar without conceiving it stained with spots of human blood, conveyed a just notion of the cruel disposition, of any who make light of ceasing to use it. With me it is a point of conscience, which no power upon earth can make me relinquish. I feel it my duty as sincerely to testify against the using Rum and Sugar at present, as to preach the Gospel. Among a variety of tracts which have been published, against the use of these luxuries while procured on the present plan, there is one which does peculiar honour to the principles and abilities of the writer, entitled, *An Address to the People of Great Britain, on the propriety of abstaining from West India Sugar and Rum.*

In that valuable pamphlet there is the following passage, which it concerns us, not to pass lightly over. *May we not also hope that the Methodists, who appear to feel forcibly their principles, will seriously consider it? They are so numerous, as to be able of themselves to destroy that dreadful traffic, which is the sole obstacle to their ministers spreading the Gospel in the extensive continent of Africa; and, however others may affect to degrade the negroes, they are bound to consider thousands of them as their brethren in Christ.*

That we feel forcibly our principles, will, I hope, be always evidenced by our conduct, for, however forcibly the principles of any people may be felt, it is only by the good effects of their operation, that their utility can be demonstrated. That we greatly wish to spread the Gospel, will not be doubted by any one, who considers the unequivocal proofs we have given of such a disposition.

That the *slave-trade* is the *chief*, perhaps, the *sole obstacle* to our ministers spreading it in Africa, is undeniable. If therefore every other argument were out of the question, this one sufficiently proves that it is our duty, to do every thing we can to accomplish its abolition. And if we be so numerous, as to be able of ourselves to destroy that dreadful traffic, (which I cannot deny) by only laying aside a *mere sensual gratification*, and that but for a season, are we not justly chargeable with all the consequences of its continuance, while we indulge ourselves in the use of Rum and Sugar? At least, we ought to abstain from these drugs, for a sufficient length of time, to make a fair trial.

The irresistible force of this conclusion first brought conviction to my mind, about five months ago, and I have conscientiously abstained from Sugar ever since; Rum I never liked, and therefore had not the trouble of leaving it off; my family and most of my friends have done the same: and my worthy colleague and I have borne a public testimony against using these articles, both in town and country. But my mind is still uneasy; I think something further may be done to serve the cause of Justice and Humanity, and I know of no method at present so likely to do this as the one I have adopted; which should it produce no other effect, it will be some relief to my own feelings; for to say the truth, it hurts me exceedingly to think that I, who from the ground of my heart, have always abhorred slavery in every shape, and detested the thoughts of infringing upon the just liberty of any creature, should nevertheless, have been in some degree accessory to the Bondage, Torture and Death of myriads of human beings, by assisting to consume the produce of their labour, their tears, and their blood! I ask pardon of God, and of them, and earnestly pray, that this little tract may make some restitution for my former want of attention to my duty in this respect.

I should conclude here, but that it seems necessary to take some notice of a few objections. I say a *few*, for though there may be *many*, yet I do not think above two or three of them worth an answer. For instance, who would stoop to answer a person that has the impudence to laugh at and ridicule those who wish to alleviate the calamities of oppressed innocence? Such senseless triflers must be totally destitute of the spirit of our Holy Religion, though I am sorry to add, I have found some of them among the professors of it.

Nor do I think it necessary to say anything to those who pretend to doubt these facts, which are established by such respectable evidence.

A less gentle treatment is justly due to those who are offended because these things are *searched into*: some of them are likely to sustain a temporary loss, should they appear friends to the abolition, and they are ashamed to appear against it. They therefore generally talk of *moderation*, of not pushing things to *extremes*, and of the *impossibility* of accomplishing the end by the means recommended above.

These objectors are more dangerous than the former, because there is some plausibility in what they say. For *moderation* cannot be too highly commended in speculative matters. And as every man has an equal right to think for himself, (but owing to the present frailty of our nature, that which is demonstration in the judgment of one, may be grossly absurd in the esteem of another) there are no qualities more becoming a wise and good man than Candour and Forbearance. But what has this to do with our using rational means to lessen the miseries of our fellow-creatures? I believe there is not a man upon earth more free from bigoted attachments to parties and opinions than I am, nor a greater friend to unbounded liberty of conscience; but I should be ashamed to talk of *moderation*, and not pushing things to *extremes*, on a subject that relates simply to our endeavouring to put a stop to Robbery and Murder. Saint Paul tells us that, "It is good to be zealously affected always in a good thing." And had it not been for the indefatigable zeal of the virtuous friends of civil and religions liberty, these nations might have to this day, been wandering in the darkness of pagan idolatry, or groaning under the tyrannic yoke of popish Superstition. If *moderate men*, as they affect to be called, had been attended to in France, that infernal mansion, the Bastille, had still remained; and millions of intelligent beings had continued in the galling chains of servile oppression, who are now rising to the privileges of a free people.

And as to our not accomplishing the end, by the means which have been recommended, that waits to be proved. We expect much from the *Petitions* which are preparing for the Parliament, in various parts of the kingdom. Should these fail again, we expect more powerful effects from the disuse of Rum and Sugar, which (whatever may be the determination of the Parliament) we never can be authorized to use, while slavery exists in our Islands for the purpose of supplying us with them. And should every human effort prove ineffectual, still "the Lord God omnipotent reigneth!" We have every thing to hope from an unspoken dependence upon him. We cannot pray in vain!

While we were ignorant of the iniquitous nature of the slave-trade, something might be said in our favour; but we must sin with our eyes open, if we countenance or encourage it any longer. Nor are we altogether free, that we did not consider it sooner. On many accounts, we ought to have been the first in the nation to have testified against it. That glory I believe, belongs to the people called Quakers, who in this have set us an admirable example. We have cheerfully followed them in a determined opposition to that diabolic business; let us now also cease to tempt unprincipled men to commit such horrid acts of wickedness, in order to supply us with unnecessary luxuries. For we must remember, that if the commodities were not consumed, the planters would cease to cultivate what they could not sell, slaves would not be wanted, the slave-trade would be at an end.

It has been objected, "That if all the people in *England* were to leave off using sugar, it would have no effect on slavery, or the slave-trade, as the only consequence that would result therefrom would be, that of its being consumed in foreign nations."

This certainly may be in some measure true while the disturbances in *St. Domingo* interrupt the usual supply of Europe. Yet even at present our abstinence will materially affect the happiness of the Negroes, as the lower we can keep the present enormous price, in proportion, we shall take away the temptation of breaking up the Cotton Plantations (which is the most favourable employment for the Negroes) to be planted with sugarcane which is the only source of their misery and destruction. And when the European markets shall receive their usual supply from the French West-Islands, as the quantity of Sugar used in *England* is so enormous as nearly to equal what is used in all Europe besides; how would one quarter of this overstock the foreign markets! This would lower the price so much, that in a very little time it would ruin all who have any concern in it. Besides, when it is known abroad that we have left off using Sugar from a principle of humanity, the surrounding nations are not so destitute of shame and honour, as to receive that, which we refuse from such a motive. The French have begun to leave off using it already; and it is probable that millions will quickly follow the example. The revolution in France has in some measure, affected all Europe. The spirit of Philanthropy accompanies the spirit of Liberty, and the beneficial effects of both are easily perceptible. Only persevere in refusing the produce of the Islands, and this, added to the other steps which we are taking, together with what has been mentioned above, will speedily convince the haughty slave-mongers, that it is not at their option, whether the vile traffic in their fellow-creatures shall be abolished or not!

Some artful men have endeavoured to deceive simple people, by telling them, that refusing to use Rum and Sugar would avail nothing, unless they refused *Cotton* also. But there is no man who understands this subject, who does not know that this is an absolute falsehood. For, nearly three fourths of the Cotton which is manufactured in *England*, comes from other countries, not from the West India Islands. In the year 1786, twenty millions of pounds were imported, about fifteen millions of which were bought from Foreigners, not from our own people, and though the quantity imported now be above thirty millions of pounds annually, yet the same proportion still holds. But this is not the case with the Sugar, which comes almost all from the Islands. For the duty is so great on the East India Sugar, that very little of it has ever been imported. Therefore be not deceived by those who pretend to sell you East-India Sugar; it is in general a mere imposition. Were no more Cotton ever to be imported from the

Islands, the manufacturers of that useful article need be at no loss to supply the want. So that if the West-India produce were wholly destroyed, our resources are such, that the nation would perhaps be a gainer, rather than a loser thereby. But there is not the least need of spending a moment in debating the point. The tenth part of the inhabitants of Britain abstaining from Sugar and Rum, would in three years, put a stop to the slave-trade, and be productive of such a change in the treatment of the slaves already in the Islands, as would make them happy, which is all that we design at present. So that the mentioning *Cotton*, or any thing else, is just the same sort of logic, as some of the slave-mongers have used, when they tell you "That God made the negroes to be slaves; that he allows of slavery;" and as a proof, cite some passages out of the Old Testament; not considering that the Jewish dispensation was of so peculiar a nature, that no other people have, or ever had any right to claim any of its privileges, unless they first became Jews by submitting to its institutions. Besides, the gospel has entirely abolished all national distinctions, and annulled for ever any right in one man to enslave another. Let any man that thinks he can, prove the contrary. Till then it is your duty to oppose the slave-trade.

If you say, you cannot drink your Tea without Sugar; suppose you were to lay aside Tea also? I have done so, and find many very considerable advantages by so doing. And as to your being but *one*, so may every one say. And as to your using but a *little*, would you admit of this plea on any other occasion? If a man told you that he *swore but little*, and *only told a few lies*, would you not reply, "Whosoever shall keep the whole law, and yet offend in *one point, he is guilty of all*?" Because he disregards the authority of the Legislator from whom the whole has it sanction. With regard to your paying for what you use, this is no excuse; for, many, who receive stolen goods pay for them; *but the Receiver is still as bad as the Thief.*

Never imagine that you can use these articles with a good conscience, while they are procured on the present plan. You cannot pray in faith for a blessing upon them; and whatsoever is not of

faith is sin. You generously contribute towards the support of the Missionaries who preach the gospel in the Islands. You believe that Jesus Christ is, at least, the intentional Saviour of the negroes. O! do every thing you can to forward their comfort and salvation, here and hereafter; and expect your reward in the kingdom of your heavenly Father.
FINIS.

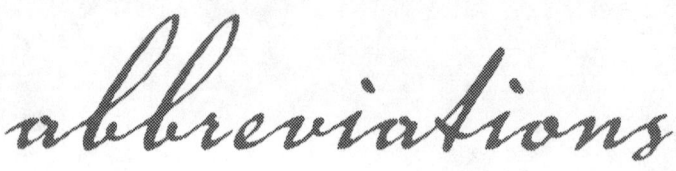

abbreviations

Jackson, *Works of Wesley*
  Thomas Jackson, ed., *The Works of John Wesley*, 3rd ed., 14 vols. (London: Wesleyan Conference Office, 1872).

Wesley, *Works*
  John Wesley, *The Works of John Wesley*, 26 vols. [various editors] (Nashville: Abingdon Press, 1984-2003).

Curnock, *Journal*
  Nehemiah Curnock, ed., *The Journal of the Rev. John Wesley, A.M.*, 8 vols. (London: Epworth Press, 1938).

Telford, *Letters*
  John Telford, ed., *The Letters of the Rev. John Wesley, A.M.*, 8 vols. (London: Epworth Press, 1931).

Wesley, *Explanatory Notes*
  John Wesley, *Explanatory Notes Upon the New Testament* (London: William Bowyer, 1765).

INTRODUCTION, pages xv to xvii

1   Robert William Fogel, *Without Consent or Contract: The Rise and Fall of American Slavery* (New York: Norton, 1989).
2   Jackson, *Works of Wesley*, I, 371, or Wesley, *Works*, XIX, *Journal* II, 267.

CHAPTER 1, pages 1 to 12
John Wesley in context: his century, relationships and spiritual journey

1   Charles Wesley believed that John had effectively separated himself from the Church of England when he began to ordain his preachers. However, Wesley was influenced by King and Stillingfleet and believed that according to the book of Acts, he had the authority, as a presbyter, to ordain. It is interesting that King had earlier seen a bishop and presbyter as the same, but later repudiated this idea. Wesley retained it.
2   Correspondence with Andrew F. Walls, May 5, 2004.
3   Curnock, *Journal*, I, 422, n.2, from 1772.
4   Curnock, *Journal*, I, 96 (Wesley's letter to Richard Morgan).
5   Curnock, *Journal*, I, 96-97. Wesley's description of these ministries is found in his letter to Richard Morgan of Dublin following the death of his son, William Morgan, in 1732. Wesley and the Holy Club were accused of bringing about his death through stringent fasting, and the letter is Wesley's explanation to William's father of their lifestyle and activities, clearing himself of encouraging Morgan to fast. His letter was obviously effective as Richard Morgan sent his other son to be tutored by Wesley in 1734. Wesley's letter is found as part of the introductory material to the first *Journal* (Ibid., 87-102), and gives Wesley's interesting description of early Methodism ("The Rise and Design of Oxford Methodism"). See also Robert G. Tuttle, *John Wesley: His life and theology* (Grand Rapids: Zondervan, 1978), 117-118, 124.
6   This is the position of Robert Tuttle (Tuttle, *John Wesley*, 290). For a very

moving description of this encounter, see Ibid., 289-292. The wedding occurred on October 3, 1749 and Wesley learned of it two days later.

7   Whitefield's pro-slavery letter was written to Wesley in 1751, but was probably not well known and certainly would not have been broadcast by Wesley. It is likely that Whitefield's pro-slavery stand was not used by the slavery lobby until many years later (the late 1780s) when the fight intensified. Whitefield died in 1770.

8   Wilberforce was nine years old when he went to live with his Methodist aunt in Wimbledon, and was eleven years old when Whitefield died.

9   In 1738 Wesley retrospectively described his experience from 1725. His practices reflect very strong commitment. He writes of meeting regularly with a friend for the purpose of mutual encouragement in their discipleship, and altering his entire lifestyle "to set in earnest upon a new life." He spent one to two hours daily in "religious retirement" (prayer and study), went to communion weekly and "began to aim at, and pray for, inward holiness." He "watched more carefully against actual sins" and acknowledges that at the time "doubted not but that [he] was a good Christian." He acknowledged that the writings of William Law "convinced me more than ever of the exceeding height and breadth and depth of the law of God" and his response was that "the light flowed in so mightily upon my soul, that everything appeared in a new view. I cried to God for help, and resolved not to prolong the time of obeying Him as I had never done before." At that time he stated: "by my continued endeavour to keep His whole law, inward and outward, to the utmost of my power, I was persuaded that I should be accepted of Him, and that I was even then in a state of salvation." Regular fasting became a part of his routine as did other forms of self denial. His goal was to conform to the image of God, "by doing His will, not my own." He was also involved in practical ministries to the poor, sick and those in prison. From his own description, there is no doubt that Wesley had become deeply committed to his Christian faith and was conscientiously trying to grow as a Christian. This description is found in his *Journal* (Curnock, *Journal*, I, 467-468).

10 Tuttle, *John Wesley*, 109.

11 Wesley, *Works*, XVIII, 136, n.4. Wesley wrote Dr. John Burton: "I hope to learn the true sense of the gospel by preaching it to the heathens" (Ibid., 137, n.5). See also Tuttle, *John Wesley*, 129.

12 Curnock, *Journal*, I, 112, 146, 257, n.1, 413, 432. The following dates are given: sailing from England (Gravesend) on October 21, 1735, arriving in America on February 6, 1736; Charles left America on August 11, 1736 and John left on December 22, 1737, arriving in England (Deal) on February 1, 1738.

13 Ibid., 418.

14 Wesley, *Works*, XVIII, *Journal* I, 228. This is from his entry on March 4, 1738, Wesley's italics.

15 Wesley, *Works*, XVIII, *Journal* I, 241-249, especially n.76.

16 Wesley, *Works*, XVIII, *Journal* I, 249-250.

17 Curnock, *Journal*, I, 422, n.2.

18 Letter dated June 27, 1766 (Telford, *Letters*, V, 16). The paragraph in which those statements occur reads: "In one of my last I was saying I do not feel the wrath of God abiding on me; nor can I believe it does. And yet (this is the mystery) [I do not love God. I never did!]. Therefore [I never] believed in the Christian sense of

the word. Therefore [I am only an] honest heathen, a proselyte of the Temple...." "If I ever had that faith, it would not be so strange." The words in brackets were in Wesley's shorthand, according to Telford, *Letters*, 15.

19   Wesley, *Works*, XVIII, *Journal* I, 41. Editor W. Reginald Ward sees a similarity between the Moravian style of journal writing and that of Wesley, where both utilize a comparatively brief conversion narrative to introduce a much lengthier account of service (42). The point is that the "spiritual experience" is not the focal point, but the life of service that follows is. The conversion narrative serves merely as an introduction.

20   Tuttle sees Aldersgate as the fitting and inevitable climax (an actual evangelical conversion), of the intense seeking process that Wesley had experienced from at least 1725. He also quotes Albert Outler (Tuttle, *John Wesley*, 76, n.13) who describes Wesley's 1725 change of heart as "a conversion if ever there was one." For Tuttle's excellent and sensitive treatment see his analysis section, 215-229, especially 227-228. While I appreciate Tuttle's comprehensive treatment of Wesley's process, eventuating in Aldersgate, I would posit that Wesley's "conversion" in fact began in 1725, and had several components, the component of assurance occurring in 1738. I concur with Ward that Wesley's emphasis was clearly on his obedient service to God's kingdom and thus the components of his conversion, evangelical experience and assurance are best understood as the necessary steps to enable that service.

CHAPTER 2, pages 13 to 43
John Wesley's antislavery journey

1   Aphra Behn was a controversial English woman, born probably in 1640. As a young woman she lived in Surinam and was involved in a slave rebellion. After varied adventures, far beyond what most seventeenth century women experienced, including serving as a Dutch spy for Charles II, she began to write. She produced some thirteen novels and seventeen plays. Her novel on slavery was named after the African prince who led the slave rebellion. See Kirstin Olsen, *Remember the Ladies*, (Oklahoma: University of Oklahoma Press, 1988), 62.

2   Curnock, *Journal*, I, 255. Note 1 states: "one of the rules drawn up by the Trustees forbade the employment of Negroes; this was soon set aside — a fact which reached the ears of the Trustees before Wesley sailed for Georgia." This note is attached to the end of Wesley's journal entry for August 2, 1736, but is not in the Abingdon edition.

3   Letter from John Burton to Wesley on September 18, 1735 (Curnock, *Journal*, VIII, 287). It appears that the people of Purrysburg were some of the first to begin purchasing Negroes. Curnock notes that Burton mentions the people of Purrysburg as those who "began the buying of negroes" (Curnock, *Journal*, I, 409, n.4). The Abingdon edition (Wesley, *Works*, XVIII, 181) does not mention Purrysburg as the place slavery was introduced.

4   Curnock, *Journal*, I, 244, n.1. See also Wesley's *Journal*, April 23, 1737 and May 27, 1737 (Jackson, *Works of Wesley*, I, 40, 48-49, 70, 72).

5   Curnock, *Journal*, I, 244, n, or, Wesley, *Works*, XVIII, 164, n.12, describes Tailfer as a "ringleader for the importation for liquor and slaves."

6   Thomas Jackson, ed., *The Journal of the Rev. Charles Wesley, M.A.* (London: Wesleyan Methodist Book Room, 1849), I, 36-37. John and Charles had reached Charleston two days earlier, on July 31, 1736 (Curnock, *Journal*, I, 254).

7   Jackson, *Journal of Charles Wesley*, I, 36-37. Reginald Ward agrees that this experience in South Carolina as Charles was leaving America was the brothers' first exposure to the cruelties of slavery (Wesley, *Works*, XVIII, *Journal and Diaries* I, 181, n.74).

8   Wesley, *Works*, XVIII, *Journals and Diaries* I, 169.

9   Wesley, *Works*, XVIII, 410. See also Curnock, *Journal*, I, 260 (Friday, August 20, 1736) and Frank Baker, "The Origins, Character and Influence of John Wesley's *Thoughts Upon Slavery*," *Methodist History*, XXII (January 1984), 75.

10   Wesley, *Works*, XVIII, *Journals and Diaries* I, 180 (April 23, 1737).

11   Although the term "Negro" has been replaced in accepted common usage by "African-American" and other terms, it was the common word in the eighteenth century. Because it is the word mostly used by Wesley, it is used throughout this book. Normally it is capitalized, but in quotations the lowercase or capitalized form of the original author is retained.

12   Curnock, *Journal*, I, 352.

13   Curnock, *Journal*, I, 353, or, Wesley, *Works*, XVIII, *Journals and Diaries* I, 181.

14   Wesley, *Works*, XVIII, *Journals and Diaries* I, 207-208 (December 1737 and January 7, 1738).

15   Warren Thomas Smith, *John Wesley and Slavery* (Nashville: Abingdon, 1986), 53, citing Ralph Betts Flanders, *Plantation Slavery in Georgia* (Cos Cob, Connecticut: John E. Edwards, 1967), 13, and Betty Wood, *Slavery in Colonial Georgia, 1730-1775* (Athens: University of Georgia Press, 1984).

16   A.M. Barnes, *Proceedings of the Wesley Historical Society*, XVI, 61.

17   Curnock, *Journal*, II, 362.

18   Wesley, *Explanatory Notes*, 558. Randy Maddox indicates that Wesley was finishing the *Notes* in 1755 [Randy L. Maddox, *Responsible Grace* (Nashville: Abingdon, 1994), 294, n.98].

19   Jackson, *Works of Wesley*, II, 337-338, 354-356, 392.

20   From Wesley's tract entitled "The Doctrine of Original Sin" (Jackson, *Works of Wesley*, IX, 243).

21   January 17, 1758 and November 29, 1758 (Jackson, *Works of Wesley*, II, 433,464).

22   Stiv Jakobsson, *Am I Not a Man and a Brother?* (Uppsala: Almquist & Wiksells, 1972), 276; Edgar Thompson, *Nathaniel Gilbert: Lawyer and Evangelist* (London: Epworth Press, 1960), 24.

23   See Irv Brendlinger, *To Be Silent...Would Be Criminal: The Antislavery Influence and Writings of Anthony Benezet* (Lanham, Maryland: Scarecrow Press, 2006), 12, 27-28, 31-33.

24   Wesley, *Works*, XXII, *Journal* V, 307.

25   Benezet's letter to Sharp on May 14, 1772, in George S. Brookes, *Friend Anthony Benezet* (Philadelphia: University of Pennsylvania Press, 1937), 290-293.

26   It is almost certain that Wesley wrote to Benezet after reading his tract,

Endnotes   229

although no copies of such correspondence seem to have survived. Frank Baker agrees with this. See Frank Baker, "The Origins, Character and Influence of John Wesley's *Thoughts Upon Slavery*," *Methodist History*, XXII (January 1984), 78.

27   Letter from Sharp to Benezet dated January 7, 1774 [Roger Anstey, *The Atlantic Slave Trade and British Abolition, 1760-1810* (London: Macmillan Press Ltd, 1975), 240], citing Sharp Transcripts.

28   *The Arminian Magazine* VI (1783), 98-99, 151-153, 211-212. See Appendix 1 (175-178) for an extract of the Robin-John deposition before Lord Mansfield.

29   "The Journal" in *Monthly Review*, LI (September 1774), 234; *Gentleman's Magazine*, XLV (March 1775), 157.

30   The 1st, 3rd, 4th and 5th editions are housed in the John Rylands University Library, Manchester. Frank Baker states that there were four editions the first year. See Baker, *Methodist History*, XXII, 83, 86. A 1774 edition housed at Rylands contains 53 pages and measures approximately 4 1/4 by 7 1/2 inches. Baker mentions that the additional 1774 editions were formatted to 28 pages and sold for two pence.

31   Folarin Shyllon, *James Ramsay, The Unknown Abolitionist* (Edinburgh: Canongate Publishing, 1977), 89.

32   Shyllon, *James Ramsay*, 2-3, 125. In fact, Ramsay's writing about slavery was not always single-minded. While he seems to be opposed to slavery, he makes a very strong case for improved treatment of slaves. When discussing immediate and inadequately prepared for emancipation or continued slavery, he opts for continued slavery. See his *Essay on the Conversion and Treatment of African Slaves in the British Sugar Colonies* (London: J. Philips, 1784), 283. Ramsay's tracts were written between 1784 and 1788. His comment about writing in a "more... decisive manner" after reading Wesley might well refer to wishing he had taken an unequivocal position as had Wesley. For a thorough discussion of Ramsay's views, see Irv Brendlinger, "A Study of the Views of Major Eighteenth Century Evangelicals on Slavery and Race, With Special Reference to John Wesley" (Ph.D. thesis, Edinburgh University, 1982), 81-96.

33   Telford, *Letters*, VIII, 277, to Samuel Hoare, August 18, 1787.

34   A letter from Granville Sharp to Benjamin Rush, February 21, 1774, in Brookes, *Friend Anthony Benezet*, 446-447. Baker mistakenly dates this letter February 2, rather than 21, no doubt a clerical error (Baker, *Methodist History*, XXII, 82).

35   See Rush's letter to Sharp on May 1, 1773 in Brookes, *Friend Anthony Benezet*, 445-446.

36   John S. Simon, *Proceedings of the Wesley Historical Society*, XIII, 1.

37   Jackson, *Works of Wesley*, XIV, 79.

38   Frank Baker says that Wesley utilized about thirty per cent of Benezet's tract. However, when considering ideas, his own summaries of Benezet's material, paraphrases and direct quotations, it seems to be closer to fifty per cent. See Baker, *Methodist History*, XXII, 79.

39   Letter from Sharp to Wesley, used by permission of Dairmaid MacCulloch, formerly of Wesley College, Wesley College Library, Bristol, fo. 314. The letter is part of a collection in a bound volume made by Mary Ann Smith, daughter of Adam Clark; it is undated, but probably from late 1773 or early 1774. (The college is now closed; I am not aware of the present location of this letter.)

40   Baker, *Methodist History*, XXII, 79.

41   See Brendlinger, *To Be Silent*, 20-21.

42   See Brendlinger, *To Be Silent*, 92-104, for Benezet's letters to Selina, Countess of Huntingdon, May 20,1774 and March 10, 1775.

43   From Wesley's sermon, "The Ministerial Office" in Jackson, *Works of Wesley*, VII, 271-272. Wesley disagreed with these three on human ability to act beneficently, apart from the assistance of grace.

44   Sharp to Wesley, early 1774 (Wesley College Library, Bristol, fo. 314). See note 39 above.

45   See letter from Sharp to Benjamin Rush, February 21, 1774 (Brookes, *Friend Anthony Benezet*, 446-447).

46   Letter from Benezet to Moses Brown, May 9, 1774, in the Haverford Archives, Haverford College, Collection 852 (see also, Brendlinger, *To Be Silent*, 88-89). Benezet explains to Brown that Granville Sharp "also writes me that the celebrated Methodist preacher John Westly [sic] had sent him a [indecipherable word] manuscript of a piece he was on the point of publishing on the same subject for his. When either of these come to my hand I purpose to communicate them to thee."

47   Frank Baker states that Wesley sent the tract, however conclusive evidence is not cited (Baker, *Methodist History*, XXII, 82.) Baker cites Vaux's 1817 edition of Anthony Benezet's memoirs (Roberts Vaux, *The Memoirs of Anthony Benezet* [Philadelphia: W. Alexander, 1817], 53). In fact, Vaux does not indicate that Wesley sent the tract.

48   Letter from Benezet to Wesley, May 23, 1774 in *The Arminian Magazine*, X (1787), 44-48. Brookes also republishes the letter (Brookes, *Friend Anthony Benezet*, 318-321) with very slight modifications, also citing the *Arminian Magazine*. The complete letter is contained in Appendix 1.

49   Letter from Wesley to Benezet, no date, but probably 1774 (Vaux, *Memoirs*, 44).

50   Frank Baker agrees that the letter was from Wesley to Benezet, but states it arrived as a cover letter with Wesley's tract, *Thoughts Upon Slavery*. However, Baker cites no evidence that it was a cover letter. Baker cites Vaux (Vaux, *Memoirs*, 53), and Vaux does quote this letter under the heading, "From John Wesley," but makes no mention of its accompanying Wesley's tract. Unfortunately, Vaux gives no source for or location of the letter in question. To confuse matters further, it appears that Vaux's *Memoirs* was produced in two forms in 1817 — a 136 page form and one with 156 pages. The letter is found on page 44 in one of them and on page 53 in the other. Brookes cites the Vaux source, but makes no mention of it being sent with the tract (Brookes, *Friend Anthony Benezet*, 86). Butterworth also says the letter was from Wesley to Benezet but says nothing about its being a cover letter. See *Proceedings of the Wesley Historical Society*, V (1905), 45-46.

51   Stanley Ayling, *John Wesley* (London: Collins, 1979), 283. Ayling comments that Wesley "had come to regard all suitable writing as grist to his own ...mill."

52   Benezet to Wesley, May 23, 1774 in *The Arminian Magazine* X (1787), 44-48. See also Brookes, *Friend Anthony Benezet*, 318, and Brendlinger, *To be Silent*, 77-79.

53   February 6, 1776 in Curnock, *Journal*, VI, 67, n.

54   Benezet to Sharp, May 5, 1772 in Brookes, *Friend Anthony Benezet*, 290-291.

55   Sharp to Benezet, August 21, 1772 in Brookes, *Friend Anthony Benezet*, 418-419.

56   The first copyright act was passed in Britain in 1709 but only applied to works recorded in the register of the Stationers' Company. It was not until the nineteenth century that the rules of copyright were generally established and applied. See Stanley Sadie, ed., *The New Grove Dictionary of Music & Musicians* (London: Macmillan, 1980), IV, 736ff. Brookes concurs with my assessment of Wesley's use of Benezet's material, stating that Wesley lived in "a century free of plagiarism" (Brookes, *Friend Anthony Benezet*, 84).

57   When commenting on verbose writers, Wesley asked why they "write so much larger books?" and then answered, "to get money [whereas] my only [purpose] is to do good" (journal entry for February 17, 1769 in Jackson, *Works of Wesley*, 353).

58   The same practice and principle can be observed in music. It was not uncommon for composers of the seventeenth and eighteenth centuries to borrow from one other. The melody of "O Sacred Head, Now Wounded," so often attributed to J.S. Bach, was actually written by someone else, but arranged by Bach. As publishing and printing developed, copyright rules were refined and the conventions changed.

59   Wesley is quoting from Benezet's letter of May 23, 1774 (Telford, *Letters*, VI, 126).

60   Jackson, *Works of Wesley*, XI, 125-126.

61   Wilberforce Museum (Hull) exhibit, noted in a personal visit on March 9, 2001. The decade of those particular figures were not specified, but such volume for any decade indicates the significance of the city of Liverpool to the slave trade.

62   From April 14, 1777 (Jackson, *Works of Wesley*, IV, *Journal*, 95-96).

63   Jackson, *Works of Wesley*, XI, 145. See full quotation in chapter 3, at n.26.

64   Baker, *Methodist History*, XXII, 84, citing "A citation of Minutes of the Methodist Conferences" (Philadelphia: Tuckniss, 1795), 38; *Virginia United Methodist Heritage* (Fall 1977), 27-28.

65   *The Arminian Magazine* IV (December 1781), 676-677, 680. Wesley spells her name both "Wheatly" and "Wheatley."

66   Telford, *Letters*, VII, 195, 201. Smith mentions that they were never published (Smith, *Wesley and Slavery*, 103).

67   See Appendix 1 for the extract of deposition.

68   *Minutes of the Methodist Conferences, 1744-1798*, I (London, 1862), 187.

69   *Proceedings of the Wesley Historical Society*, XX (1935-1936), 158. F. Deaville Walker's fascinating article, "A Newly-Discovered Pamphlet by Dr. Coke," explores the relationship of Coke's 1786 tract to this appointment.

70   David Brion Davis, *The Problem of Slavery in Western Culture* (Ithaca: Cornell University Press, 1975), 220. The actual name was the "Society Instituted in 1787 for Effecting the Abolition of the Slave Trade."

71   Telford, *Letters*, VIII, 275-276. Wesley's letter was addressed to Samuel Hoare, August 18, 1787. Pages 6-7 of *Letters* indicates that Clarkson read Wesley's letter to the Abolition Committee on August 21, 1787.

72   Telford, *Letters*, VIII, 23, to Thomas Funnell, November 24, 1787.

73   Telford, *Letters*, VIII, 16-17, to Granville Sharp, October 11, 1787.

74   Telford, *Letters*, VIII, 277, to Granville Sharp, November 14, 1787.

75 Wesley to William Thompson, January 12, 1788. This letter is in the holdings of Cambridge University, not in Telford (personal correspondence with Randy Maddox, summer 2003).

76 Diary entry for Monday, March 3, 1788 (Curnock, *Journal*, VII, 359).

77 From March 3rd, 4th and 6th, 1788 (Jackson, *Works of Wesley*, IV, *Journal*, 408).

78 Baker suggests it was a thunderstorm (Baker, *Methodist History*, XXII, 86).

79 Rupert E. Davies, personal correspondence, August 21, 1981. Ward concurs (personal conversation with the author, June 22, 2001).

80 Curnock, *Journal*, VII, 360. With no apparent hint of contradiction the diary for that Friday includes references to dinner and supper. Probably the intention was to call Methodist people to a day of prayer for slaves rather than a description of Wesley's activity.

81 *The Arminian Magazine* XI (1788), 208-209 ("Resolutions of the Society for the purpose of effecting the abolition of the Slave Trade"). The petition letter is included in Appendix 1.

82 Ibid., (January), 263-264; (October), 558-560; (November) 612-616. The stanza mentioned is included in Appendix 1.

83 Telford, *Letters*, VIII, 207 (March 14, 1790).

84 *The Arminian Magazine*, XIII, 307-309.

85 Ibid., (March), 156; (June), 307-309; (September), 502-503. Samuel Paynter heard Nathaniel Gilbert speak around 1770. Excerpts from his story include: "The many severe conflicts I have had with the world are well known to the brethren; for, being at that time a Slave, and my owner holding the Methodists in the light of a deceitful Sect, just started up in the island, and their ringleader Mr. Gilbert as a fanatick, because he sacrificed his honours and profits in the Community (for he stood high in the Legislature, and as a Lawyer was a President) to preach to a set of ignorant low people; he therefore laid every stumbling-block he could find in the way betwixt me and the means, and sometimes proceeded to open violence against me; but the 28th verse of the 10th chapter of St. Matthew's gospel, being uppermost in my mind, carried me through the whole of this trying scene with very great fortitude; though at the same time I behaved with all humility, from St. Paul's exhortation to that effect, till it pleased God to soften the rigour of the treatment, so that by degrees it abated, and at last subsided. Through many shifting scenes of life, during the period of the nineteen years that I was in the Society, I at last obtained my freedom, by purchasing it for a sum of money, which, by industry in my profession as a Wheel-right, and frugality, with the blessing of God upon my labours, I obtained. But my wife and children continuing Slaves to this day, and subject to the vicissitudes of the state I escaped from I still suffer on their account; and find the necessity there is for my cleaving close to God, and to receive out of his fullness."

86 Curnock, *Journal*, VIII, 118 (journal entry for December 31, 1790). Randy Maddox suspects that the book referred to was *The Reigning Abominations, especially the Slave Trade, considered as Causes of Lamentation*, published in 1788 (personal correspondence with the author, December 18, 2000). The strong feeling indicated in this diary entry would be consistent with his response to slavery.

87   Letter to Wilberforce, dated February 24, 1791 (Telford, *Letters*, VIII, 264-265).
88   Wilberforce's note (or docket) on the letter: "John Wesley, his last words. Slave Trade" (Telford, *Letters*, VIII, 265). *The Watchman*, June 22, 1870, contains a letter to the editor by George J. Stevenson indicating that the letter to Wilberforce was, in fact, Wesley's last letter. Immediately following Stevenson's letter is a note of confirmation by Thurnley Smith. In July of 1981 I discovered this edition of *The Watchman* in loose leaf form on the top shelf of the safe in Wesley Chapel, City Road, London. A bound copy is in the John Rylands University Library, Manchester (March 6, 2001).

CHAPTER 3, pages 45 to 71
A brief excursion into Wesley's position on slavery and Negro inferiority

1   James Ramsay, *An Essay on the Treatment and Conversion of African Slaves in the British Sugar Colonies* (London, 1784), 292-293. Beginning with a caution, Ramsay observes that "the feelings of benevolence have been forced to give way to the suggestions of narrow policy [he is referring to immediate and unprepared for emancipation]; and even a sense of the public interest has been made to yield to private prejudice. Yet, if our slaves were once accustomed to taste only a few of the sweets of society, a little of the security of being judged by known laws, they would double their application to procure the comforts and conveniences of life; and, with their additional property, would naturally rise in their rank in society. Many, especially if our plan of working them by task were to take place, would, in time, be able to purchase their own freedom. Their demands for manufactures would increase, and extend our trade; they would acquire a love for the country and government that shewed this attention to them. The labour of such as become free might, for some time, be regulated on the same plan as that of labourers in England. Under the awe of, or rather assisted by, a few regular troops, they might safely be trusted with arms for the defense of themselves, their families, their own, and patron's property. Then would the colonies enjoy a security from foreign attacks that no protection from Europe can afford them." Obviously from Ramsay's perspective, slavery can be made gentle and freedom should come through a gradual process of slaves purchasing their freedom — with the end result being happiness and financial and military security for all, black and white persons alike.

2   On his journey back to England from Africa where he had experienced something akin to white slavery, he was involved in a horrific storm at sea. Exhausted from unrelieved hours at the helm, the captain called upon Newton to guide the ship. In the wee hours, with the storm at its crescendo, and all the crew assured of impending death, he shocked himself by a sudden exclamation of "Oh, God!" He was surprised because he didn't even believe in God. This experience was a factor in his conversion, and upon safely reaching England he set about discovering a meaningful faith and reordering his life. One aspect of this involved seeking new employment.

3   From "Authentic Narrative" in John Newton, *Letters, Sermons, and a Review of Ecclesiastical History* (Philadelphia: William Young, 1795-1797), I, 95, and "Letters to a Wife" (August 18, 1754) in John Newton, *The Works of the Rev. John Newton*

(London, 1816), V, 486. His retrospective *Journal* reveals his later confusion and anguish over how he could have worked in the slave trade as a Christian with no difficulty of conscience, but he acknowledges that he had.

4   These misunderstandings of Newton's life and actual position on slavery continue to be perpetuated. Warren Thomas Smith calls Newton "the reformed slave ship captain" with no clarification. In discussing the relationship between Wesley and Newton, Smith laments the fact that they did not dialogue about slavery "in view of their staunch opposition to slavery." Only Wesley's opposition was staunch. See Warren Thomas Smith, *John Wesley and Slavery* (Nashville: Abingdon, 1986), 68-69. For Newton's views see his "Thoughts Upon the African Slave Trade," bound with his *Journal of a Slave Trader 1750-1754* (London: Epworth Press, 1962).

To a lesser extent Frank Baker generalizes without clarification by referring to "the converted slave ship captain, John Newton" and to some text that Benezet possibly took from Newton (Baker, *Methodist History*, XXII, 84, n.52). As recently as 2001, in a Bill Moyers documentary about "Amazing Grace," Newton is portrayed as reforming his attitudes about slavery, the slave trade and his involvement in it directly from his conversion.

5   This plan is developed in Benezet's *Short Account of that Part of Africa Inhabited by the Negroes* (Philadelphia, 1762), 70-71, and *Some Historical Account of Guinea* (Philadelphia: Joseph Cruikshank, 1771), 139-140. See also Brendlinger, "Views of Evangelicals on Slavery and Race," 168-169.

6   Letter from Benezet to Fothergill, April 28, 1773 (Haverford Collection 852).

7   Because freedom was simply their right Benezet was completely opposed to slaves working to purchase their freedom. He called freeing them in "halves," (where some of their labour time was for their owner and some for the purchase of their own freedom) similar to Ananias and Sapphira trying to deceive the apostles (Acts 5). See Benezet's *Observations on Slave Keeping* (Philadelphia, 1772), 18-19 and Brendlinger, "Views of Evangelicals on Slavery and Race," 170.

8   *Thoughts Upon Slavery* in Jackson, *Works of Wesley*, XI, 70. Natural rights will be dealt with in Chapter 4.

9   Jackson, *Works of Wesley*, XI, 79, author's italics.

10   Jackson, *Works of Wesley*, XI, 70. This position is also maintained by Benezet (Benezet, *Some Historical Account*,131-132) and Sharp (Granville Sharp, *Appendix to the Representation against Slavery* (London: Benjamin White, 1772).

11   "Thoughts Upon Liberty" in Jackson, *Works of Wesley*, XI, 34,37.

12   Ibid., 37.

13   Ibid., 41.

14   Ibid., 37.

15   Ibid., 37-38. See also Wesley's "Observations on Liberty" from 1776 (Jackson, *Works of Wesley*, XI, 92).

16   "Calm Address to the Inhabitants of England" in Jackson, *Works of Wesley*, XI, 136. A number of Wesley's references to slavery are of this sort and not about Negro slavery. Missing that distinction, it is easy, as some authors have done, to misuse such Wesley quotations as if they were about Negro slavery. The Wesley quotations do make a point about hypocrisy, but Wesley's supporting evidence is the political

slavery of his targets, not Negro slavery.

17   "A Calm Address to our American Colonies" in Jackson, *Works of Wesley*, XI, 80-90.

18   Ibid., 81.

19   "Observations on Liberty" from 1776 in Jackson, *Works of Wesley*, XI, 97.

20   Jackson, *Works of Wesley*, XI, 70, 97.

21   *Thoughts Upon Slavery* in Jackson, *Works of Wesley*, XI, 72.

22   Ibid., 72-73.

23   Ibid., 73.

24   Letter to the Trustees of Georgia, December 1748 [Arnold Dallimore, *George Whitefield* (Edinburgh: Banner of Truth Trust, 1980), II, 367]. Three years later, on March 22, 1751, Whitefield expressed the same opinion to Wesley: "it is plain to a demonstration that hot countries cannot be cultivated without Negroes" [quoted in Benezet's letter to Selina, Countess of Huntingdon, March 1775 (Haverford Collection 852); also in David D. Thompson, *John Wesley as a Social Reformer* (New York: Eaton and Mains, 1898), 44]. Wesley addresses this in *Thoughts Upon Slavery* (Jackson, *Works of Wesley*, XI, 73).

25   *Thoughts Upon Slavery* in Jackson, *Works of Wesley*, XI, 74.

26   "A Serious Address to the People of England With Regard to the State of the Nation" from 1788, in Jackson, *Works of Wesley*, XI, 145.

27   John Wesley, *A Serious Address to the People of England With Regard to the State of the Nation* (London, 1788, first edition), postscript (located at John Rylands University Library).

28   John Wesley to Granville Sharp, October 11, 1787 (Telford, *Letters*, VIII, 16-17).

29   See "A Summary View of the Slave Trade" edited by John Wesley, in two parts in *The Arminian Magazine*, XI (August 1788), 379-381, 437-440. Wesley gives an excellent rationale of the fiscal deficit that the continued slave trade causes England (on 438, before "Part II"):

"V. The negroe-trade (i.e.) a branch of it, by enabling the French to clear and cultivate new land in St. Domingo (which they are unable to do to the extent of their wishes without our assistance) is replete with the most pernicious consequences to the British nation.

This island, if fully cultivated, can produce more sugar than all our islands together. Every lot of slaves, which we import there, enables them to clear an additional acre. Every acre so gained supplies additional produce. This produce employs additional ships to old France. Nor does the evil stop here, a new fleet of ships is raised for them in exporting this produce to other countries. Now, if we consider that French ships carry double the number of men that ours of the same burthen do, we shall find that we are enabling our enemies by this branch of the trade, to dispute with us the sovereignty of the seas."

30   Robert Fogel describes Wilberforce's change in strategy (Fogel, *Without Consent or Contract*, 214). Frustrated that he and his colleagues were not having success in ending the slave trade, in 1805 Wilberforce decided that it would be better to at least end part of it — the foreign slave trade. He persuaded William Pitt to ban the trade to the French Islands (captured by the British in 1803) and Dutch

Guiana. It was within Pitt's power to do this by administrative decree. This was deemed economically prudent because the Dutch islands' production of sugar could threaten the English sugar market. Not to curtail the foreign production, made possible by slaves, would assist the enemy. As Fogel states, "Pitt could quite reasonably base his decree on grounds of economic and military expediency." The point here is that nearly twenty years before this plan, which proved very effective, Wesley articulated both the economic issue and its effectiveness as a strategy.

31 In his "Introduction" to Philemon (Wesley, *Explanatory Notes*, 580), Wesley asserts: "It seems Philemon, not only pardoned, but gave him his liberty; seeing Ignatius makes mention of him, as succeeding Timothy at Ephesus."

32 Wesley, *Explanatory Notes*, 521 (Ephesians 6:5); Ibid., 578 (Titus 2:9-10).

33 *Thoughts Upon Slavery* in Jackson, *Works of Wesley*, XI, 77.

34 Ibid., 71.

35 Ibid., 68.

36 Ibid., 75.

37 See Benezet's *Short Account*, 27-28, 66.

38 *Thoughts Upon Slavery* in Jackson, *Works of Wesley*, XI, 72.

39 "A Seasonable Address to the Inhabitants of Great Britain" from 1776, in Jackson, *Works of Wesley*, XI, 125.

40 Letter from Whitefield to Wesley on March 22, 1751 in Thompson, *John Wesley as a Social Reformer*, 43-45. The majority of this letter is also contained in a letter Anthony Benezet wrote to Selina, Countess of Huntingdon, on March 10, 1775 (Haverford Collection 852).

41 See Irv Brendlinger, "Wesley, Whitefield, A Philadelphia Quaker, and Slavery," *Wesleyan Theological Journal* XXXVI (Fall 2001).

42 Jackson, *Works of Wesley*, XI, 78.

43 Frank Baker, *From Wesley to Asbury* (Durham, North Carolina: Duke University Press, 1976), 121-122. In a footnote Baker quotes Asbury's Journal, February 23, March 27 and April 23, 1779: "I have lately been impressed with a deep concern for bringing about the freedom of slaves in America, and feel resolved to do what I can to promote it. If God in His providence hath detained me in this country to be instrumental in so merciful and great an undertaking, I hope He will give me wisdom and courage sufficient, and enable me to give Him all the glory. I am strongly persuaded that if the Methodists will not yield on this point and emancipate their slaves, God will depart from them ... I have just finished my feeble performance against slavery; if our conference should come into the measure, I trust it will be one of the means toward generally expelling the practice from our Society. How would my heart rejoice if my detention in these parts should afford me leisure in any measure in so desirable a work ... I was employed according [to] the desire of the conference in preparing a circular letter, to promote the emancipation of slaves, and to be read in our Societies." Baker indicates that these passages were in Asbury's original journal, but unfortunately they have been deleted from the modern edition. The result is that the clarity of Asbury's early opposition to slavery is obscured.

44 See Walker, "A Newly-Discovered Pamphlet by Dr. Coke," *Proceedings of the Wesley Historical Society* XX (1935-1936), 158 (see also Chapter 2, page 36, footnote 69). Two years earlier, in January 1784, Coke had published a plan for such missions:

"Plan of the Society for the Establishment of Missions among the Heathens."

45 Baker, *From Wesley to Asbury*, 151-152.

46 John Vickers, *Thomas Coke, Apostle of Methodism* (London: Epworth Press, 1969), 98, citing Coke's *Journal*, American edition, 397ff. Coke and Asbury visited influential people to continue to push the antislavery agenda. George Washington even received them (May 26, 1786?): "He received us very politely, and was very open to access. He is quite the plain country gentleman and he is a friend to mankind. After dinner we desired a private interview, and opened to him the grand business on which we came, presenting to him our petition for the emancipation of the negroes, and intreating his signature, if the eminence of his station did not render it inexpedient for him to sign any petition. He informed us that he was of our sentiments, and had signified his thoughts on the subject to most of the great men of the State: that he did not see it proper to sign the petition, but if the Assembly took it into consideration, would signify his sentiments to the Assembly by a letter. He asked us to spend the evening and lodge at his house, but our engagement at Annapolis the following day, would not admit of it. I was loth to leave him, for I greatly love and esteem him and if there was no pride in it, would say that we are kindred Spirits, formed in the same mould. O that God would give him the witness of his Spirit!"

47 Ibid., 96. Vickers notes that even so there was at least one attempt on Coke's life in Halifax County and legal proceedings were begun against him.

48 James Weldon Johnson, *God's Trombones* (New York: The Viking Press, 1927), 13.

49 Baker, *From Wesley to Asbury*, 84.

50 See also William B. Gravely, "Early Methodism and Slavery: the Roots of a Tradition," *Wesleyan Quarterly Review*, II (1965), 84-100, especially 87, and Baker, *From Wesley to Asbury*, 121, 151-152.

51 Frederick Douglass, *Narrative of the Life of Frederick Douglass* (New York: Dover Publications, 1995), 32. First published in 1845 by the Anti-Slavery Office.

52 Ibid., 46.

53 See note 43 above regarding Asbury's *Journal* entry that if the Methodists did not "emancipate their slaves, God will depart from them."

54 "Causes of the Inefficacy of Christianity" in Jackson, *Works of Wesley*, VII, 287.

55 Ibid.

56 Ibid.

57 Ibid., 288.

58 Philip D. Curtin, *The Image of Africa, British Ideas and Action, 1780-1850* (Madison: The University of Wisconsin Press, 1964), 30, 386.

59 Davis, *The Problem of Slavery in Western Culture*, 453. He quotes Morgan Godwyn from 1680. Thomas Gossett developed the thesis that Negro slavery was extremely important in generating race theories and such theories were only developed when the institution, slavery, came under attack. See Thomas F. Gossett, *Race: The History of an Idea in America* (New York: Schocken, 1965), 29.

60 Curtin, *The Image of Africa*, 378, quoting Robert Knox, *The Races of Man: a Fragment*, 2nd ed. (London: Henry Renshaw, 1862), v.

238   SOCIAL JUSTICE THROUGH THE EYES OF WESLEY

61   For very fascinating examples of how Wesley describes the same group of people differently, depending on his purpose, see his negative view (for depravity) in Jackson, *Works of Wesley*, IX, 209-210, or in Jackson, *Works of Wesley*, VI, 278. His positive view (for slavery) can be seen in Jackson, *Works of Wesley*, XI, 63-66, 74, 76, 78. A very positive view, not in the context of fighting slavery is found in Jackson, *Works of Wesley*, V, 365 ("Sermon on the Mount, Discourse VIII") and 17-18 ("The Almost Christian").

62   Jackson, *Works of Wesley*, VII, 145 ("On Pleasing All Men").

63   Jackson, *Works of Wesley*, VII, 62 ("On Zeal").

64   Matthew Prior's *Solomon* (ii, 242) quoted in Telford, *Letters*, V, 127, 133 (to Mrs. Woodhouse, February 15, 1769 and to Jane Salkeld, August 9, 1772, respectively). The levelling accusation is reported by Lecky's, *History of England in the Eighteenth Century*, III, 122 and Maldwyn Edwards, *John Wesley and the Eighteenth Century* (London: George Allen & Unwin, 1933), 194.

65   Telford, *Letters*, I, 188.

66   Jackson, *Works of Wesley*, I, 59 (*Journal*, October 7, 1737).

67   Jackson, *Works of Wesley*, I, 66. This last description is also used by Wesley in his discourse on "The Doctrine of Original Sin," Jackson, *Works of Wesley*, IX, 212.

68   Jackson, *Works of Wesley*, IV, 180.

69   Jackson, *Works of Wesley*, XI, 68, 76, 78.

70   Ibid., 74.

71   Jackson, *Works of Wesley*, VII, 383 (Sermon, "Causes on the Inefficacy of Christianity").

72   Jackson, *Works of Wesley*, IX, 222 ("The Doctrine of Original Sin").

73   Jackson, *Works of Wesley*, 64-65.

74   Note his support at the 1786 Conference of sending missionary workers to Antigua, as well as Northern Scotland and Nova Scotia.

75   Jackson, *Works of Wesley*, VII, 197 (Sermon, "On Faith").

76   Ibid., 48.

77   Ibid., 353.

78   Jackson, *Works of Wesley*, I, 522 (journal entry for October 11, 1745). Wesley was referring to Marcus Aurelius Antoninus, who was emperor of Rome from A.D. 161-180. Taught by Stoic teachers, his reign reflected a clear integration of his religion and philosophy with all of life. His administration was marked by self-discipline and benevolence and his *Meditations* form a record of what he did, not merely what he believed. Because love of fellows was paramount in his thinking, John Stuart Mill considered his *Meditations* to approach the Sermon on the Mount in ethical significance [*Encyclopaedia Britannica*, XVII (1911 edition), 694-696]. Obviously, Wesley also held him in very high esteem.

CHAPTER 4, pages 73 to 128
The relationship between Wesley's theology and his position on slavery

1   An excellent current study is Maddox, *Responsible Grace*. Helpful older studies include: Colin W. Williams, *John Wesley's Theology Today* (London: The Epworth Press, 1960); William R. Cannon, *The Theology of John Wesley* (Nashville: Abingdon, 1946);

George Croft Cell, *The Rediscovery of John Wesley* (New York: Henry Holt, 1935).
2   This was in Wesley's *Pamphlets*, Original, IV, no.3 of the Hobill Collection, H 179.
3   Jackson, *Works of Wesley*, V, 54 (Sermon, "Justification By Faith").
4   Such a high view of original humankind and these same traits are found in other of Wesley's writings. Of particular interest is his early sermon from 1730 on Genesis 1:27 (manuscript sermon on Genesis 1:27, John Rylands Library, 3-5). Also in Wesley, *Works*, IV (Sermon 141, "The Image of God"). It contains the following lofty statements: "Understanding was just. ... It never was betrayed in any mistake; Whatever he perceived, he perceived as it was. He thought not at all of many things, but he thought wrong of none. ...nothing appeared in a false light... Light and darkness there were, but no twilight... He was equally a stranger to error and doubt; Either he saw not at all, or he saw plainly and hence arose that other excellence of his understanding. Being just and clear, it was swift in its motion."

"Far greater and nobler was his second endowment, namely a will equally perfect. It could not but be perfect while it followed the dictates of such an understanding. His affections were rational, even just and regular..."

"Man was what God is, love. What made his Image yet plainer in his human offspring was the liberty he enjoyed; the perfect freedom implanted, interwoven in his nature, and interwoven with all its parts."

"... His own choice was to determine him in all things. The balance did not incline to one side or the other, unless by his own deed..."

"... he was the sole Lord and sovereign judge of his own actions."

"The results of all these, an unerring understanding, an uncorrupt will and perfect freedom, gave the last stroke to the image of God in man by crowning all these with happiness. Then indeed, to live was to enjoy. When every faculty was in its perfection, amidst abundance of objects which infinite wisdom had purposely suited to it. When man's understanding was satisfied with truth, as his will was with good: when he was at full liberty to enjoy the Creator or the creation; to indulge in rivers of pleasure, ever new, ever pure from any mixture of pain."

This sermon manuscript (in Wesley's hand) was found and transcribed in the John Rylands library in 1981. It has since been published in Wesley, *Works*, IV, 290-303 (Sermon 141, "The Image of God"). It is significant that this high view of original humankind was written early, but was not departed from in his later writings. Similar passages can be found in later sermons, including "On the Fall of Man" and "The End of Christ's Coming" (Jackson, *Works of Wesley*, VI, 215ff, 270).

5   Jackson, *Works of Wesley*, IX, 435 ("The Doctrine of Original Sin").
6   Jackson, *Works of Wesley*, VIII, 284-285 ("Minutes of Some Late Conversations," 1745).
7   Quoted by John W. Fletcher, *A Vindication of the Rev. Mr. Wesley's Last Minutes*, (Bristol, 1771), 21. See also Jackson, *Works of Wesley*, XII, 137. Fletcher maintains "I have heard him [Wesley] ... steadily maintain the total fall of man in Adam, and his utter inability to recover himself, or take any one step towards his recovery..." [John Fletcher, *The Works of the Rev. John Fletcher*, 8 vols. (London: John Mason, 1837), II, 205-206].
8   Jackson, *Works of Wesley*, IX, 381 ("The Doctrine of Original Sin").

9   Jackson, *Works of Wesley*, IX, 381 ("The Doctrine of Original Sin").

10   Wesley's sermon on Genesis 1:27, 9-10. The rest of the quotes in this paragraph are from the same location. Wesley actually suggested physical changes in the brain that resulted from the Fall. These were passed on to offspring. This is extremely interesting in light of the recent advance of genetic understanding as related to the Human Genome Project with resultant gene testing and gene therapy.

11   This attitude was, no doubt, fostered by Wesley's mother — an amazingly capable woman who refused to teach her daughters to sew until they could read. In "The Reward of the Righteous," Wesley despairs of the current attitude that many women are brought up "as if they were only designed for agreeable playthings." He encouraged women to "yield not to that vile bondage any longer! You as well as men, are rational creatures. You, like them, were made in the image of God; you are equally candidates for immortality; you too are called of God, as you have time, to 'do good unto all men'" (Jackson, *Works of Wesley*, VII, 126). See also Jackson, *Works of Wesley*, VI, 218, "On the Fall of Man." Maddox briefly addresses this and points out that Wesley accepted the view of his day that women "should be subordinate to men in social structures." See Maddox, *Responsible Grace*, 72. My point here is that Wesley subscribed to a basic equality of the sexes and attributed the notion of female inferiority to the Fall.

12   Jackson, *Works of Wesley*, VI, 246 (Sermon, "The General Deliverance"). See also Ibid., 212 (Sermon, "God's Approbation of His Works").

13   Jackson, *Works of Wesley*, IX, 335 ("Doctrine of Original Sin"). For a helpful discussion of the transmission of original sin and Wesley's position, see Maddox, *Responsible Grace*, 75-81.

14   Jackson, *Works of Wesley*, IX, 57 ("Doctrine of Original Sin").

15   Jackson, *Works of Wesley*, VI, 508 (Sermon, "On Working Out Our Own Salvation"). See also Jackson, *Works of Wesley*, V, 73, 257 (Sermons, "The Righteousness of Faith" and "Sermon on the Mount, Discourse I").

16   Jackson, *Works of Wesley*, VI, 231 (Sermon, "God's Love To Fallen Man").

17   Jackson, *Works of Wesley*, IX, 429-430.

18   Jackson, *Works of Wesley*, VI, 63 (Sermon, "Original Sin").

19   It may be helpful to point out that Wesley scholars have disagreed on Wesley's view of depravity. Representative of the debate are Cell, *The Rediscovery of John Wesley* and Cannon, *The Theology of John Wesley*. Cell believes that Wesley's position was simply a renewal of the Luther-Calvin position that there is no human ability in or even toward salvation, so God's activity is everything (Cell, *The Rediscovery of John Wesley*, 271). William Cannon disagrees, believing that Wesley's rejection of predestination implied some human ability (Cannon, *The Theology of John Wesley*, 105-106). In fact the idea that salvation depends either on predestination or human ability misses the truly Wesleyan perspective, which is not a synthesis. Wesley's understanding, developed in the following section, is based on his understanding of prevenient grace.

20   Jackson, *Works of Wesley*, VII, 346 (Sermon, "The Heavenly Treasure in Earthen Vessels"). This theme is widespread in Wesley's sermons and tracts. See Jackson, *Works of Wesley*, V, 70, 74, 86, 141, 169, 184, 203, 224, 241, 256, 267, 269, 294, 359, 363, 388-389, 402, 427; VI, 64-65, 222-223, 506; VII, 230, 233, 346, 353,

430, 486, 491, 509; VIII, 47; IX, 308.

21 Jackson, *Works of Wesley*, VI, 275, 223 (Sermons, "The End of Christ's Coming," "The Fall of Man'). In light of the loss of understanding, Wesley did believe that the purpose of education was to "supply the loss of original perfection" as much as possible. Education should be viewed as the "art of recovering man to his rational perfection" [Jackson, *Works of Wesley*, VII, 87 (Sermon, "On the Education of Children")].

22 Jackson, *Works of Wesley*, VI, 224 (Sermon, "The Fall of Man").

23 Thomas Nugent, trans., *The Spirit of the Laws*, 2nd ed. (New York/London: Hafner Publishing Co., 1949) I, 238-239 (originally published in 1748). On 238 Montesquieu also satirically notes evangelization as justification for slavery. This is a fascinating insight that would be demonstrated in the years following Montesquieu. Since the eighteenth century various groups have evangelized from the unrecognized motive of "assisting" the "inferior;" therefore any means became justified.

24 Jackson, *Works of Wesley*, IV, 296 (journal entry for January 25, 1785).

25 Jackson, *Works of Wesley*, I, 411 (journal entry for January 24, 1743).

26 See Allan Lamar Cooper, "John Wesley: A Study in Theology and Social Ethics" (Ph.D. diss., Columbia University, 1962), 121.

27 See Jackson, *Works of Wesley*, XI, 97. See also "Thoughts Concerning the Origin of Power," "Thoughts Upon Liberty," "Some Observations on Liberty," "A Calm Address to Our American Colonies," "A Seasonable Address to the Inhabitants of Great Britain" and "A Calm Address to the Inhabitants of England" (Ibid.).

28 Wesley would have taken issue with Reinhold Niebuhr's statement: "Man's capacity for justice makes democracy possible; but his inclination for injustice makes democracy necessary" (*The Children of Light and the Children of Darkness*). At the same time, Wesley remained somewhat open to different forms of government because the locus of power was God who could confer authority on another form of government. See Jackson, *Works of Wesley*, XI, 47.

29 See Wesley's sermon "What is Man?" (Jackson, *Works of Wesley*, VII, 171-172).

30 Gordon Rupp, *Principalities and Powers* (London: Epworth Press, 1952), 77.

31 Michael Joseph Scanlon addresses this in "The Christian Anthropology of John Wesley" (STD. thesis, The Catholic University of America, 1969), 91.

32 E.J. Bicknell, *A Theological Introduction to the Thirty-nine Articles of the Church of England* (London: Longmans, Green & Co., 1919, 1953), 219.

33 Some excellent work on this topic has been done by Charles A. Rogers, "The Concept of Prevenient Grace in the Theology of John Wesley" (Ph.D. thesis, Duke University, 1967) and Maddox, *Responsible Grace*.

34 Rogers, "Prevenient Grace," 129, 142-143.

35 Jackson, *Works of Wesley*, V, 167 (Sermon, "The Repentance of Believers").

36 Jackson, *Works of Wesley*, VI, 512 (Sermon, "On Working Out Our Own Salvation").

37 Ibid., 44. See also Scanlon, "Christian Anthropology," 94.

38 Jackson, *Works of Wesley*, VI, 354-355 (Sermon, "The Case of Reason Impartially Considered").

39 Ibid., 354-359.

40 Ibid., 507 (Sermon, "On Working Out Our Own Salvation"). See also Jackson, *Works of Wesley*, V, 436 ("The Original Nature ... of the Law").

41 Jackson, *Works of Wesley*, VII, 187 (Sermon, "On Conscience"). On the following page Wesley states that the conscience acts as "witness" (testifying regarding our actions), "judge" (passing sentence) and then it "executes the sentence" (with feelings of satisfaction or uneasiness).

42 Jackson, *Works of Wesley*, VII, 187. This is Wesley's consistent, mature position. The one time he allows that it could possibly be natural is found in a sermon preached five months before his death (September 1790), entitled "The Heavenly Treasure in Earthen Vessels" (Ibid., 345). One senses that regardless of how it is termed, Wesley believed conscience was God's gift to all humankind as a result of the atonement, through prevenient grace. He always maintained that all people know good from evil.

43 Jackson, *Works of Wesley*, VI, 512, 44.

44 Maddox concurs, stating that "Prevenient grace effects a partial restoring of our sin-corrupted human faculties, sufficient that we might sense our need and God's offer of salvation, and respond to that offer" (Maddox, *Responsible* Grace, 87).

45 See Maddox, *Responsible* Grace, 88-93. For a less comprehensive treatment see Brendlinger, "Views of Evangelicals on Slavery and Race," 258-265.

46 In a statement that does not diminish depravity, but defines it in order to show how prevenient grace affects it and how depraved human beings can respond to God, Maddox explains, "depravity is not the obliteration of our human faculties, but their debilitation when devoid of God's empowering Presence." This shifts the dynamic from human *possession* to *relationship* and its accompanying power. He continues: "With God's approach our faculties are increasingly empowered, to the point that we can recognize our need and God's offer of renewed relationship and respond to it. The key point, of course, is that our response is made possible by grace..." (Maddox, *Responsible Grace*, 90). Dealing with Divine initiative contrasted to human initiative, Rogers distinguishes between a "gift offered" and a "gift given" (Rogers, "Prevenient Grace," 217). A somewhat helpful, but limited analogy is that of someone making a deposit in another's chequing account. There is no need for the recipient's initiative or action and therefore no place for pride. The resources are simply there. However, the recipient can then draw on those funds or refuse to access them. When this analogy is recast in the context of God's empowering Presence rather than a possession it is even more appropriate. God, through prevenient grace, is with us, relating to us and making us aware, or awakening us to his Presence. This is the "gift given." We then can "draw" on God as our resource or refuse to even acknowledge the relationship or the Presence.

47 Jackson, *Works of Wesley*, XI, 68.

48 Jackson, *Works of Wesley*, VII, 189. While Wesley agrees on this description of conscience it is not surprising that he disagrees with Hutcheson about the origin. Wesley sees these senses as supernatural gifts, through prevenient grace, whereas Hutcheson sees them as natural. Wesley is quick to point out the difference.

49 Jackson, *Works of Wesley*, XI, 70.

50 Ibid., 79.

51 This is particularly true of Granville Sharp, who, by comparison appealed

more to fear of judgement.

52   Another interesting contrast is between Wesley and Edmund Burke. Burke believed that people took a strange sort of "pleasure" in the hardships of others. This was the basis for empathy and without it people would avoid others in difficulty and have no capacity for benevolence. Seeing benevolence as a result of prevenient grace, Wesley would have considered this ludicrous. Davis describes Burke's explanation of benevolence (Davis, *The Problem of Slavery in Western Culture*, 356-359).

53   Jackson, *Works of Wesley*, VII, 378-379.

54   Whitefield's published letter responding to Wesley's preaching of "Free Grace," December 24, 1740, is printed in Dallimore, *George Whitefield*, II, 552-569.

55   The name "Drogheda" has lived on in the memories of the Irish for centuries because of Oliver Cromwell's merciless annihilation of the enemy after his victory. It is a classic example that one's theology greatly affects one's human relationships, for good or ill. The fact that Cromwell's action was based on his theology casts even greater light — contrasting light — on Wesley's antislavery position, derived from his belief in a universal atonement.

56   Jackson, *Works of Wesley*, V, 104 (Sermon, "The Spirit of Bondage and Adoption") and X, 392 ("Some Remarks on Mr. Hill's Review of All the Doctrines Taught By Mr. John Wesley").

57   Jackson, *Works of Wesley*, VI, 311 (Sermon, "The Signs of the Times").

58   Telford, *Letters*, VI, 263 (To Miss March, April 1777).

59   In "The Doctrine of Original Sin" Wesley asserted, "I believe none ever did, or ever will, die eternally, merely for the sin of our first father" (Jackson, *Works of Wesley*, IX, 315).

60   Wesley consistently maintained two threads throughout his teaching on free will: God is sovereign, and the individual is responsible. Robert Chiles comments that Wesley was "quite content, on the basis of scripture and experience, to affirm both that God does everything in salvation, and that man is responsible for his own salvation. It is being quite true to Wesley simply to state this tension between divine initiative and human responsibility and let it stand" [Robert Chiles, "From Free Grace to Free Will" in *Religion in Life*, XXVII (Summer 1958), 440]. While this is true, it seems helpful to attempt to work through how the two threads interface and that is the purpose of this section.

61   Jackson, *Works of Wesley*, X, 350. In "The End of Christ's Coming," Wesley explains that Adam "was endued with a will, with various affections; (which are only the will exerting itself various ways;) that he might love, desire, and delight in that which is good: Otherwise, his understanding had been to no purpose. He was likewise endued with liberty; a power of choosing what was good, and refusing what was not so. Without this, both the will and the understanding would have been utterly useless. Indeed, without liberty, man had been so far from being a free agent, that he could have been no agent at all. For every unfree being is purely passive; not active in any degree."

62   Jackson, *Works of Wesley*, VIII, 52-53 ("A Farther Appeal To Men of Reason and Religion"). Wesley is quoting Article X of the *Articles of the Church of England*.

63   Jackson, *Works of Wesley*, VII, 345 (Sermon, "The Heavenly Treasure in Earthen Vessels"). See also "What is Man?" (Ibid., 227-228) and "The General

Deliverance" (Jackson, *Works of Wesley*, VI, 242-243).

64 Jackson, *Works of Wesley*, X, 467, 463 ("Thoughts Upon Necessity"). See also "A Thought Upon Necessity" (Ibid., 475).

65 Ibid., 457.

66 In Wesley's "Thoughts Upon God's Sovereignty," (Ibid., 361-363) he discusses God "under a two-fold character," Creator and Governor. When speaking of God as Creator he relates characteristics of sovereignty and portrays God's actions as irresistible. When speaking of God as Governor he speaks of God's mercy, particularly when "mercy rejoices over justice." Thomas Madron believes that Wesley came closest to the Calvinists when speaking of God as Creator, and moved farthest from them when dealing with God as Governor [Thomas William Madron, "The Political Thought of John Wesley" (Ph.D. thesis, Tulane University, 1965), 36].

67 Jackson, *Works of Wesley*, X, 350 ("Remarks on a Defence of Aspasio Vindicated").

68 Ibid., 229 ("Predestination Calmly Considered").

69 Ibid., 350.

70 Ibid., 229 ("Predestination Calmly Considered").

71 Ibid., 473 ("Thoughts Upon Necessity").

72 Ibid., 474 ("Thoughts Upon Necessity"). At another time Wesley explains, "I have not an *absolute* power over my own mind, because of the corruption of my own nature..." [Jackson, *Works of Wesley*, VII, 128-129 (Sermon, "What is Man?")], author's italics.

73 Jackson, *Works of Wesley*, X, 474.

74 Although different from the concept of relinquishing control, Cushman describes the "inactivation of the will through despair." See "Salvation For All" by Robert E. Cushman in William K. Anderson, ed., *Methodism* (Methodist Publishing House, 1947), 111-115. See also Rogers, "Prevenient Grace," 15, 239.

75 Another way of stating this would be that through prevenient grace and subsequent freedom, the working of human death is transformed into the death of human ego-driven working. It is the presence of God that shifts the locus.

76 While Wesley may not agree with every facet of my analogy to describe his view of free will, he was not opposed to such analogies. See his remarkable story of the toad that was "buried alive" in a tree that grew around it, and emerged alive (!) some 100 years later when the tree was felled [Sermon, "On Living Without God," in Jackson, *Works of Wesley*, VII, 349 or Wesley, *Works*, IV, 169 (Sermon 130)].

77 Jackson, *Works of Wesley*, VIII, 286 ("Minutes of Some Late Conversations").

78 Wesley states: "This doctrine neither dishonours the grace of God, nor does too much honour to nature, in that it supposed nature to work only in the power and efficacy of grace itself" (manuscript sermon on Philippians 2:12-13). This is one of two sermons preached on this text, both adapted from William Tilly [William Tilly, *Sixteen Sermons* (London, 1712), 86].

79 Jackson, *Works of Wesley*, VI, 512.

80 Wesley makes it clear that it is only by God's grace that we can do outward works of mercy for others (feeding the hungry, clothing the naked). If such acts are done apart from grace they would only serve to condemn us because our motive would be self serving. See "Predestination Calmly Considered," Jackson, *Works of*

Wesley, X, 221-222.

81   Wesley, manuscript sermon on Philippians 2:12-13.

82   Wesley, manuscript sermon on Philippians 2:12-13.

83   This kind of thinking would be a good foundation for later trusteeship attitudes and policies. The Codrington Estates (owned by the SPG) and George Whitefield are examples of justifying slavery as a means of evangelizing.

84   See Jackson, *Works of Wesley*, XI, 34ff, "Thoughts Upon Liberty."

85   Thomas Clarkson used this same argument in *An Essay on the Slavery and Commerce of the Human Species* ... *1785*, 2nd ed. (London: J. Phillips, 1788) 56, 160, 162-163. It is conceivable he picked up the idea from Wesley.

86   For a fuller description of Benezet's response to Whitefield's position on slavery see Brendlinger, "Wesley, Whitefield, A Philadelphia Quaker, and Slavery," *Wesleyan Theological Journal*, XXXVI (Fall 2001), 170 -172.

87   Wesley deals with this theme in numerous places. In his sermon "On Visiting the Sick" (Jackson, *Works of Wesley*, VII, 117-118) he writes: "Surely there are works of mercy as well as works of piety, which are real means of grace." He goes on, "'Inasmuch as ye have done it to the least of these my brethren, ye have done it unto me.' If this do not convince you that the continuance in works of mercy is necessary to salvation, consider what the Judge of all says to those on the left hand: 'Depart, ye cursed, into everlasting fire, prepared for the devil and his angels'...Is it not strange, that this important truth should be so little understood, or, at least, should so little influence the practice of them that fear God?" In "On Working Out Our Own Salvation" (Jackson, *Works of Wesley*, VI, 510ff) Wesley portrays works of mercy, made possible by prevenient grace, as part of the entire process of salvation, from justification through sanctification. See also Jackson, *Works of Wesley*, VI, 51; X, 221-222, 466.

88   Jackson, *Works of Wesley*, XIII, 9 (Letter to Robert Brackenbury, September 15, 1790).

89   Frank Whaling, ed., *John and Charles Wesley, Selected Writings and Hymns* (London, 1981), xv (preface by Albert Outler).

90   Williams, *John Wesley's Theology Today*, 168. It is interesting and paradoxical that the "doctrine" of Christian Perfection has fostered more misunderstanding of Wesley and his followers and more conflict between his followers than any other topic. However, it is my contention that when viewed as the full development of Wesley's doctrine of grace, not as a separate doctrine, the facets that tend to divide can be harmonized. Among other facets, debate has centred on how instantaneous, complete, biblical, practical, and even honest, sanctification is.

91   Jackson, *Works of Wesley*, V, 21 (Sermon, "The Almost Christian").

92   Telford, *Letters*, III, 167 (To William Dodd, 1756).

93   Telford, *Letters*, V, 93, 314.

94   Jackson, *Works of Wesley*, VIII, 285 ("Minutes of Some Late Conversations").

95   Jackson, *Works of Wesley*, VI, 45 (Sermon, "The Scripture Way of Salvation").

96   Jackson, *Works of Wesley*, VI, 65-66 (Sermon, "The New Birth"), Wesley's italics. Later in the same sermon he reiterates: "When we are born again, then our sanctification, our inward and outward holiness, begins" (74). See also Jackson, *Works of Wesley*, VII, 205; VIII, 285; IX, 310.

97 Jackson, *Works of Wesley*, V, 56 (Sermon, "Justification By Faith").
98 Jackson, *Works of Wesley*, V, 212ff (Sermon, "The Marks of the New Birth").
99 Jackson, *Works of Wesley*, VIII, 279 ("Minutes of Some Late Conversations").
100 Jackson, *Works of Wesley*, XII, 333 (Letter to Mrs. A.F., October 12, 1764).
101 Jackson, *Works of Wesley*, VIII, 286 ("Minutes of Some Late Conversations").
102 Jackson, *Works of Wesley*, VI, 51 (Sermon, "The Scripture Way of Salvation").
103 Jackson, *Works of Wesley*, VI, 50.
104 Jackson, *Works of Wesley*, VI, 48, Wesley's italics.
105 Jackson, *Works of Wesley*, VI, 51-52, Wesley's italics.
106 Telford, *Letters*, IV, 71.
107 These contrasts are seen in Jackson, *Works of Wesley*, XI, 420; V, 56; VII, 314. Authors italics.
108 Jackson, *Works of Wesley*, VII, 486 (Sermon, "On Grieving the Holy Spirit").
109 Jackson, *Works of Wesley*, VI, 509 (Sermon, "On Working Out Our Own Salvation"). See also Jackson, *Works of Wesley*, V, 224 and VI, 65. Wesley's emphasis on both faith and ethical holiness led George Croft Cell to call Wesley's teaching a "synthesis of the Protestant ethic of grace with the Catholic ethic of holiness" (Cell, *The Rediscovery of John Wesley*, 361). But the element of merit is completely absent in Wesley with his unequivocal insistence that faith is the only condition and it is God's free gift. Others disagree with Cell's assessment, including W.D. Allbeck ["Plenteous Grace With Thee Is Found," *Religion in Life*, XXIX (Autumn 1960), 503] and Colin Williams (Williams, *John Wesley's Theology Today*, 174-175, 187). Gordon Rupp's comment is particularly insightful. Noting that Wesley's theology contains a "certain combination of Christian truths," he states that this "has sometimes been explained by saying that John Wesley combined the Protestant teaching of justification by faith with the Catholic conception of holiness. I do not find this an enlightening statement at all. [...] I do not think it bears close inspection. [...] What he had to say about holiness was bound together with what he believed about justification by faith: it was not an afterthought, but the original starting point of his search for Christian perfection. [...] For him the Pauline doctrine of justification was closely linked with the Epistles of John and the doctrine of love" [Gordon Rupp, *Principalities and Powers* (London: Epworth Press, 1952) 82]. On this issue see also J. E. Rattenbury, *The Evangelical Doctrines of Charles Wesley's Hymns* (London: Epworth Press, 1941) 300 and John L. Peters, *Christian Perfection and American Methodism* (Nashville: Abingdon Press, 1956), 20-21.
110 Jackson, *Works of Wesley*, XI, 369. Also, on May 14, 1765 he asserted in a letter to John Newton: "the sermon on the Circumcision of the Heart ... contains all that I now teach concerning salvation from all sin and loving God with an undivided heart" (Telford, *Letters*, IV, 299).
111 Jackson, *Works of Wesley*, XI, 444, author's italics. Rob Lyndal Staples points out Wesley's debt to the devotional writers he had studied. From Jeremy Taylor came purity of intention, from Thomas A'Kempis came the mind of Christ and from William Law came loving God and neighbour (Rob Lyndal Staples, "John Wesley's Doctrine of Christian Perfection; A Reinterpretation" [Th.D. thesis, Pacific School of Religion, 1963], 10). See also Peters, *Christian Perfection and American Methodism*, 21.

112 See "Justification By Faith" in Jackson, *Works of Wesley*, V, 54.

113 In the context of prevenient grace, Maddox speaks of the "pardon" and "power" dimensions of God's grace (Maddox, *Responsible Grace*, 87). The power issue there relates to the partial restoration of the natural image of God, partly rehabilitating the intellect and conscience. In the present discussion of sanctification, God's power is even more lavishly demonstrated as the moral image is fully restored.

114 Jackson, *Works of Wesley*, V, 56 (Sermon, "Justification By Faith").

115 Wesley, *Works*, IV (Sermon 141, "The Image of God").

116 In "The New Birth," Wesley states: "Gospel holiness is no less than the image of God stamped upon the heart." In "Working Out Our Own Salvation" he says: "by sanctification ... we are restored to the image of God." In "Sermon on the Mount, Discourse I" righteousness is defined as "the image of God stamped upon the heart, now renewed after the likeness of Him that created it" (Jackson, *Works of Wesley*, VI, 71; VI, 509; V, 256). The pervasiveness of the renewed image as the essence of sanctification is seen throughout Wesley's sermons and writings. Some references include: Jackson, *Works of Wesley*, V, 70, 74, 86, 169, 184, 203, 241, 267, 269, 294, 363, 388-389, 402, 426, 430; VI, 416, 422-423; VII, 230, 233, 346, 353, 430, 486, 491, 513; VIII, 47, 48, 279, 357; IX, 289, 308, 313; X, 364; XI, 378, 381, 424, 444, 523; XII, 416.

117 What a tragedy and travesty that this teaching has at times been emasculated by the attempt to limit it to the correct verbiage. When that happens, once again the "wild truth" of orthodoxy is tamed, to use Chesterton's metaphor, and the power of such truth is lost [Gilbert K. Chesterton, *Orthodoxy* (Westport, CT: Greenwood Press, [reprint]), 187].

118 Jackson, *Works of Wesley*, VII, 67 (Sermon, "On Redeeming the Time").

119 Jackson, *Works of Wesley*, VI, 46 (Sermon, "The Scripture Way of Salvation"); Telford, *Letters*, V, 223 (to Walter Churchey, February 21, 1771); Telford, *Letters*, VII, 120 (to Ann Loxdale, April 12, 1782). Although the implications of Wesley's view of Christian Perfection will be addressed below, the biblical texts cited here (as Wesley's description of perfection) are completely antithetical to the eighteenth century practice of slavery. It would be ludicrous to try to reconcile such passages to slave owning!

120 Jackson, *Works of Wesley*, XI, 430 ("Plain Account").

121 Jackson, *Works of Wesley*, V, 207 (Sermon, "The Circumcision of the Heart," from 1733). This early sermon is prototypic of Wesley's mature theology. He states that the circumcision of the heart is comprised of humility, faith, hope and love. His description of humility is very similar to his later description of repentance, the first step of response in the process of salvation. His concept of faith is not as developed as his mature view where faith is the only condition of salvation, but he does speak of it as God's gift. His view of hope is similar to his later doctrine of assurance. His view of love, both for God and neighbor is remarkably close to how he develops it in the context of Christian perfection.

122 Jackson, *Works of Wesley*, VI, 71 (Sermon, "The New Birth").

123 Jackson, *Works of Wesley*, XI, 440 ("Plain Account").

124 Jackson, *Works of Wesley*, V, 219 (Sermon, "Marks of the New Birth"), 22 (Sermon, "The Almost Christian"). See also Jackson, *Works of Wesley*, XI, 418 ("Plain

Account"). At another point Wesley cautioned against "bigotry," encouraging his followers not to restrict their loving actions to Methodists, particularly sanctified Methodists (Jackson, *Works of Wesley*, XI, 431). See also Jackson, *Works of Wesley*, V, 79; VI, 413.

125 Jackson, *Works of Wesley*, VI, 413-414 (Sermon, "On Perfection").

126 Ibid.

127 Telford, *Letters*, VII, 120 (to Ann Loxdale, April 12, 1782). Also, Jackson, *Works of Wesley*, XI, 430 ("Plain Account").

128 Jackson, *Works of Wesley*, VI, 51 (Sermon, "The Scripture Way of Salvation").

129 Ibid., 284-285 (Sermon, "The General Spread of the Gospel").

130 Jackson, *Works of Wesley*, VIII, 352 ("Advice to the People Called Methodists"). The same theme occurs in his sermon "On Charity": "such a love of our neighbour... can only spring from the love of God. And whence does this love of God flow? Only from that faith which is of the operation of God" (Jackson, *Works of Wesley*, VII, 47). In a statement that seems to blend holiness with love of neighbour Wesley says, "no true holiness can exist without that love of God for its foundation" ["Minutes on Some Late Conversations" (Jackson, *Works of Wesley*, VIII, 290)]. In "The Scripture Way of Salvation" he states more overtly: "We are inwardly renewed by the power of God. We feel 'the love of God shed abroad in our heart by the Holy Ghost which is given unto us;' producing love to all mankind, and more especially to the children of God" (Jackson, *Works of Wesley*, VI, 45) See also V, 60, 86; VII, 38, 269.

131 Jackson, *Works of Wesley*, VII, 271-272 (Sermon, "The Ministerial Office").

132 Jackson, *Works of Wesley*, V, 462 (Sermon, "The Law Established Through Faith"). In a letter to John Smith on June 25, 1746, Wesley described faith "not as an end, but a means only" (Telford, *Letters*, II, 75). As far back as 1738 Wesley described the necessity of balancing faith with other components. He commented on some whose "confused" accounts "magnified faith to such an amazing size that it quite hid all the rest of the commandments." In reflective retrospect he analyzed: "I did not then see that this was the natural effect of their overgrown fear of Popery; being so terrified with the cry of merit and good works, that they plunged at once into the other extreme" (Curnock, *Journal*, I, 419).

133 Jackson, *Works of Wesley*, V, 464 (Sermon, "The Law Established Through Faith"). See also VIII, 513; XI, 416.

134 It has been the peripheral issues, such as when sanctification occurred, its tenure and how it is related to sin, from which the holiness dogmas have taken root and spawned various holiness groups.

135 Jackson, *Works of Wesley*, VIII, 338 ("Minutes of Some Late Conversations"), author's italics.

136 Seeing perfection as a state is closer to seeing it as a possession. Such a view increases the possibility of objectifying the experience rather than seeing it as a meaningful part of a dynamic relationship. Martin Buber's paradigm of "I/It" compared to "I/Thou" explores the nature of relationships as objectifying or as mutual. Perceptions and various teachings of Christian perfection can be explored in light of this paradigm. Rob Staples examines Wesley's view in this context and feels the "possession" emphasis fits Buber's "I/It" model. He clarifies that Wesley transcends the possession idea, holding that perfection is a dialogical relationship, fitting the

"I/Thou" model (Staples, "John Wesley's Doctrine of Christian Perfection," 146, 149ff).

137 Rob Staples suggests that from 1725 to 1738 Wesley exclusively emphasized gradual sanctification. From 1738 to 1758 he held to both, sometimes emphasizing one, sometimes the other. From the late 1750s on he posited a "working synthesis," involving "an instantaneous moment of entire sanctification as a definite point within the gradual process" (Staples, "John Wesley's Doctrine of Christian Perfection," 94-95).

138 Jackson, *Works of Wesley*, XI, 382-383, 393, 423 ("Plain Account of Christian Perfection"). See also Jackson, *Works of Wesley*, XII, 275.

139 Jackson, *Works of Wesley*, XI, 442. This passage presents several issues for examination, one of which is the nature of sin. Wesley seems to imply that sin is an entity that has an existence, but its existence can be ended. It may be that he is simply using a metaphor to address the issue of instantaneousness because his broader understanding seems to be that sin is a choice or disability that destroys relationship with God. On the issue of instantaneousness, Wesley also uses the analogy of birth, indicating that the work of sanctification occurs, but must be followed by gradual growth ["The Wilderness State" in Jackson, *Works of Wesley*, VI, 91).

140 Jackson, *Works of Wesley*, XI, 417.

141 For a helpful discussion of the relationship of crisis to process, in light of the modern linear view of time, see Lawrence W. Wood, *Pentecostal Grace* (Kentucky: Francis Asbury, 1980), 117-118.

142 Among the numerous passages where Wesley contended for both the instantaneous and the gradual aspects of sanctification, see, Jackson, *Works of Wesley*, VI, 5, 75, 91, 490-491, 509; VII, 205, 212; VIII, 329; XI, 382-383, 393, 402, 423, 442; XII, 207, 275, 333-334, 416. It should be further noted that in the 1760s Wesley questioned the instantaneous nature of sanctification. See his letters to his brother Charles (Jackson, *Works of Wesley*, XII, 132, 136) and (Telford, *Letters*, IV, 187). See also Harald Lindström, *Wesley and Sanctification: A Study in the Doctrine of Sanctification* (Stockholm: Nya Bokforlags Aktiebolaget, 1946), 121ff.

143 Maddox, *Responsible Grace*, 189-190.

144 In "A Plain Account of Christian Perfection" he asks and answers, "Can those who are perfect grow in grace? Undoubtedly they can; and that not only while they are in the body, but to all eternity" (Jackson, *Works of Wesley*, XI, 426). The same concept of growth is seen in Ibid., 442 and IX, 310. Maddox points out, with apparent surprise, that Wesley "even suggested that the perfect would grow in grace to all eternity (i.e. beyond paradise)!" (Maddox, *Responsible Grace*, 191). But this can be assumed as reasonable and normal in light of seeing Christian Perfection as a relationship, not as a state or a possession. A healthy relationship continues to progress and grow and God's proximate eternal Presence would intensify that process.

145 Jackson, *Works of Wesley*, VI, 412 (Sermon, "On Perfection"). See also XI, 383.

146 Jackson, *Works of Wesley*, VI, 413 (Sermon, "On Perfection"). It seems that Wesley describes humankind differently, depending on the context. In the context of refuting absolute perfection, he mentions the disabilities, probably referring to the political and natural dimensions of the image of God that are not yet fully restored.

But in another context he indicates that it is possible, because of the atonement, for persons to be more holy than had there been no Fall (Ibid., 232-233). He is probably referring to the complete restoration of the moral image.

147 Ibid., 413.

148 Regarding Wesley's discouraging the use of the term, see Jackson, *Works of Wesley*, XI, 396, 418, 442, 446.

149 Wesley was careful to not treat sin lightly. He acknowledges that at an earlier period he believed it was not possible for a sanctified person to fall into sin. However, over time his opinion changed (Jackson, *Works of Wesley*, XI, 426). In his sermon "On Sin In Believers" he addresses the concepts of "inward" and "outward" sin (Jackson, *Works of Wesley*, V, 144ff.). See also "The Repentance of Believers," Jackson, *Works of Wesley*, V, 156ff. Controversy did develop and has continued. Wesley's lack of specific definitions for relevant terms makes resolution more difficult. He spoke of sin being "destroyed." Some interpreted this as "eradicated," which clearly indicates the impossibility of return. Others interpreted it as "suppressed," indicating the possibility of return. For a good introduction to this topic see Peters, *Christian Perfection and American Methodism*, 57-58. However, understanding sanctification in the perspective of relationship rather than a state or possession, and seeing sin as ego-centricity and that which breaks relationship rather than as a state or an entity, changes the entire dynamic and elicits a different set of questions.

150 Jackson, *Works of Wesley*, VI, 237 (Sermon, "God's Love to Fallen Man"). He further believed that this kind of holiness (doing good to others) produces happiness.

151 For example, see Maddox, *Responsible Grace*, 87, 168.

152 Jackson, *Works of Wesley*, VI, 415 (Sermon, "On Perfection"). See also V, 313.

153 Jackson, *Works of Wesley*, V, 313-314 ("Sermon on the Mount, Discourse V").

154 William Cannon speaks of an "ethics of realization, not aspiration" (Cannon, *The Theology of John Wesley*, 225).

155 Jackson, *Works of Wesley*, V, 464. See also VIII, 513 and XI, 416. Maddox deals helpfully with the concept of God's presence engendering the power of transformation. See Maddox, *Responsible Grace*, 88-90, passim.

156 Jackson, *Works of Wesley*, V, 317. An interesting comparison could be made between Wesley's concept of giving Christ the "kiss of Judas" and Dietrich Bonhoeffer's understanding of "cheap grace" in *The Cost of Discipleship*. Both relate to disregarding or discounting the law in the presence of and in the name of Christ. Wesley addresses the role and power of Christ in enabling us to fulfill the law.

157 Telford, *Letters*, III, 122.

158 Jackson, *Works of Wesley*, VI, 124ff (Sermon, "The Use of Money").

159 Jackson, *Works of Wesley*, VII, 216 (Sermon "On Riches"). See also "The Danger of Riches" (Ibid., 9-11, 14.)

160 Jackson, *Works of Wesley*, VII, 282-290, especially 286-287 (Sermon, "Causes of the Inefficacy of Christianity").

161 Jackson, *Works of Wesley*, VII, 20 (Sermon, "On Dress"). See also 21, 25. He also opposed apparel that engendered pride or provoked lust (17, 19).

162 Jackson, *Works of Wesley*, VII, 500.

163 Jackson, *Works of Wesley*, VII, 305ff.

164 Jackson, *Works of Wesley*, VII, 220 (Sermon, "On Riches").

165 Wellman Joel Warner, *The Wesleyan Movement in the Industrial Revolution* (London: Longmans, Green & Co, 1930), 209.

166 Jackson, *Works of Wesley*, VI, 139 (Sermon, "The Good Steward").

167 Jackson, *Works of Wesley*, VI, 126 (Sermon, "The Use of Money"). See also 134-135, 146-147, 332, 334; V, 374-375; VII, 37, 360.

168 Wellman Warner contrasts the prevailing eighteenth century view of poverty with that held by Wesley. Most believed that poverty was the result of insufficient material goods, idleness of the poor due to their depravity, and Providence. Wesley contended that poverty was the responsibility of the entire community, not just the poor. There were sufficient goods but inequitable consumption by a few, produced poverty for the rest, and this was immoral because all goods belonged to God. Further, he believed that lack of employment was often the result of injustice and that laziness could be found in all classes. See Warner, *The Wesleyan Movement*, 155-164.

169 Jackson, *Works of Wesley*, VI, 126-129 (Sermon, "The Use of Money").

170 Ibid., 131-132.

171 It seems that as the first generation of Methodists began to prosper from industry and conservation they eventually began to reduce their giving. Wesley was adamant in his condemnation of their not giving all they could. He attributed the decreased Methodist success in Bristol to "love of money" and "love of ease," characteristics of accumulating rather than giving. See Wesley's sermon on "Dives and Lazarus," (Jackson, *Works of Wesley*, VII, 250) and "Sermon on the Mount, Discourse VIII" (Jackson, *Works of Wesley*, V, 374-375). See also Jackson, *Works of Wesley*, VII, 84, 248 and Warner, *The Wesleyan Movement*, 192-193, 197.

172 Jackson, *Works of Wesley*, VI, 137ff (Sermon, "The Good Steward"). In an interesting contrast, John Locke held that persons could have a "right" to property. Wesley disagreed, believing that persons were only "trustees." However, Wesley defended the use of property as a civil liberty, but not an absolute. See also Warner, who states Wesley's view that "no human authority was competent to alienate the divine title" to property (Warner, *The Wesleyan Movement*, 208).

173 For a greater development of this theme, see Madron, "The Political Thought of John Wesley," 78ff.

174 John Deschner's *Wesley's Christology* is the most thorough study of his doctrine of Christ. Deschner states that Wesley used verbatim the Anglican Article II for the second of his "Twenty-Five Articles": "two whole and perfect natures, that is to say, the Godhead and Manhood, were joined together in one person, never to be divided; whereof is one Christ, very God and very Man" [John Deschner, *Wesley's Christology: An Interpretation* (Dallas: Southern Methodist University Press, 1960), 15].

175 Maddox, *Responsible Grace*, 116. Pages 114-118 provide an excellent and succinct summary of Wesley's Christology, giving both the Eastern and Western contexts and showing Wesley's view more closely aligned with the Eastern position. Maddox suggests that Wesley's overemphasis on the divine nature borders on monophysitism (117).

176 Maddox states that Wesley was more interested in Christ as the locus of God's work than the example of restored human nature. It seems to me that Wesley

does emphasize the role of Christ as the example of what we can become through God's grace. In "Plain Account of Christian Perfection" he states that holiness is "all the mind which was in Christ, enabling us to walk as Christ walked." In this concise statement Wesley points to Christ as both the example of being fully human and the means of experiencing such humanity (Jackson, *Works of Wesley*, XI, 444). This statement reflects the dynamic process and the resulting product: Christ's mind enabling our minds so that we can live as he lived.

177   At times Wesley advises that acts of mercy begin within the "household of faith," but they are never to remain there. At other times, he makes no distinction about the recipients of Christian beneficence.

CHAPTER 5, pages 129 to 146
The larger context: Wesley's social ethic and philosophy of social change

1   William Ernest Sweetland, "A Critical Study of John Wesley as Practical Thinker and Reformer" (Ph.D. thesis, Michigan State University, 1955), 165, citing Rousseau's *Social Contract*.

2   See sermon "On Visiting the Sick," in Jackson, *Works of Wesley*, VII, 124. Maddox, *Responsible Grace*, 118, cites and concurs with liberation theologian José Miguez Bonino that Wesley did not utilize Jesus as a model for challenging unjust laws and liberating the oppressed. On the other hand, even though Wesley's Christology did not provide such a "model," his teaching of Christianity required action against oppression, not complacent acceptance of it. His overall theology did move him to serve the oppressed and work on their behalf.

3   Jackson, *Works of Wesley*, V, 256. The use of this definition for righteousness is not unique to this sermon. It also appears in "Discourse IX," V, 387.

4   Jackson, *Works of Wesley*, V, 258-260.
5   Jackson, *Works of Wesley*, V, 265.
6   Jackson, *Works of Wesley*, V, 270, 284-285.
7   Jackson, *Works of Wesley*, V, 387-390.
8   Jackson, *Works of Wesley*, V, 336-337.
9   Jackson, *Works of Wesley*, V, 404.
10 See Warner, *The Wesleyan Movement*, 215.
11 Jackson, *Works of Wesley*, V, 413
12 Jackson, *Works of Wesley*, VI, 104-105, 112.
13 Jackson, *Works of Wesley*, V, 424-433, quotation, 430-431.

14 For sermon passages where the social dimension is obvious in what Wesley calls "true religion," see Jackson, *Works of Wesley*, V, 141, 219, 256, 265, 296-297, 299, 334, 375ff., 381, 465, 498; VI, 112, 498-499; VII, 263, 269, 353. Among Wesley's sermons that have a particularly strong appeal to social action, see Jackson, *Works of Wesley*, VI, 103ff ("Self-Denial"); 124ff ("The Use of Money"); 136ff ("The Good Steward"); 149ff ("Before the Society for the Reformation of Manners"); VII, 1ff, especially 14 ("The Danger of Riches"); 281ff ("Causes of the Inefficacy of Christianity"); 360-362 ("On the Danger of Increasing Riches").

15 Jackson, *Works of Wesley*, VII, 61, 65 (Sermon, "On Zeal").
16 Jackson, *Works of Wesley*, V, 360.

17   Jackson, *Works of Wesley*, VI, 464ff.
18   Jackson, *Works of Wesley*, XIV, 320-321 (Wesley's preface to *The Poetical Works of John and Charles Wesley*). Similar statements are made in his "Sermon on the Mount, Discourse IV." For instance, he states that "Christianity is essentially a social religion; and that to turn it into a solitary one is to destroy it," and a "solitary Christian [is]... little less than a contradiction in terms" (Jackson, *Works of Wesley*, V, 296, 298).
19   Jackson, *Works of Wesley*, VI, 259 (Sermon, "The Mystery of Iniquity").
20   It must be remembered that sociology as a discipline was not yet established. While there were emerging theories, an understanding of the structural issues was not yet fully developed or accepted. Wesley was assessing the ills of society from his understanding of the nature of sin and the individual. His views should be seen in this context rather than assuming the principles and theories of sociology were available to him.
21   Warner, *The Wesleyan Movement*, 138. See also Cooper, "John Wesley: A Study in Theology and Social Ethics."
22   Jackson, *Works of Wesley*, VI, 155 (Sermon, "Before The Society for the Reformation of Manners").
23   S. Paul Schilling, *Methodism and Society in Theological Perspective* (New York: Abingdon, 1960), 61.
24   Jackson, *Works of Wesley*, VI, 155.
25   Jackson, *Works of Wesley*, VI, 253, 255-256 (Sermon, "The Mystery of Iniquity").
26   Jackson, *Works of Wesley*, VI, 284. For a helpful study on Wesley's approach to economics regarding the Christian community, and his own practice, see Theodore W. Jennings, Jr., *Good News to the Poor: John Wesley's Evangelical Economics* (Nashville: Abingdon Press, 1990).
27   Jackson, *Works of Wesley*, VII, 424. The same passage can be found in Wesley's "Earnest Appeal to Men of Reason and Religion" in Jackson, *Works of Wesley*, VIII, 3-4.
28   Jackson, *Works of Wesley*, V, 299.
29   Jackson, *Works of Wesley*, V, 300.
30   Jackson, *Works of Wesley*, VI, 284 (Sermon, "The General Spread of the Gospel").
31   Whaling, *John and Charles Wesley, Selected Writings and Hymns*, 57. It would be an oversimplification to attribute the averting of a revolution to Wesley alone. However, his philosophy of quiet and subtle infiltration with gradual influence did produce a combination and coalescing of factors, not the least of which was the change in values, produced by the revival, of a significant portion of the English masses.
32   Emile Durkheim (1858-1917) was a French sociologist. His theory of "collective representation" opposed and suggested an alternative to the assumed individualistic approach to society.
33   Jackson, *Works of Wesley*, III, 33. This is a journal entry on January 2, 1761, citing his letter to the *London Chronicle*.
34   Jackson, *Works of Wesley*, III, 33-34.
35   Luke Tyerman, *The Life and Times of the Rev. John Wesley, M.A.*, 3 vols. (London: Hodder and Stoughton, 1890), III, 495.

36   Jackson, *Works of Wesley*, I, 251, journal entry for November 27, 1739. Elie Halevy concurred in this description of miners in general [Elie Halevy, *A History of the English People in the Nineteenth Century*, 2nd ed., trans. E. I. Watkins and D.A. Barker, 6 vols., (London: Ernest Benn, 1949), I, 262].

37   Jackson, *Works of Wesley*, I, 251-252.

38   Author's correspondence with Reginald Ward, October 12, 2001.

39   Jackson, *Works of Wesley*, XI, 75-76 (*Thoughts Upon Slavery*).

40   Jackson, *Works of Wesley*, VI, 149-167. Professor Ward describes Wesley's sermon as somewhat "bizarre" because usually the "Pietist movements sought to jack up the religious performance of the elite rather than use the state to chastise the sinners" (personal correspondence, October 12, 2001).

41   Jackson, *Works of Wesley*, II, 446 (journal entry for May 27, 1758).

42   Jackson, *Works of Wesley*, IV, 468 (journal entry for August 18, 1789).

43   Telford, *Letters*, VIII, 276-277 (August 18, 1787).

44   *The Arminian Magazine*, XI (1788), 263-264. This is an open letter, "On the Slave-Trade," from January 1, 1788. The letter was written by Thomas Walker, chairman of the Manchester Antislavery Committee. See complete text of letter in Appendix 1.

45   H. Richard Niebuhr, *The Social Sources of Denominationalism* (New York: Henry Holt & Co., 1929), 66.

46   Niebuhr, *Social Sources*, 67.

47   After the Council of Nicaea (A.D. 325) the empire under Constantine acquiesced to the Arian position, adopting a position that Christ was less than divine. This was in opposition to the decision of Nicaea. Athanasius, the champion of Nicaea, remained steadfast even though he stood "against the world," or, *Athanasius contra mundum*, as Wesley quoted to Wilberforce in his final letter.

48   Telford, *Letters*, VII, 276 (August 18, 1787, to Samuel Hoare).

49   Schilling, *Methodism and Society*, 62-63.

50   In 1790 the *Arminian Magazine*, supported a boycott of articles produced by slaves. See Warner, *The Wesleyan Movement*, 244, citing *The Arminian Magazine*, XIII (1790), 502.

51   Schilling, *Methodism and Society*, 62-63.

52   See Madron, "The Political Thought of John Wesley," 336.

CHAPTER 6, pages 147 to 170
The significance of John Wesley's antislavery influence

1   Edwards, *John Wesley and the Eighteenth Century*, 112. Allen Lamar Cooper gives a very similar, but unreferenced statement: "...there is hardly a person whose influence was more considerable. The name of John Wesley must be included along with Wilberforce, Clarkson, and Granville Sharp" [Cooper, "John Wesley: A Study in Theology and Social Ethics," 208].

2   Richard K. MacMaster, "Thomas Rankin and the American Colonists" (*Proceedings of the Wesley Historical Society*, XXXIX (June 1973), 26-27.

3   See Chapter 3, 49-50.

4   Some interesting manuscript correspondence is housed in the John Rylands

University Library, Manchester. Published letters are in Jackson, *Works of Wesley*, XIII, 123-126 and Telford, *Letters*.

5   Samuel Bradburn, *An Address to the People Called Methodists; Concerning the Wickedness of Encouraging Slavery* (London: G. Paramore, 1792), 19. Bradburn's tract is included in Appendix 3.

6   Thompson, *John Wesley as a Social Reformer*, 63-69.

7   Benezet's letter to Wesley in May 1774 reports Gilbert's death, but also quotes Gilbert's recent account of his own work for and among the slaves. The letter is included in Appendix 1. See also Stiv Jacobsson, *Am I Not a Man and a Brother?* (Uppsala: Almquist and Wiksells, 1972), 276 and Thompson, *Nathaniel Gilbert*, 24.

8   Frank Baker's "The Origins of Methodism in the West Indies, The Story of the Gilbert Family," *London Quarterly and Holborn Review*, vol. 185 (1960) is a helpful and concise introduction to Gilbert and also traces his family. Andrew F. Walls, *Proceedings of the Wesley Historical Society*, XXXIV (June 1964), VI, 151, mentions the chaplaincy of Gilbert's son in Sierra Leone.

9   Richard Watson, *The Religious Instruction of the Slaves in the West India Colonies Advocated and Defended* (London, 1824). The sermon is based on 1 Peter 2:17: "Honour all men."

10   Margaret Hodgen states that without Wesley's influence regarding equality, "emancipation might well have been long delayed" ["The Negro in the Anthropology of John Wesley," *Journal of Negro History*, XIX (July 1934), 323].

11   Roger Anstey's "The Pattern of British Abolitionism" in Christine Bolt and Seymour Drescher, eds., *Anti-Slavery, Religion and Reform: Essays in Memory of Roger Anstey* (Hamden: Archon Books, 1980), 27 [Anstey cites the *Anti-Slavery Reporter*, 61 (June 1830 report of the May meeting)].

12   Anstey, "The Pattern of British Abolitionism" in Bolt, *Anti-Slavery, Religion and Reform*, 26. Anstey lists the following sources for the early nineteenth century Wesleyan position against slavery and its encouraging of petitions: *Wesleyan Methodist Magazine*, 3rd ser., II (July 1823), 461-465; III (January 1824), 49-53; III (October 1824), 618, 687-692; IV (February 1825), 115-119; (November 1825), 628-643; V (February 1826), 121-125; IX (June 1830), 435; IX (September 1830), 608-610; *Minutes of the Wesleyan Methodist Conference* (1825, 1829, 1830); *Anti-Slavery Reporter* (August 20, 1830), 65, 349ff.

13   Representative of this position is Stuart Andrews, *Methodism and Society* (London: Longmans, 1970), 52.

14   Anstey, *The Atlantic Slave Trade*, 240-241. Anstey quotes the *Dictionary of National Biography* that Wesley "was the earliest religious leader of the first rank to join the protest against slavery." Fogel, *Without Consent or Contract*, 212, relates almost the same phrase.

15   Lucius C. Matlack, *The Anti-Slavery Struggle and Triumph in the Methodist Episcopal Church* (New York: Phillips & Hunt, 1881), 242, 245, 95; Lucius C. Matlack, *The History of American Slavery and Methodism from 1780 to 1849* (New York: Wesleyan Book Room Office 1849), 21-23, 111-112.

16   Charles Elliott, *History of the Great Secession from the Methodist Episcopal Church in the Year 1845* (Cincinnati: Swormstedt & Poe, 1855), 31. Some may consider Elliott's description to be an overstatement, however, it demonstrates the extremely

high regard many continued to have for the tract and Wesley's influence through it.

17   Jackson, *Works of Wesley*, II, 531 (journal entry for March 13, 1760).

18   An excellent source on the Clapham Sect is E.M. Howse, *Saints in Politics: The "Clapham Sect" and the Growth of Freedom* (Toronto: University of Toronto Press, 1952).

19   On March 21, 1754 Henry Venn wrote to Wesley: "Very shortly ... I am to be placed in a cure near this city... And as I have often experienced your words to be as thunder to my drowsy soul, I presume, though a stranger, to become a petitioner, begging you would send me a personal charge, to take heed to feed the flock committed to me." Quoted in John Telford, *A Sect That Moved the World* (London: W. Phillips, 1804), 19.

20   Robin Furneaux, *William Wilberforce* (London: Hamish Hamilton Ltd., 1974), 5, 8-10.

21   Part of the house survives, known as Lauriston Cottage. In the late twentieth century it was owned by a Mr. Whitehead, 6 South Side Common, Wimbledon. It was Mr. Whitehead's opinion that this was the yard where the famous conversation with Pitt occurred. During modifications of the house during the twentieth century a signal bell was discovered with the label, "Mr. Pitt's room" (conversation with Mr. Whitehead, June 1980).

22   Robin Furneaux gives a lucid account of Wilberforce's conversion and spiritual pilgrimage (Furneaux, *William Wilberforce*, 32-53). Roger Anstey points out that Wilberforce had been in contact with Newton since 1777, a fact that Furneaux misses (Anstey, *The Atlantic Slave Trade*, 251).

23   Telford quotes Henry Venn, "Mr. Wilberforce has been seen at the [Surrey] chapel, and attends the preaching constantly. Much he has to give up! And what will be the issue, who can say?" (Telford, *A Sect That Moved The World*, 100).

24   Furneaux, *William Wilberforce*, 41, citing Wilberforce's journal entry for June 12, 1786.

25   Jackson, *Works of Wesley*, IV, 445-446 (journal entry for February 24, 1789). Wilberforce's comment for the day was: "I called on John Wesley, — a fine fellow" (Telford, *A Sect That Moved The World*, 107).

26   "The Evangelicals of Hull" (no author cited) in *Proceedings of the Wesley Historical Society*, XII, 130.

27   Richard Butterworth, *Wesley Studies by Various Writers* (London: Charles H. Kelly, n.d. [probably 1903 or 1904]), 190.

28   This point is made by E.M. Hunt, "The North of England Agitation for the Abolition of the Slave Trade, 1780-1800" (M.A. thesis, Manchester University, 1959), ii, 156, 107. Hunt describes the religious motivation of this move indicating that the nonconformists and evangelicals east of the Pennines had nothing financially to gain by the ending of the trade. For them it was simply the Christian thing to do.

29   Furneaux, *William Wilberforce*, 268-271, writes about the closeness of this election. Stuart Andrews states that without the Methodists Wilberforce may have lost the election (Andrews, *Methodism and Society*, 52). Although this may be true, it is difficult to verify.

30   See Sweetland, "A Critical Study of John Wesley as Practical Thinker and Reformer," 111.

31   In his "Calm Address to Our American Colonies" he stated: "No governments under heaven are so despotic as the republican; no subjects are governed in so arbitrary a manner as those of a commonwealth," and "Republics show no mercy" (Jackson, *Works of Wesley*, XI, 87). His most direct statements about democracy can be found in his "Thoughts Concerning the Origin of Power," "Thoughts Upon Liberty" and "Some Observations on Liberty" (Jackson, *Works of Wesley*, XI, 46ff, 34ff, 90ff).

32   See Chapter 3 where Wesley's view of government is rooted in his view of human nature, especially depravity. As indicated on page 50, Wesley believed that in a constitutional monarchy the constitution held the monarch and his depravity in check and the monarch enforced the constitution and law, holding the people and their depravity in check.

33   Jackson, *Works of Wesley*, XI, 45 ("Thoughts Upon Liberty"). See also "Free Thoughts On Public Affairs" in Jackson, *Works of Wesley*, XI, 33.

34   Jackson, *Works of Wesley*, VII, 145.

35   Warner, *The Wesleyan Movement*, 364-365.

36   Warner, *The Wesleyan Movement*, 276-277. Warner states that Wesleyanism was "liberal in its tendencies" but "combated the particular doctrines advanced by early radicals." He explains: "its liberalism was unlabeled, and therein lay its power, for, unperceived, it spread a germinating influence. Priestly, the radical, gauged accurately what but few others saw when he predicted that Wesleyan Methodism would accomplish far more than its leaders could foresee, even while clothed in its conservative disguise" (277).

37   Bernard Semmel, *The Methodist Revolution* (London: Heineman, 1973), 195 and also John Richard Green, *A Short History of the English People* (London: Macmillan, 1885). Green makes the point, "No man ever stood at the head of a great revolution whose temper was so anti-revolutionary" (Green, *A Short History*, 772).

38   "Methodism; The French Revolution: The Industrial Revolution," no author cited, from *Proceedings of the Wesley Historical Society*, XXV, 219-220.

39   R.W. Dale represents the nineteenth century view that Methodism was primarily responsible for the decline of Calvinism among evangelical Nonconformists. He states, "John Wesley rendered us immense service by the vigour with which he asserted the moral freedom of man against the Calvinistic doctrine of the Divine decrees, and the universality of the Atonement as against the Calvinistic doctrine which limited the relations of the death of Christ to the elect" [R.W. Dale, *The Evangelical Revival and Other Sermons* (London: Hodder and Stoughton, 1880), 21-22]. See also Alfred H. Pask, "The Influence of Arminius on John Wesley," *London Quarterly and Holborn Review*, vol. 185 (1960), especially 259. Duncan Rice speaks of the influence evangelicals had on the English abolitionists through the "leveling impact of Wesley's thought within the Church of England" [C. Duncan Rice, *The Rise and Fall of Black Slavery* (London and Basingstoke: Macmillan, 1975), 161].

40   Anstey, "The Pattern of British Abolitionism" in Bolt, *Anti-Slavery, Religion and Reform*, 20. Anstey also commented that "the evangelical was likely to be a formidable force if he turned to political action against the slave trade" (22) and that is precisely what happened even more in the years leading to the 1833 victory of British emancipation, when Wesley's message had been assimilated across Britain.

41 Anstey, *The Atlantic Slave Trade*, 94-95.

42 The growing trend of Arminianism continued and can be seen even more clearly in attitudes in America in the early nineteenth century. Anne Loveland relates that religious leaders of that period, some of whom were followers of Jonathan Edwards "unwittingly adopted certain humanistic, Arminian doctrines of their opponents." The change is demonstrated in the shift from assuming human inability to asserting human ability and moving from a piety that focused on God alone to a piety that included benevolence to humanity [Anne C. Loveland, "Evangelicalism and 'Immediate Emancipation' in American Antislavery Thought," *Journal of Southern History*, XXXII (May 1966), 175-176]. The idea of piety including benevolence is certainly consistent with Wesley's thought, and some may consider it one of his major legacies.

43 A good example is Henry Venn's 1789 letter to his daughter in which he took issue with Wesley on perfection. He had fallen into the common misunderstanding that Wesley meant absolute or "sinless" perfection. See Telford, *A Sect That Moved the World*, 56-58. This was the common misunderstanding of Wesley's opponents.

44 Warner concurs, stating that the "unique theme of every sermon [by Wesley was] the immediate moral transformation of character, authenticated not by a remotely realized salvation, but by the discernible evidences of social conduct" (Warner, *The Wesleyan Movement*, 137; see also 58-59).

45 Curtin, *The Image of Africa*, 54.

46 William Wilberforce (*Practical View*, vii), quoted in Anstey, *The Atlantic Slave Trade*, 163; Jackson, *Works of Wesley*, XI, 418 ("Plain Account of Christian Perfection"). A similar statement occurs in Wesley's sermon, "The Way to the Kingdom," where he describes loving one's neighbour with an "invariable thirst after his happiness" (Jackson, *Works of Wesley*, V, 79).

47 For a closer examination of Sharp's hermeneutic, especially in his tracts, "The Just Limitation of Slavery in the Laws of God" (1776) and "The Law of Liberty" (1776), see Brendlinger, *Views of Evangelicals on Slavery and Race*, 129-137.

48 Anstey, *The Atlantic Slave Trade*, 189-90.

49 Anstey, *The Atlantic Slave Trade*, 96ff.

50 Fogel, *Without Consent or Contract*, 209. For the following information on the relationship of popular opinion to the final passage of the Emancipation Act in 1833 I am indebted to Robert Fogel. His chapter on the British Campaign (chapter 7) is concise but comprehensive and his appropriation of statistical information gives the necessary substance to my argument of the impact of Wesley's influence.

51 Fogel indicates that "politics was no longer confined to Parliament" once the "new public" "emerged as a political force" (Fogel, *Without Consent or Contract*, 209).

52 Fogel, *Without Consent or Contract*, 212.

53 Seymour Drescher, *From Slavery to Freedom: Comparative Studies in the Rise and Fall of Atlantic Slavery* (New York: New York University Press, 1999), 49.

54 Part of the appeal reads: "It is the opinion, not only of the Manchester Subscribers, but of the London Committee, who stand first in this cause, that applications to Parliament, from different parts of the kingdom, representing the nature of the grievance, and praying redress, will prove most effectual in tending to remove

the causes of offence. The intention of the present Address, is to invite you to join with them and us in this measure [...]" (*The Arminian Magazine*, XI (May 1788), 208-209). Read the complete letter in Appendix 1.

55 Seymour Drescher, "Two Variants of Anti-Slavery: Religious Organization and Social Mobilization in Britain and France, 1780-1870" in Bolt and Drescher, *Anti-Slavery, Religion and Reform*, 56.

56 Fogel, *Without Consent or Contract*, 217.

57 Fogel, *Without Consent or Contract*, 225.

58 Fogel, *Without Consent or Contract*, 225-226.

59 Fogel, *Without Consent or Contract*, 219.

60 Anstey, "The Pattern of British Abolitionism" in Bolt and Drescher, *Anti-Slavery, Religion and Reform*, 28. Anstey cites the Brougham MSS 10544, Macaulay to Brougham, May 13, 1833.

61 Fogel, *Without Consent or Contract*, 227. Anstey, "The Pattern of British Abolitionism" in Bolt and Drescher, *Anti-Slavery, Religion and Reform*, 28. Anstey indicates that this resulted in a bloc of 140-200 candidates returning to office in 1832.

62 Anstey, "The Pattern of British Abolitionism" in Bolt and Drescher, *Anti-Slavery, Religion and Reform*, 29-30.

63 Fogel, *Without Consent or Contract*, 229-230.

64 Fogel states that Prime Minister Grey was referring "especially to the Methodists" when he "spoke of needing to cement an alliance with 'the real and efficient mass of public opinion'" (Fogel, *Without Consent or Contract*, 230).

65 Fogel, *Without Consent or Contract*, 230. The Methodists were seen by the Grey government as the means to counter and defeat the radicals who were a threat to the Grey government.

66 Fogel, *Without Consent or Contract*, 228. The bill was signed by the King on August 28, 1833.

67 Fogel points out that the actual cost to Britain was more than double the £20 million because of the increased cost of sugar in the amount of about £21 million (Fogel, *Without Consent or Contract*, 229).

68 Fogel, *Without Consent or Contract*, 231.

69 Drescher, *From Slavery to Freedom* 37.

70 Drescher, *From Slavery to Freedom*, 38. Graph used by the permission of Seymour Drescher and New York University Press.

71 Drescher, *From Slavery to Freedom*, 40. These figures are based on Drescher's chart.

72 Reginald Ward notes that extra-parliamentary pressure was not a consistently successful factor and except for the first decade of the Reformed system, Parliament was "extraordinarily resistant to pressure from the outside." However, "the abolition of slavery was carried through in the brief period when there was a sympathetic government with a majority to enable it to act" (personal correspondence, October 12, 2001). Ward's position attributes the success of abolition less to outside pressure on Parliament than does Fogel. He sees it more as the coalescing of numerous factors. My position sees Wesley as at least partly related to those factors. Fogel's statistical analysis reflects the collective role of individuals and bolsters my thesis of Wesley's significance.

73   Anstey, "The Pattern of British Abolitionism" in Bolt and Drescher, *Anti-Slavery, Religion and Reform*, 36.
74   Fogel, *Without Consent or Contract*, 205.
75   Jackson, *Works of Wesley*, V, 274, 303 ("Sermon on the Mount" Discourses II and IV, respectively).
76   Jackson, *Works of Wesley*, XI, 79 (*Thoughts Upon Slavery*).

EPILOGUE, pages 171 to 173

1   In the early 1820s Wilberforce had passed the leadership of the cause to Thomas Fowell Buxton (Fogel, *Without Consent or Contract*, 219).
2   Telford, *Letters*, VIII, 265 (letter to Wilberforce, February 24, 1791): "Go on, in the name of God and in the power of His might, till even American slavery (the vilest that ever saw the sun) shall vanish away before it."
3   Irv Brendlinger, Visiting Fellow lecture, "Christians and the Clash of Values: Whitefield, Wesley and Benezet on Slavery," University of Edinburgh, New College, March 15, 2001.
4   Parker Palmer, *Let Your Life Speak* (San Francisco: Jossey-Bass Inc., 2000), 76.
5   Palmer, *Let Your Life Speak*, 76.
6   Eric Williams was a former Prime Minister of Trinidad and author of *Capitalism and Slavery*. His book appeared in 1944 and was the first significant threat to the long held romantic assumption that the overthrow of slavery was motivated by magnanimous human altruism. His position was that slavery ended not because of human good will, but only when it was no longer a viable economic institution. This view was largely unchallenged until the solid work of Roger Anstey, and others in the 1970s, examined the fiscal realities. Those facts coupled with the lives and actions of individuals such as those mentioned in this study (Wesley, Benezet, Wilberforce and others), reflect the greater truth of Havel's belief that human history is affected by the non-material, the idea. These lives also demonstrate Anstey's counter to Williams that beneficence through human agency, not materialism, was the causative factor. See Anstey, *The Atlantic Slave Trade*, passim.
7   Jackson, *Works of Wesley*, XI, 79 (*Thoughts Upon Slavery*).

APPENDIX 1, pages 175 to 192
A sampling of original source material

1   Extract from the Deposition of Little Ephraim Robin-John and Ancona Robin Robin-John of Old Town, Old Calabar, on the coast of Africa. In the Court of King's Bench [*The Arminian Magazine*, VI (1783), 151-153, 211-212].
2   *The Arminian Magazine*, X (1787).
3   John Wesley, *Thoughts on Slavery*, published in 1774; reprinted with considerable additions by Anthony Benezet (Philadelphia: Hugh Gaine, Robert Bell, & John Dunlap, 1774).
4   "A Treatise upon the Trade from Great-Britain to Africa, etc.," by an African Merchant (London, 1772), deals with Anthony Benezet in Appendix D.

5   See Anthony Benezet's letter to Benjamin Franklin (April 27, 1772) in Brendlinger, *To Be Silent*, 62, and his letter to Richard Shackleton (June 6, 1772) in Brookes, *Friend Anthony Benezet*, 293.
6   Telford, *Letters*, VIII, 275.
7   *The Arminian Magazine*, XI (1788); located in the John Rylands University Library, Manchester. Later the same year, the July and August issues of *The Arminian Magazine* contained "A Summary View of the Slave Trade." It was a seven-page article based on material from Benezet and Wesley's *Thoughts Upon Slavery*.
8   *The Arminian Magazine*, XI (1788), 558-560 (October), 612-616 (November); Wesley's editorial footnote is on 615.
9   Wesley's footnote: "Author of the Tragedy of Oroonoko." [Reference is being made to Aphra Behn.]
10   Wesley's footnote: "Besides many valuable productions of the soil, cloths and carpets of exquisite manufacture are brought from the coast of Guinea."
11   This refers to followers of William Penn (Quakers). Wesley adds the following footnote: "Not so. Vast multitudes in Great Britain and Ireland are, at present, as great enemies to Slavery as ever the Quakers were."

APPENDIX 2, pages 193 to 199
Not only the slave, but wherever Jesus showed his face in the form of human need

1   This essay by the author is included to further develop the theme of Wesley's understanding of the social aspect of Christianity and to show how that extended to *many* aspects of his ministry, not just the antislavery movement.
2   Jackson, *Works of Wesley*, VI, 259 (Sermon, "The Mystery of Iniquity").
3   Telford, *Letters*, VI, 230 (September 1776).
4   Jackson, *Works of Wesley*, VII, 21 (Sermon, "On Dress").
5   Jackson, *Works of Wesley*, VII, 36 (Sermon, "The More Excellent Way").
6   Eric McCoy North, *Early Methodist Philanthropy* (New York: Privately Published, 1914), 122.
7   Telford, *Letters*, V, 108-109 (October 6, 1768).
8   Jackson, *Works of Wesley*, I, 9-11 (Journal).
9   Jackson, *Works of Wesley*, I, 309.
10   Warner, *The Wesleyan Movement*, 219.
11   Warner, *The Wesleyan Movement*, 219.
12   North, *Early Methodist Philanthropy*, 67-68.
13   Jackson, *Works of Wesley*, VIII, 267 ("A Plain Account of the People Called Methodists").
14   North, *Early Methodist Philanthropy*, 76-81.
15   Jackson, *Works of Wesley*, VIII, 265-6. See also North, *Early Methodist Philanthropy*, 83-88.
16   Jackson, *Works of Wesley*, VIII, 263.
17   William C. Dowling, "Wesley and Social Care" in *Proceedings of the Wesley Historical Society*, XXXVI (June 1968), 131.
18   Jackson, *Works of Wesley*, VIII, 264.

19 Thompson, *John Wesley as a Social Reformer*, 16.
20 Jackson, *Works of Wesley*, VIII, 264-265.
21 Jackson, *Works of Wesley*, II, 59 (Journal, June 6, 1747).
22 North, *Early Methodist Philanthropy*, 42.
23 I discovered a copy of Wesley's medical book in 2000, in the collection of Anthony Benezet's personal books archived at Haverford College.
24 Telford, *Letters*, VI, 225-226 (July 20, 1776).
25 Jackson, *Works of Wesley*, VIII, 271 ("General Rules of the United Societies").
26 Tyerman, *The Life and Times of the John Wesley*, I, 337.

APPENDIX 3, pages 201 to 223
An Address to the People called Methodists; Concerning the Wickedness of Encouraging Slavery

1 Samuel Bradburn, *An Address to the People Called Methodists; Concerning the Wickedness of Encouraging Slavery* (London: G. Paramore, 1792).

2 Bradburn's footnote reads:

"That SLAVE-DEALER is a proper rendering of the Apostle's word, ANDRAPODISTHS, is plain from the best Lexicographers and Critics I forbear to heap up testimonies, and shall only cite a few to prove my assertion. Thus Scapula: *Qui liberum hominem in servitutem redigit: qui furatur hominem é libero statu suo.* – He who reduces a freeman into slavery: he who steals a man from his free state.

Thus also Parkhurst: A man-stealer, a kid-napper, one who steals men to make them slaves, or sell them into slavery.

So Suidas: The barbarians violate covenants, reducing men openly into slavery. *Edit. Kuster. sub voce Andrapodizw*.

See likewise Poole: *Hominum fures, qui vel servos, vel liberos abdu cunt, retinent, vendunt, vel emunt, - qui vel fraude, vel aperta vi, homines suffurantur ut pro mancipiis vendant; &c. Synop. Critic. in loc.* – Stealers of men, who take away either servants or freemen, detain, sell, or buy them. – Those who either by fraud, or by open violence, steal men that they may sell them for slaves, &c.

In plain English, Slave-Dealers of every description."

select bibliography

The Arminian Magazine
Andrews, Stuart. *Methodism and Society*. London: Longmans, 1970.
Anstey, Roger. *The Atlantic Slave Trade and British Abolition 1760-1810*. London: Macmillan Press Ltd, 1975.
Anstey, Roger. "The Pattern of British Abolitionism in the Eighteenth and Nineteenth Centuries" in Christine Bolt and Seymour Drescher, eds. *Anti-Slavery, Religion and Reform: Essays in Memory of Roger Anstey*. Hamden: Archon Books, 1980.
Ayling, Stanley. *John Wesley*. London: Collins, 1979.
Baker, Frank. "The Origins, Character and Influence of John Wesley's *Thoughts Upon Slavery*" in *Methodist History*, XXII, January 1984.
Baker, Frank. *From Wesley to Asbury*. Durham, NC: Duke University Press, 1976.
Benezet, Anthony. *Some Historical Account of Guinea*. Philadelphia: Joseph Cruikshank, 1771.
Brendlinger, Irv. *To Be Silent…Would be Criminal: The Antislavery Influence and Writings of Anthony Benezet*. Lanham, Maryland: The Scarecrow Press, Inc., 2006.
Brendlinger, Irv. "Wesley, Whitefield, A Philadelphia Quaker, and Slavery" in *Wesleyan Theological Journal*. Fall 2001.
Brendlinger, Irv. "A Study of the Views of Major Eighteenth Century Evangelicals on Slavery and Race, With Special Reference to John Wesley." Ph.D. thesis, Edinburgh University, 1982.
Brendlinger, Irv. "Christans and the Clash of Values; Whitefield, Wesley and Benezet on Slavery." Visiting Fellow Lecture. University of Edinburgh, New College, March 15, 2001.

Brookes, George S. *Friend Anthony Benezet*. Philadelphia: University of Pennsylvania Press, 1937.

Cannon, William R. *The Theology of John Wesley*. New York, Nashville: Abingdon, 1946.

Cell, George Croft. *The Rediscovery of John Wesley*. New York: Henry Holt, 1935.

Chesterton, Gilbert K. *Orthodoxy*. Westport, CT: Greenwood Press, 1974.

Curnock, Nehemiah, ed. *The Journal of the Rev. John Wesley, A.M.* 8 vols. London: Epworth Press, 1938.

Curtin, Philip D. *The Image of Africa, British Ideas and Action, 1780-1850*. Madison: The University of Wisconsin Press, 1964.

Dallimore, Arnold. *George Whitefield*. 2 vols. Edinburgh: Banner of Truth Trust, 1980.

Davis, David Brion. *The Problem of Slavery in the Age of Revolution, 1770-1823*. Ithaca: Cornell University Press, 1975.

Davis, David Brion. *The Problem of Slavery in Western Culture*. Ithaca: Cornell University Press, 1966.

Douglass, Frederick. *Narrative of the Life of Frederick Douglass*. Boston: The Anti-Slavery Office, 1845 (republished Mineola, NY: Dover Publications Inc., 1995).

Drescher, Seymour. *From Slavery to Freedom: Comparative Studies in the Rise and Fall of Atlantic Slavery*. New York: New York University Press, 1999.

Drescher, Seymour. "Two Variants of Anti-Slavery: Religious Organization and Social Mobilization in Britain and France, 1780-1870" in Christine Bolt and Seymour Drescher, eds. *Anti-Slavery, Religion and Reform: Essays in Memory of Roger Anstey*. Hamden: Archon Books, 1980.

Edwards, Maldwyn. *John Wesley and the Eighteenth Century*. London: George Allen & Unwin, 1933.

Elliot, Charles. *History of the Great Secession from the Methodist Episcopal Church in the Year 1845*. Cincinnati: Swormstedt & Poe, 1855.

Flanders, Ralph Betts. *Plantation Slavery in Georgia*. Cos Cob, CT: John E. Edwards Press, 1967.

Fogel, Robert William. *Without Consent or Contract: The Rise and Fall of American Slavery*. New York: Norton, 1989.

Furneaux, Robin. *William Wilberforce*. London: Hamish Hamilton Ltd., 1974.

Gossett, Thomas F. *Race: The History of an Idea in America*. New York: Schocken, 1965.

Howse, E.M. *Saints in Politics: The "Clapham Sect" and the Growth of Freedom*. Toronto: University of Toronto Press, 1952.

Hunt, E.M. "The North of England Agitation for the Abolition of the Slave Trade, 1780-1800." M.A. thesis, Manchester University, 1959.

Jakobsson, Stiv. *Am I Not a Man and a Brother?* Uppsala: Alquist & Wiksells, 1972.

Jennings, Theodore W., Jr. *Good News to the Poor: John Wesley's Evangelical Economics*. Nashville: Abingdon Press, 1990.

Maddox, Randy L. *Responsible Grace: John Wesley's Practical Theology*. Nashville: Kingswood, 1994.

Matlack, Lucius C. *The History of American Slavery and Methodism from 1780 to 1849*. New York: Wesleyan Book Room Office, 1849.

Newton, John. *The Works of the Rev. John Newton.* Vol. V. London, 1816.
Palmer, Parker. *Let Your Life Speak.* San Francisco: Jossey-Bass Inc., 2000.
Peters, John L. *Christian Perfection and American Methodism.* Nashville: Abingdon, 1956.
Proceedings of the Wesley Historical Society
Rice, C. Duncan. *The Rise and Fall of Black Slavery.* London: Macmillan, 1975.
Rupp, Gordon. *Principalities and Powers.* London: Epworth Press, 1952.
Schilling, S. Paul. *Methodism and Society in Theological Perspective.* New York: Abingdon, 1960.
Semmel, Bernard. *The Methodist Revolution.* London: Heineman, 1973.
Shyllon, Folarin. *James Ramsay, The Unknown Abolitionist.* Edinburgh: Canongate Publishing, 1977.
Smith, Warren Thomas. *John Wesley and Slavery.* Nashville: Abingdon Press, 1986.
Thompson, Edgar. *Nathaniel Gilbert, Lawyer and Evangelist.* London: Epworth Press, 1960.
Tuttle, Robert G. *John Wesley: His Life and Theology.* Grand Rapids: Zondervan, 1978.
Tyerman, Luke. *The Life and Times of the Rev. John Wesley, M.A.* 3 vols. London: Hodder and Stoughton, 1890.
Vickers, John. *Thomas Coke, Apostle of Methodism.* London: Epworth Press, 1969.
Warner, Wellman Joel. *The Wesleyan Movement in the Industrial Revolution.* London: Longmans, Green & Co., 1930.
Wesley, Charles. *The Journal of the Rev. Charles Wesley, M.A.* 2 vols. Edited by Thomas Jackson. London: Wesleyan Methodist Book Room, 1849.
Wesley, John. *Explanatory Notes Upon the New Testament.* London: William Bowyer, 1765.
Wesley, John. *The Letters of the Rev. John Wesley, A.M.* 8 vols. Edited by John Telford. London: The Epworth Press, 1931.
Wesley, John. *The Works of John Wesley.* 3rd ed., 14 vols. Edited by Thomas Jackson. London: Wesleyan Conference Office, 1872.
Wesley, John. *The Works of John Wesley.* 26 vols. (various editors). Nashville: Abingdon Press, 1984-2003.
Wesley, John, ed. "A Summary View of the Slave Trade" in *The Arminian Magazine.* XI, August 1788, 379-381, 437-440.
Williams, Colin W. *John Wesley's Theology Today.* London: Epworth Press, 1960.
Williams, Eric. *Capitalism and Slavery.* London: Andre Deutsch, 1964.
Wood, Betty. *Slavery in Colonial Georgia, 1730-1775.* Athens: University of Georgia Press, 1984.
Wood, Lawrence W. *Pentecostal Grace.* Wilmore, Kentucky: Francis Asbury, 1980.

index

abolition, 53-54, 63, 167, 182, 205, 215
Act of Assembly, 33
Africa, Africans, 22, 24, 29, 33, 34, 35, 39, 53, 56, 58, 64-66, 69, 82, 90, 118-119, 125, 126, 171, 183, 216
A'Kempis, Thomas, 6
Antigua, 19, 36, 149-150, 166, 180
Antoninus, Marcus, 70
Anstey, Roger, 161, 163, 169
Arminianism, Arminius, 5, 84-85, 156, 159-161
Asbury, Francis, 58-59, 61-62, 148
Asia, 34
Athanasius, 78
Athanasius contra mundum, 42
Augustine, 78, 84
Ayling, Stanley, 30
Baker, Frank, 26
Baltimore, 35, 59
Barbados, 16, 207
Baxter, J., 36
Behn, Aphra, 13
Benezet, Anthony, 19-23, 24, 25, 30-33, 38, 46, 56, 63, 65, 89, 99, 150, 151, 156, 162, 178-182, 182
Bennett, John, 4
Bethesda, 57
Black Harry, 59
Blackstone, William, 26, 48

Böhler, Peter, 8
Bradburn, Betsy, 149
Bradburn, Samuel, 149, 201-223
Bristol, 22, 88, 139, 177, 178, 196
Bunting, Jabez, 150
Burton, Dr. John, 7
Calvinism, 5, 76, 160
Castlereagh, Viscount, 165
Charleston, 14, 16
Clapham Sect, 153, 166
Clark, Mr., 32
Clarkson, Thomas, 19, 36, 37, 41, 63, 65, 143, 147, 156, 161, 162, 171, 182, 209
Coke, Thomas, 36, 58-59, 148
constitutional monarchy, 50, 81
Continental Congress, 148
Cromwell, Oliver, 90
Curnock, Nehemiah, 9
Curtin, Philip, 65
Dagge, Abel, 139-140
Davies, Rupert, 38
Davies, Samuel, 18
Dilwyn, William, 178
Doddridge, Philip, 154
Douglass, Frederick, 60
Drogheda, 90
Dublin, 24
Durkheim, Emile, 138
Edgar, 176

Edwards, Jonathan, 93
Edwards, Maldwyn, 147
Elliott, Charles, 151
emancipation, 36, 59, 167
Emancipation Act, 167, 171
Ethiopians, 57
Enlightenment, 27
Evangelical Awakening, xvi, 6
Franklin, Benjamin, 19
Frederica, 18
Fogel, Robert, xv, 164, 165, 167, 169
Fothergill, John, 32, 47
Fuller, Thomas, 39
Georgia, 5, 6, 8, 11, 14, 30, 52, 57-58, 67, 99, 159
grace, 74-75, 79-80, 83-97, 113, 117, 119, 126, 128
Gilbert, Nathaniel, 19, 29, 39, 149-150, 180
Gilbert, Nathaniel (son), 150
Godwyn, Morgan, 16, 65
Grey, Prime Minister, 167
Greyhound, 22, 177
Gruber, Jacob, 149
Hargrave, Francis, 26
Harris, Raymund, 54
Havel, Vaclav, 172
Hawes, William, 198
Holy Club, 2, 7, 14, 159, 194
House of Commons, 41
House of Lords, 81
Howard, John, 140
Hume, 26, 110
Hutcheson, Francis, 88
Indian Queen, 176
Industrial Revolution, 1, 144
Ireland, 36, 39
James Somerset case of 1772, 20, 22, 32
Jennings, Dr., 18
John Rylands University Library, xii, 74
Johnson, Samuel, 30-31
Justinian, 48
Kingswood, 138, 140, 157, 196
Kinlaw, Dennis, xi

Knox, Robert, 65
Law, William, 6
Liverpool, 34, 35, 88
London Antislavery Society, 38
Long, Edward, 65
Luther, Martin, 9
Macaulay, Zachary, 166
Maddox, Randy, 87, 113, 115, 126
Mahometan (muslim), 21, 52, 70
Manchester, 38, 74, 149, 165, 184
Mansfield, Lord, 22, 36, 177
Maryland, 149
Matthews, Richard, 150
Methodist Conference, 36, 59
Methodist Societies, Methodism, 24, 35, 58-59, 61, 121, 130, 138, 141, 148, 150-152, 154-155, 159, 166, 169, 200
Milner, Isaac, 153
monogenesis, 80
Montesquieu, Charles de, 80
Moore, Henry, 39, 195
Moravians, 7, 8, 9, 162
More, Hannah, 38, 39, 185-192
Morgan, William, 2
Mosely, John, 34, 181
Murray, Grace, 4
Native Americans, 7, 14, 66, 67
Newcastle, 196
Newgate, 139
Newton, John, xiv, 22, 46, 56, 152, 154
Niebuhr, Richard, 144
North Carolina, 33, 180
Nova Scotia, 59, 69
Oglethorpe, General James, 7, 14, 29
Oxford, 2, 7, 105, 194
Paynter, Samuel, 39
Pelagianism, 84
Penn, William, 39
Pitt, William, 153, 154, 156
planter class, 41, 51, 52, 141, 203
polygenesis, 80
predestination, 83, 89
Prior, Matthew, 67
Purrysburg, 14, 17
Quakers, 20, 21, 39, 47, 62, 63, 104

Quincy, Rev., 7, 14
Ramsay, James, 24, 45-46, 56, 163
Rankin, Thomas, 148, 151
Robin-John, Amboe, 175, 176
Robin-John, Ancona Robin, 21, 22, 36, 175-178
Robin-John, Little Ephraim, 21, 22, 35, 175-178
Rogers, Carl, 74
Ross, Andrew, iii
Rousseau, Jean-Jacques, 26, 67, 110, 129, 135
Rush, Benjamin, 19, 24, 28, 39
Scottish Highlands, 58, 69
Senegal, 179
Sharp, Granville, 19-23, 26-28, 30-33, 36, 46, 53, 63, 147, 151, 156, 162, 169, 182
Sierra Leone, 150
sociology, 1
Society for the Abolition of the Slave Trade (Abolition Committee), 36, 37, 41, 53, 62, 143-144, 150
Society for the Propagation of the Gospel in Foreign Parts (SPG), 7, 14, 90
Society for the Reformation of Manners, 142
sola fide, 110
Somerset, James, 20, 22, 32
South Carolina, 16, 17, 58, 61, 180
Southerne, Thomas, 13
Strong, Jonathan, 20
Tailfer, Dr., 14
Taney, Roger, 149
Taylor, Jeremy, 6
theories justifying slavery, 18, 25, 45, 47-48, 55, 57-59, 64-65, 80, 82
Thirty-Nine Articles, 84, 126
Thompson, Rev. (South Carolina), 16
Thompson, William, 37
Truro, 142
Tuttle, Robert G., iii
University of Edinburgh, xii, 171
Vassa, Gustavus, 42
Venn, Henry, 153, 154, 166

Virginia, 22, 33, 177, 180
Voltaire, 26, 110, 135
Walker, Thomas, 38, 183-184
Walls, Andrew, iii, xi
Wandsworth, 19, 149
War for Independence, 34
Warrender, William, 36, 58, 166
Ward, W. Reginald, iii, xi, 10
Warner, W.J., 159
Washington, George, 24, 151
Watson, Richard, 150
Wesley, Charles, 3, 4, 8, 9, 14-18, 22, 25, 39, 154, 164, 177

Wesley, John
   Aldersgate experience, 6, 8-11, 84, 105
   antislavery writings, 21-26, 39, 48, 49, 53, 87, 143
   books that influenced him, 6, 13, 16, 39, 70
   Christology, 79, 126
   correspondence, 18, 26-29, 36-37, 47, 53, 149, 152, 182-183
   death of, 42, 171
   discouragement, 8, 11
   doctrine of creation, 126-127
   doctrine of free will, 100
   doctrine of original sin and human depravity, xiv, 18, 74-83, 91-98, 107, 118
   doctrine of prevenient grace, 83-97
   doctrine of sanctification, justification, 6, 101-104, 106-107, 112-114, 119-120
   education, 2
   evangelism, 69, 71, 109
   faith, 10
   family background, xvi, 2
   first Christian leader to challenge slavery, xii, 12
   firsthand exposure to slavery, 7, 14-18, 33
   hermeneutic of Scripture, 54, 64, 111, 130
   his dominant message (love of God

and neighbour), 11, 55, 64, 69, 89, 102, 105-106, 108-109, 115-121, 126, 130, 132, 136-137, 157, 162, 170, 193
"holiness movement," xvi
Holy Club, 2, 7, 14, 159, 194
influence assumed, xv, 147
initial involvement in antislavery cause, xiii, xvii, 17, 23, 63, 73, 120
last letter (to Wilberforce), xvii, 42, 159
leadership, 61, 63, 159, 169
legacy, xvii
Methodism, xvi, 4, 58, 121, 141, 155, 158-159, 165, 169
  open air preaching, 4
ordination as deacon, 6
preaching, 37, 55, 66, 134, 140
question of plagarism, 30-33
relationship and influence of Benezet and Sharp, 19-23, 26-30, 178-182
relationship with Whitefield, xiv, 3-6
romance, 4, 7
support for legislative means of ending slavery, 143
support for Negro schools, 18, 67
time in America, 5-8, 11, 14-18, 67
theological differences with Whitefield, 5, 52, 56-57, 89
theological distinctives, 73, 75, 77, 84, 89, 100, 107, 128, 159-160, 164
theological basis for social action, xiii, 3, 47, 55, 121, 135, 138, 139-141, 146, 157, 165, 170, 193, 199
view of Christian perfection, 98, 100-115, 161-162
view of God's sovereignty, 97
view of liberty, equality and rights, 49, 68, 71, 75, 77, 80, 99, 125, 157-158
view of money, stewardship, 51, 121-125, 194-199
witnessing to slaves, 16-17

Wesley, Sarah, 154
Wesleyan Conference, 155, 166
Wesleyan Methodist Church, 60
Wesleyan Methodist Missionary Society, 150
West Indies, 22, 24, 36, 52, 58, 149, 165-166, 180, 202-203, 208
Wheatley, Phillis, 35

Whitefield, George
  contribution to Methodism, 5-6
  election, 89
  influence, 139-140, 152-153, 196
  letter about slavery, 57
  position on slavery, 5, 26, 52, 57
  predestination, 5, 89
  relationship with Wesley, xiv, 3-6, 56, 99

Wilberforce, William, 6, 11, 24, 41, 42, 65, 144-145, 147, 152-156, 159, 161, 162, 165-166, 171, 206
Wilkes, John, 164
Williams, Colin, 100
Williams, Eric, 162, 173
Williams, Richard, 35
Winchester, Mr., 41

Works of John Wesley

A Plain Account of Christian Perfection, 105, 112
A Seasonable Address to The More Serious Part of the Inhabitants of Great Britain, 34
"A Summary View of the Slave Trade," 38
"At the Foundation of City-Road Chapel," 136
Calm Address to the American Colonies, 30, 34, 49, 149
"Causes of the Inefficacy of Christianity," 122
Explanatory Notes Upon the New Testament, 18, 54
"Free Grace," 89

"In What Sense We Are to Leave the World," 134
"On Living Without God," 70
"On The New Birth," 101
"On Working Out Our Own Salvation," 96
"On Worldly Folly," 122
Original Sin, 18
Primitive Physick: An Easy and Natural Method of Curing Most Diseases, 198
Serious Address To The People of England, With Regards To The State Of The Nation, 35
The Cirumcision of the Heart, 105
The Dignity of Human Nature, 74
"The General Spread of the Gospel," 136
"The Resolutions of the Society for the Purpose of Effecting the Abolition of the Slave Trade," 38, 165
"The Scripture Way of Salvation," 102
Thoughts Upon Slavery, xvi, 23, 25, 28, 33, 36, 38, 48, 55, 61, 69, 88-89, 143, 151, 178, 183

Other works

A Caution and Warning to Great Britain, 20
A Representation of the Injustice and Dangerous Tendency of Tolerating Slavery ... in England, 20, 26
A Short Account of that Part of Africa Inhabited by Negroes, 20, 26, 56
An Address to the People Called Methodists; Concerning the Wickedness of Encouraging Slavery, 149, 201-223
Capitalism and Slavery, 162
Christian Perfection, 6
Imitation of Christ, 6
Narrative of the Life of Frederick Douglass, 60
Notes on Isaiah, 201
"On the Slave Trade," 38, 39
Oroonoko, 13, 39
Rule and Exercises of Holy Living and Dying, 6
Solomon, 67
Some Historial Account of Guinea, 20, 23, 25, 179
Spirit of Laws, 80
Taxation No Tyranny, 30
The History of Jamaica, 65
The Negro's and Indian's Advocate, suing for their admission into the church, 16
The Races of Man, 65
The Rise and Progress of Religion in the Soul, 154
Trade from Great Britain to Africa, 179

Periodicals

Arminian Magazine, 35, 38, 53, 61, 143, 165
Evening Post, 198-199
General Post, 35
Gentleman's Magazine, 24
Monthly Review, 24, 33
Williamsburg Gazette, 33, 181
Zion's Herald, 151
Zion's Watchman, 151

Scripture references

Genesis 9:24-27 *18*, *37*
Deuteronomy 25:2-3 *56*
Psalm 130:1-4,7-8 *9*
Isaiah 58:6 *133*
Matthew 25 *131*, *196*
Mark 12:34 *9*
Luke 12:20 *122*
1 Corinthians 13 *109*
Ephesians 6:5 *54*
1 Timothy 1:9-10 *211*
Titus 2:9-10 *54*
2 Peter 1:4 *9*
James 1:25 *163*

Deo Optimo et Maximo Gloria
To God, best and greatest, be glory

Typeset in Sansa Condensed and Janson Text
Cover and book design by Janice Van Eck

© 2006 by Joshua Press Inc.

www.ingramcontent.com/pod-product-compliance
Lightning Source LLC
Chambersburg PA
CBHW020640230426
43665CB00008B/258